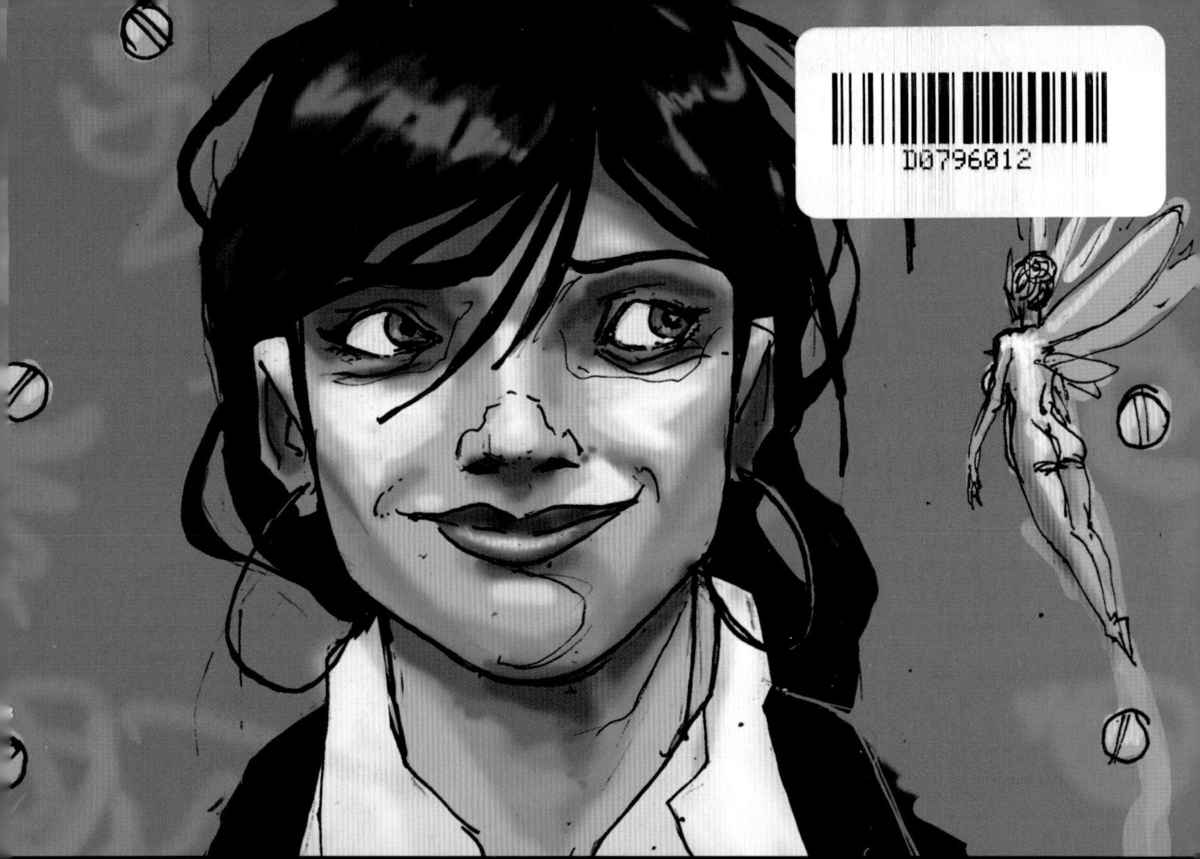

PROOF™ GOATSUCKER

CREATED BY **ALEXANDER GRECIAN** & **RILEY ROSSMO**

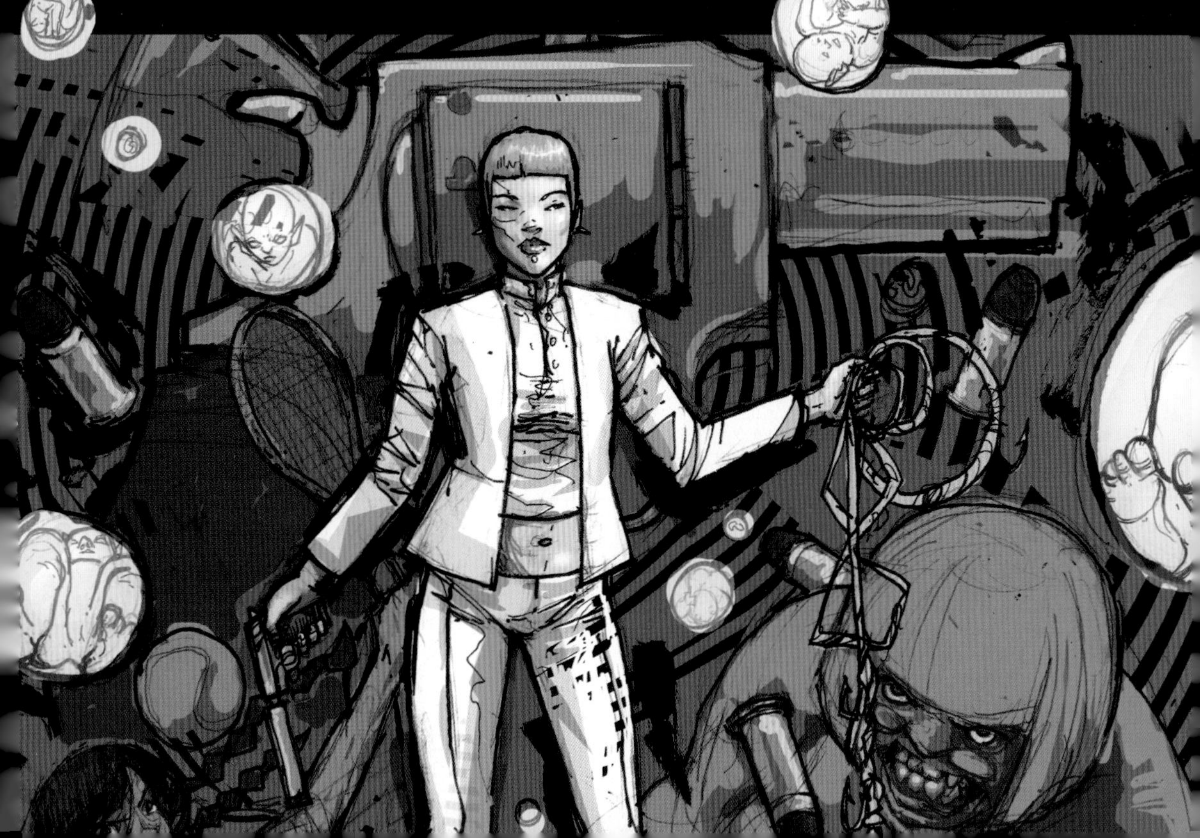

For Christy, Graham and Riley.
-Alex

For Robin and my family.
-Riley

PROOF, BOOK 1: GOATSUCKER
ISBN: 978-1-58240-944-3
Third Printing. Published by Image Comics, Inc. Office of publication: 2134 Allston Way, 2nd Floor, Berkeley, California 94704. Copyright © 2011 Alexander Grecian and Riley Rossmo. Originally published in single magazine form as **PROOF #1-5**. All rights reserved. **PROOF**™ (including all prominent characters featured herein), its logo and all character likenesses are trademarks of Alexander Grecian and Riley Rossmo, unless otherwise noted. Image Comics® and its logos are registered trademarks of Image Comics, Inc. No part of this publication may be reproduced or transmitted, in any form or by any means (except for short excerpts for review purposes) without the express written permission of Image Comics, Inc. All names, characters, events and locales in this publication are entirely fictional. Any resemblance to actual persons (living or dead), events or places, without satiric intent, is coincidental. International Rights Representative: Christine Meyer (christine@gfloystudio.com).
PRINTED IN SOUTH KOREA.

ALEXANDER GRECIAN
script & letters

RILEY ROSSMO
art & colors

with **TYLER JENKINS**
colors

Special Thanks to: **Brian Wood, John Tinkess, Phil Grecian, Eric Stephenson, Joe Keatinge, Allen Hui, Kelly Tindall, Alison Clayton and the good people of Calgary.**

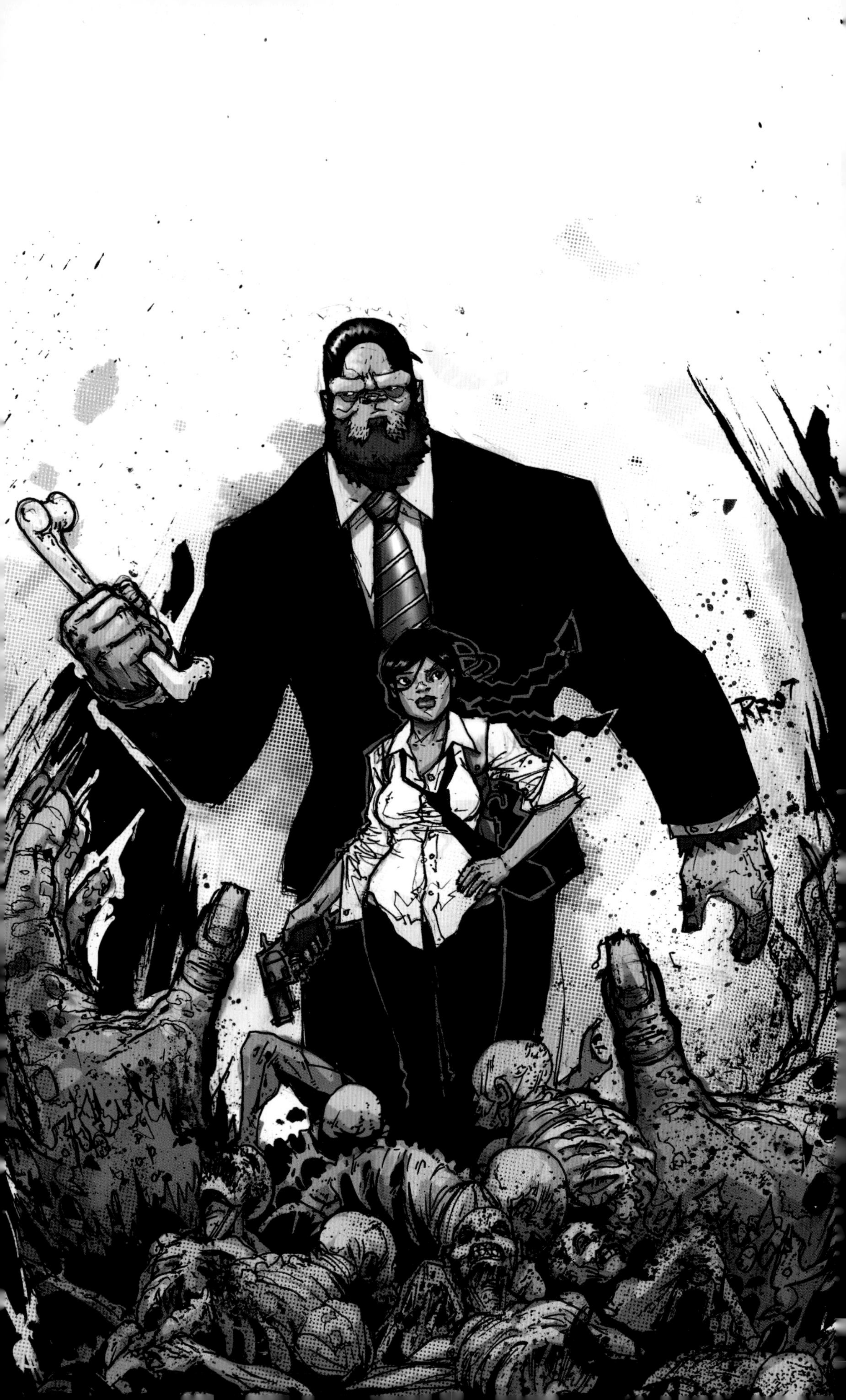

If you believe in Monsters...

Here's the original opening passage from the first issue of *Proof*...

> In the 21st century, mankind has explored nearly every corner of the Earth. But is it possible that there are creatures we haven't discovered yet? Is Bigfoot out there somewhere? What about the Loch Ness Monster? Thunderbirds? The Mothman?
>
> Is Elvis still alive?
>
> In 2006, a team of scientists found dozens of previously undiscovered animal species in New Guinea's Foja mountains, including a tree kangaroo. In the previous decade, 361 new species were discovered in Borneo. Since the late 1800s, thousands of North Americans have reported sighting a massive ape-like man roaming the wilderness.
>
> Although many of these witnesses seem credible, they all lack one thing... Proof.

As I write this, archaeologists have just uncovered fossil evidence of a species of giant frog that lived millions of years ago. There's a lot of media fuss surrounding this thing that they've decided to call a Devil Frog. It dwarfs the frogs we're currently familiar with and it apparently ate, among other things, baby dinosaurs. There's speculation that ancestors of the Devil Frog may still be alive somewhere, in some jungle we haven't adequately explored yet.

Interesting new animals have recently turned up in Madagascar and Columbia. At least once a week there's a news story about some new creature sharing this planet with us, some creature that nobody's heard of before. This, despite the notion that our world is shrinking, that our jaded human species has conquered the planet and there's nothing left to sate our natural curiosity. I beg to differ. I refer you to Columbia and Madagascar. I quietly nod toward Borneo, giant frogs and tree kangaroos.

There are wonders out there. They're waiting for us to come and find them.

Here's the definition of the monsters you'll find here:
A cryptid is a creature that's never been captured or officially documented despite multiple eye-witness accounts and un-substantiated evidence (like footprints and blurry photographs).

Cryptids...

That's what sets *Proof* apart from all the other books in which people interact with monsters. (Well, that's one of the two things, but we'll get to the other thing in a minute.) Everything between the covers of *Proof* could happen, could exist.

Okay, we'll admit it's all more than a little unlikely, but Riley and I have a real-world explanation for everything here. There's no magic. There's no futuristic technology. There might be other dimensions or ghosts or mammals that can puff themselves up like blowfish, but those things might actually, somehow, have a basis in fact.

In *Proof*'s world fairies are wild animals. They were more common a few hundred years ago. People spotted fairies flying around the woods and decided they were magical beings capable of waving wands and turning pumpkins into chariots. In *Proof*'s world, somebody witnessed a jackalope and glued antlers to a regular rabbit's head, imitating what he'd seen. In *Proof*'s world a golem lurks in the back rooms of New York's diamond district. The golem's name is Joe. There's a word tattooed on his head, but it's just a word with no more magical properties than words ever have.

Of course, words *are* freighted with magical properties, but it's a commonplace sort of magic. The kind of magic that entertains and persuades. That's the kind of magic we like.

So, the second big difference I mentioned... Our characters.

This book's called *Proof*, but Ginger and Elvis are just as important as our resident Bigfoot. The things that happen in "Goatsucker" have just as big an impact on the other agents of The Lodge as they do on Proof. Maybe more. We spend as much time letting Elvis's story play out as we do Proof's. Maybe more. Proof doesn't even make an appearance in the last 30 pages of his own book. By the end of "Goatsucker," this has clearly become Elvis's story and we've broken with standard comic book storytelling convention in order to let that story play out the way it needs to.

Because these characters *are* the story.

Another case in point: Bigfoot wears a suit and works for a government agency. Sounds a little silly on the surface, but there's more to him than that. Agent John Prufrock is just as excited to find new animal species as any explorer. The difference is that he hopes those animal species might be related to him; might, in fact, be his natural family. Because he's an orphan, he's a little more motivated than your average college professor.

Proof is the only government agent who isn't a human being and he'll always be the only monster working for The Lodge. The people around him accept him, but in the end he's not a person. He tries hard, though, and that's a little bit funny. And it's a little bit sad.

And maybe it's a little bit scary.

—*Alexander Grecian*

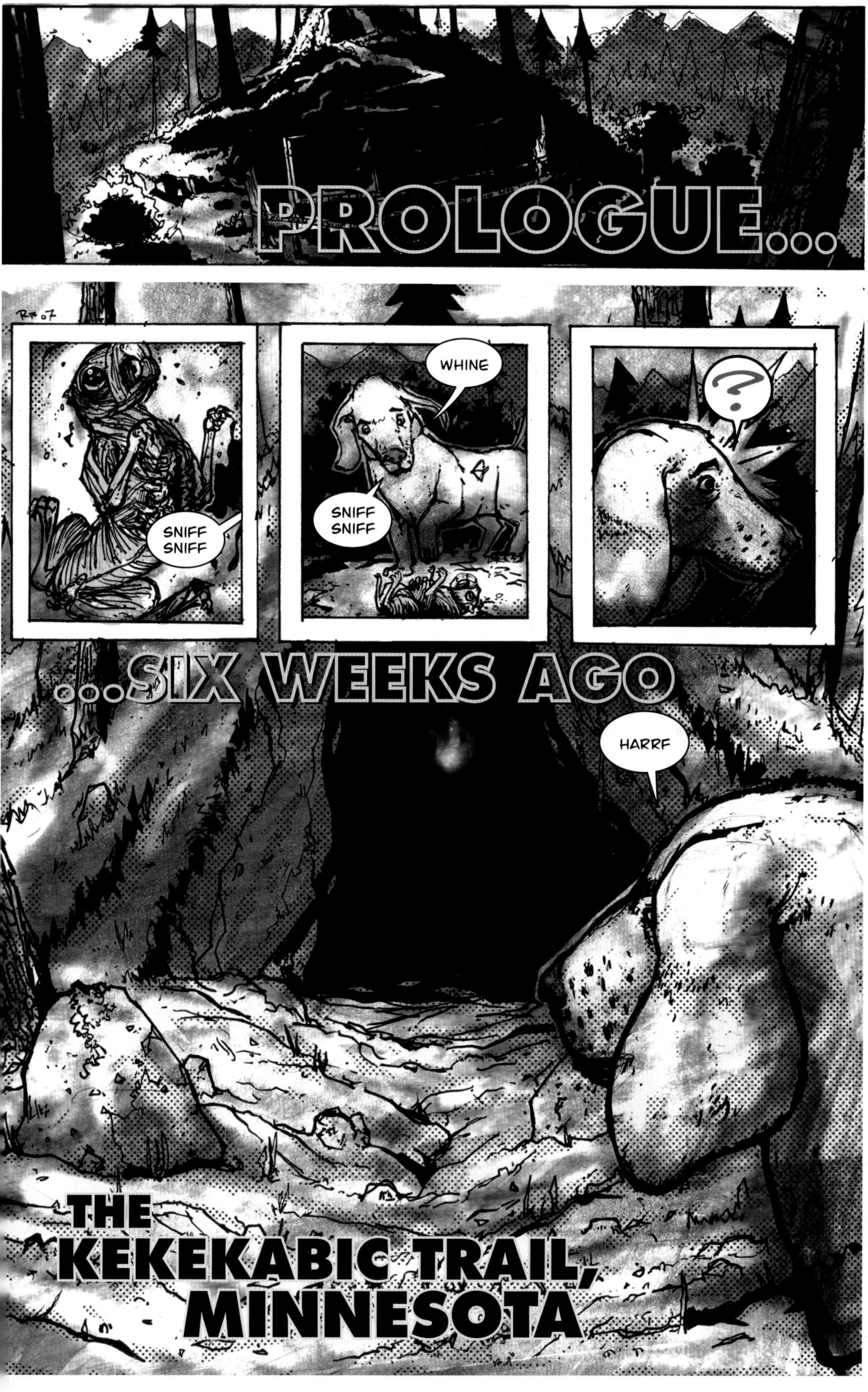
PROLOGUE...
SNIFF SNIFF
WHINE
SNIFF SNIFF
?
...SIX WEEKS AGO
HARRF
THE KEKEKABIC TRAIL, MINNESOTA

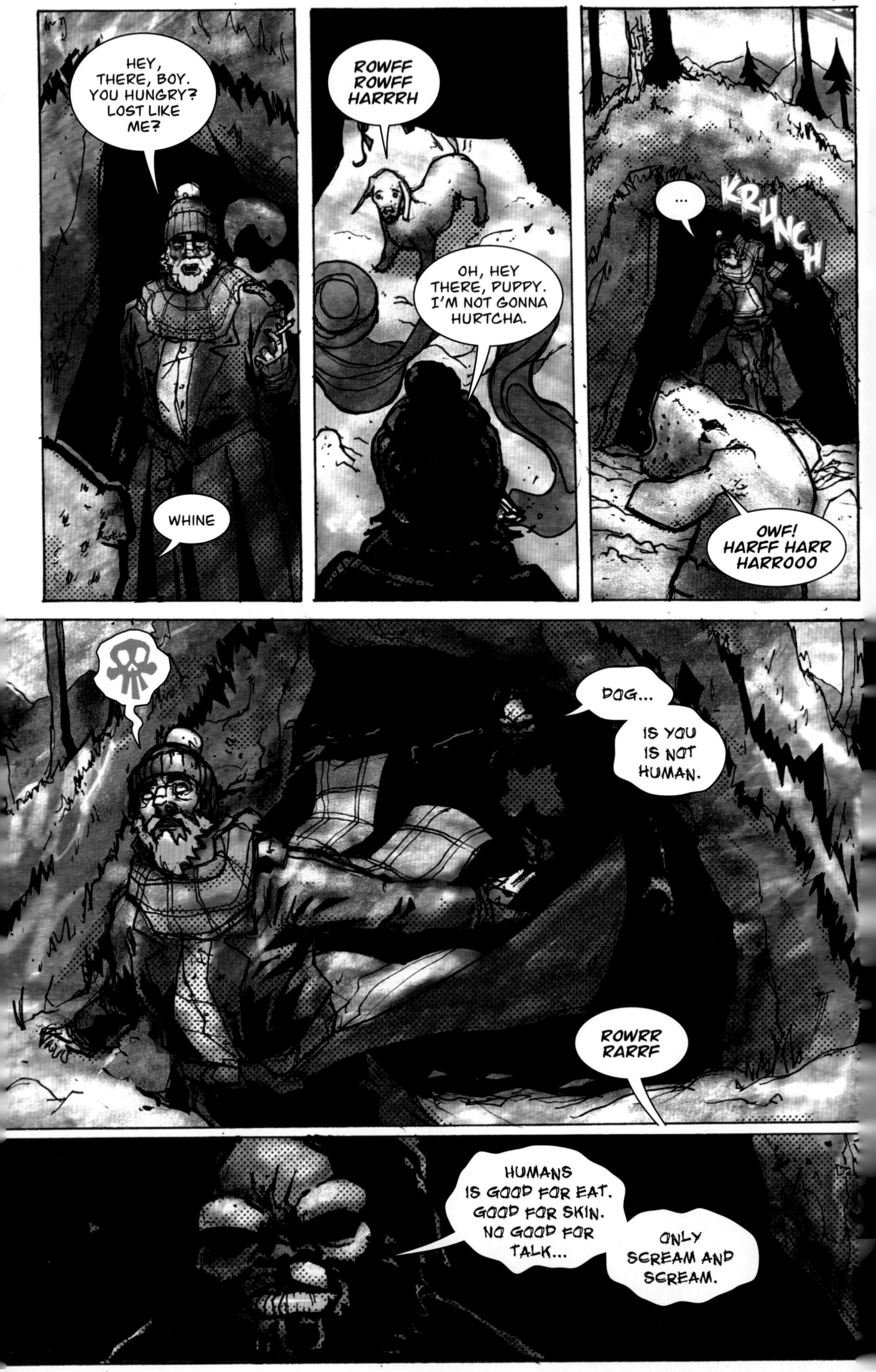
HEY, THERE, BOY. YOU HUNGRY? LOST LIKE ME?
WHINE
ROWFF ROWFF HARRRH
OH, HEY THERE, PUPPY. I'M NOT GONNA HURTCHA.
...
KRUNCH
OWF! HARFF HARR HARROOO
DOG...
IS YOU IS NOT HUMAN.
ROWRR RARRF
HUMANS IS GOOD FOR EAT. GOOD FOR SKIN. NO GOOD FOR TALK...
ONLY SCREAM AND SCREAM.

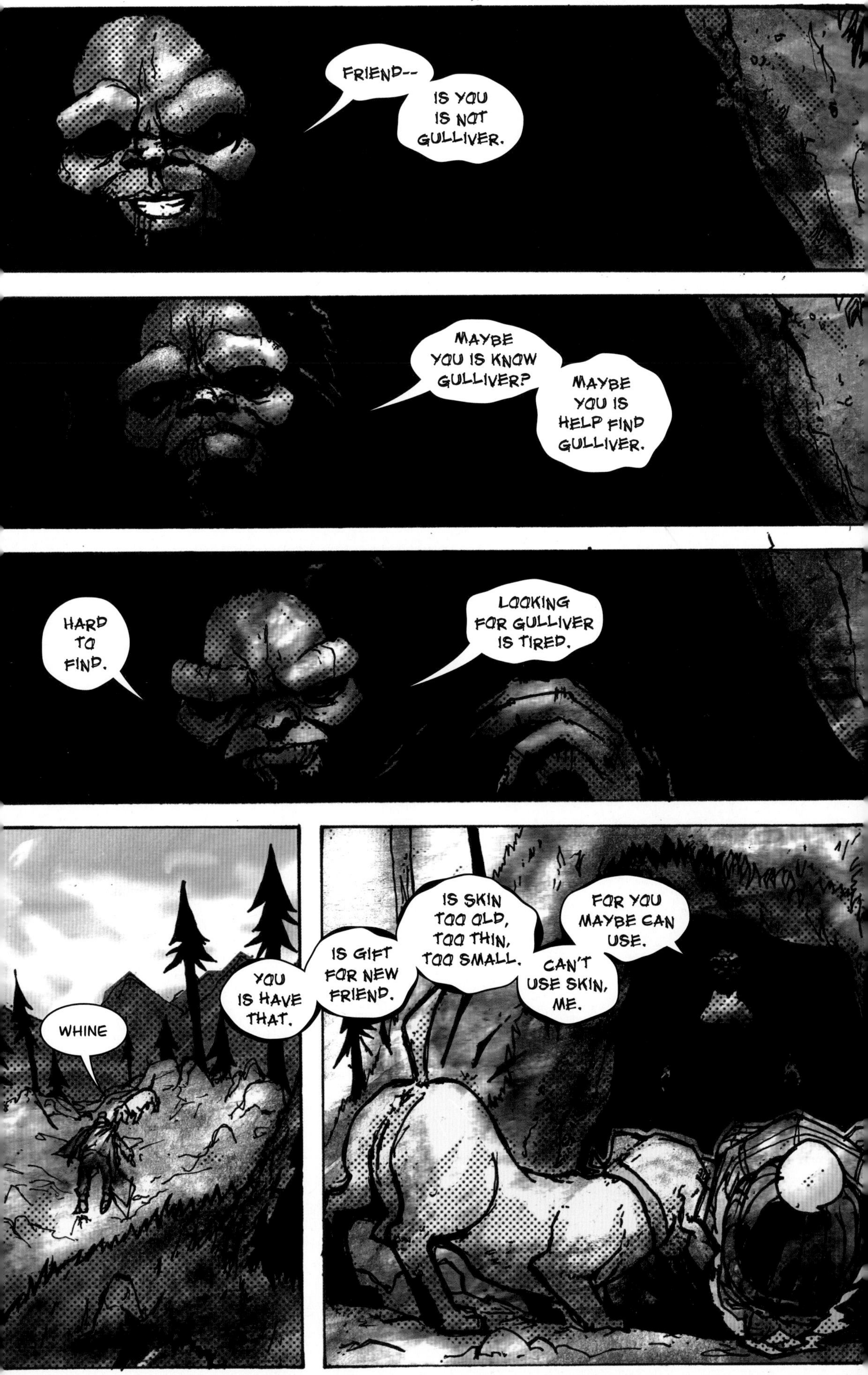
FRIEND--
IS YOU IS NOT GULLIVER.
MAYBE YOU IS KNOW GULLIVER?
MAYBE YOU IS HELP FIND GULLIVER.
HARD TO FIND.
LOOKING FOR GULLIVER IS TIRED.
WHINE
YOU IS HAVE THAT.
IS GIFT FOR NEW FRIEND.
IS SKIN TOO OLD, TOO THIN, TOO SMALL.
CAN'T USE SKIN, ME.
FOR YOU MAYBE CAN USE.

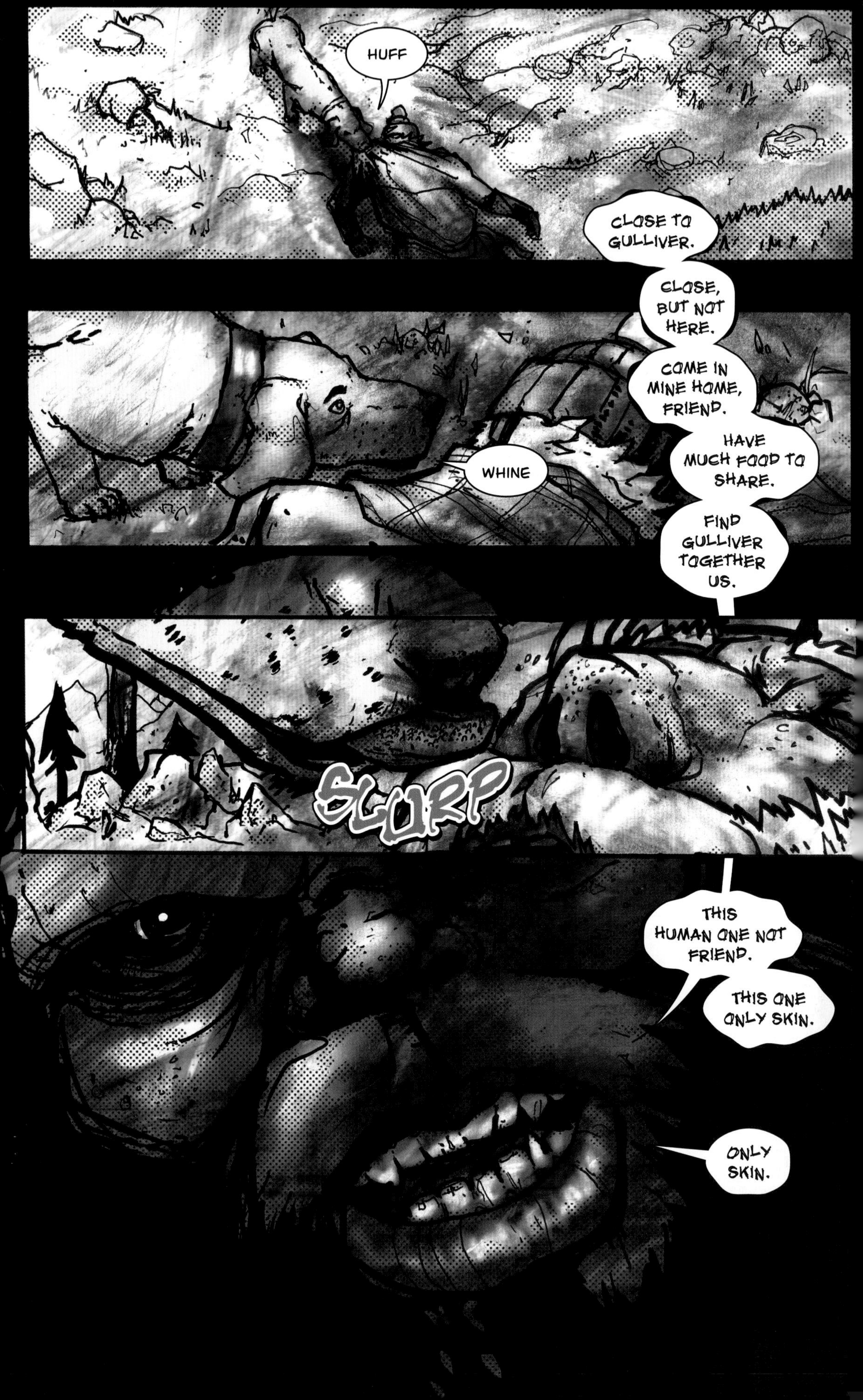
HUFF
CLOSE TO GULLIVER.
CLOSE, BUT NOT HERE.
COME IN MINE HOME, FRIEND.
HAVE MUCH FOOD TO SHARE.
FIND GULLIVER TOGETHER US.
WHINE
SLURP
THIS HUMAN ONE NOT FRIEND.
THIS ONE ONLY SKIN.
ONLY SKIN.

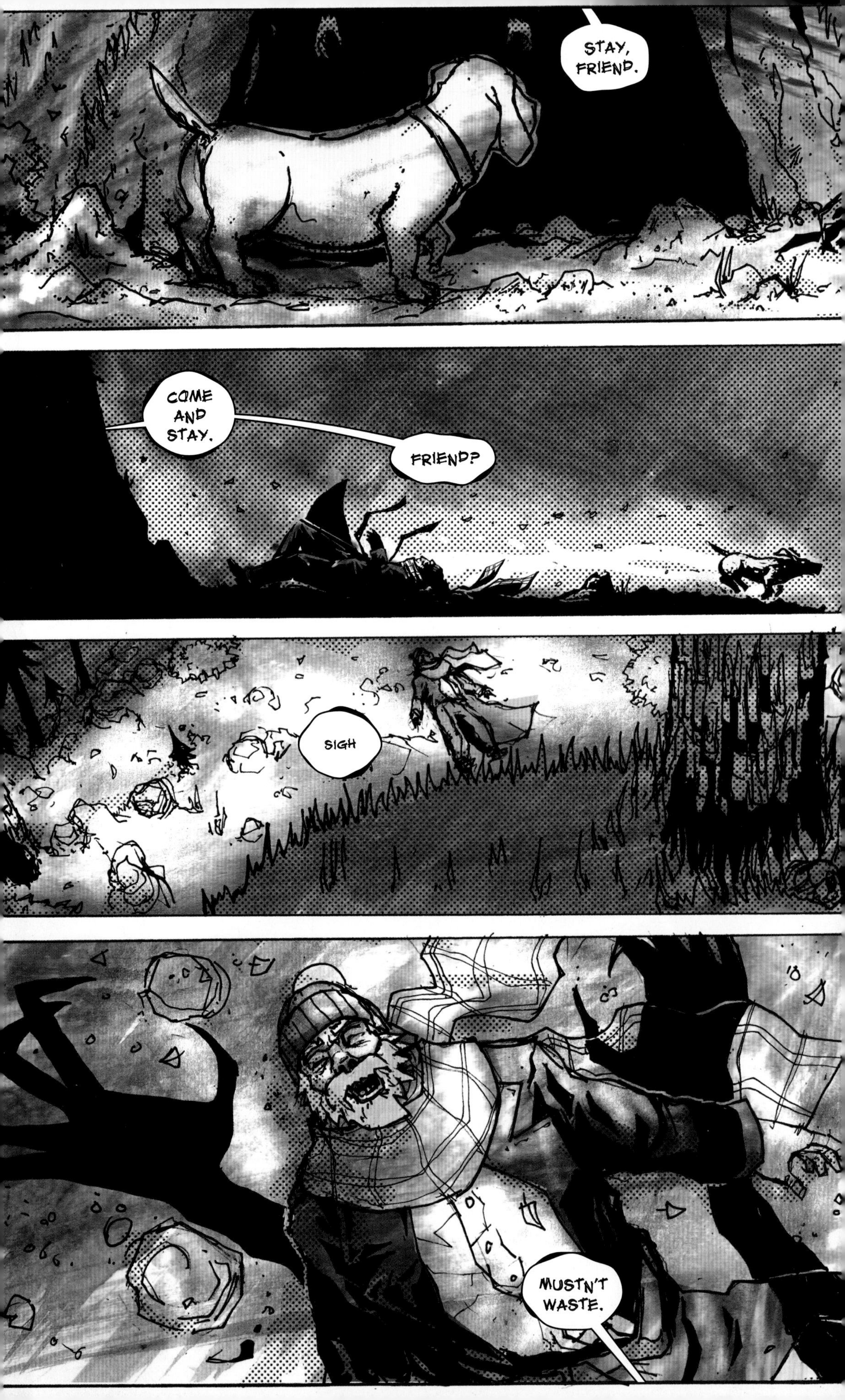
STAY, FRIEND.
COME AND STAY.
FRIEND?
SIGH
MUSTN'T WASTE.

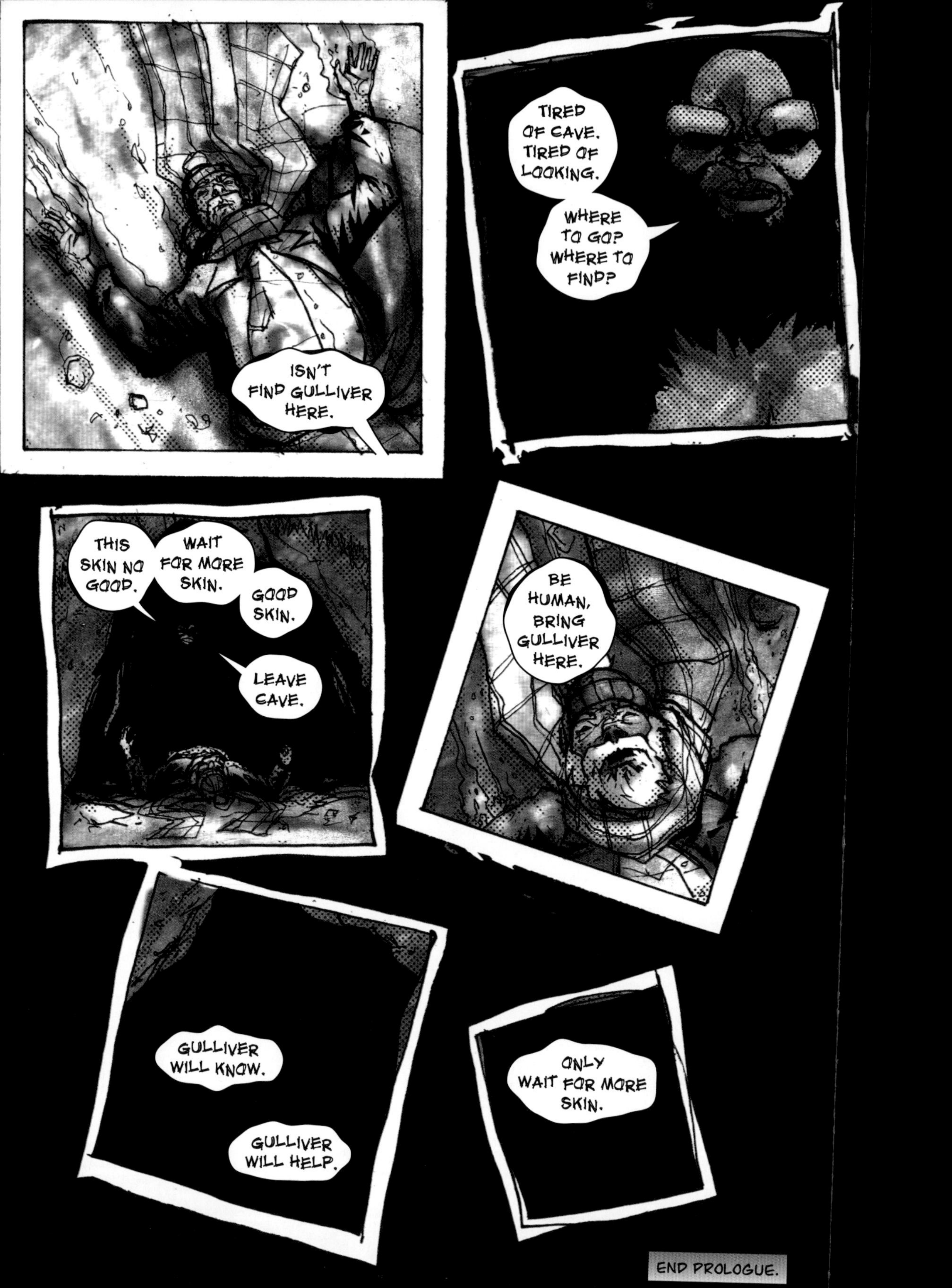
ISN'T FIND GULLIVER HERE.
TIRED OF CAVE. TIRED OF LOOKING.
WHERE TO GO? WHERE TO FIND?
THIS SKIN NO GOOD.
WAIT FOR MORE SKIN.
GOOD SKIN.
LEAVE CAVE.
BE HUMAN, BRING GULLIVER HERE.
GULLIVER WILL KNOW.
GULLIVER WILL HELP.
ONLY WAIT FOR MORE SKIN.
END PROLOGUE.

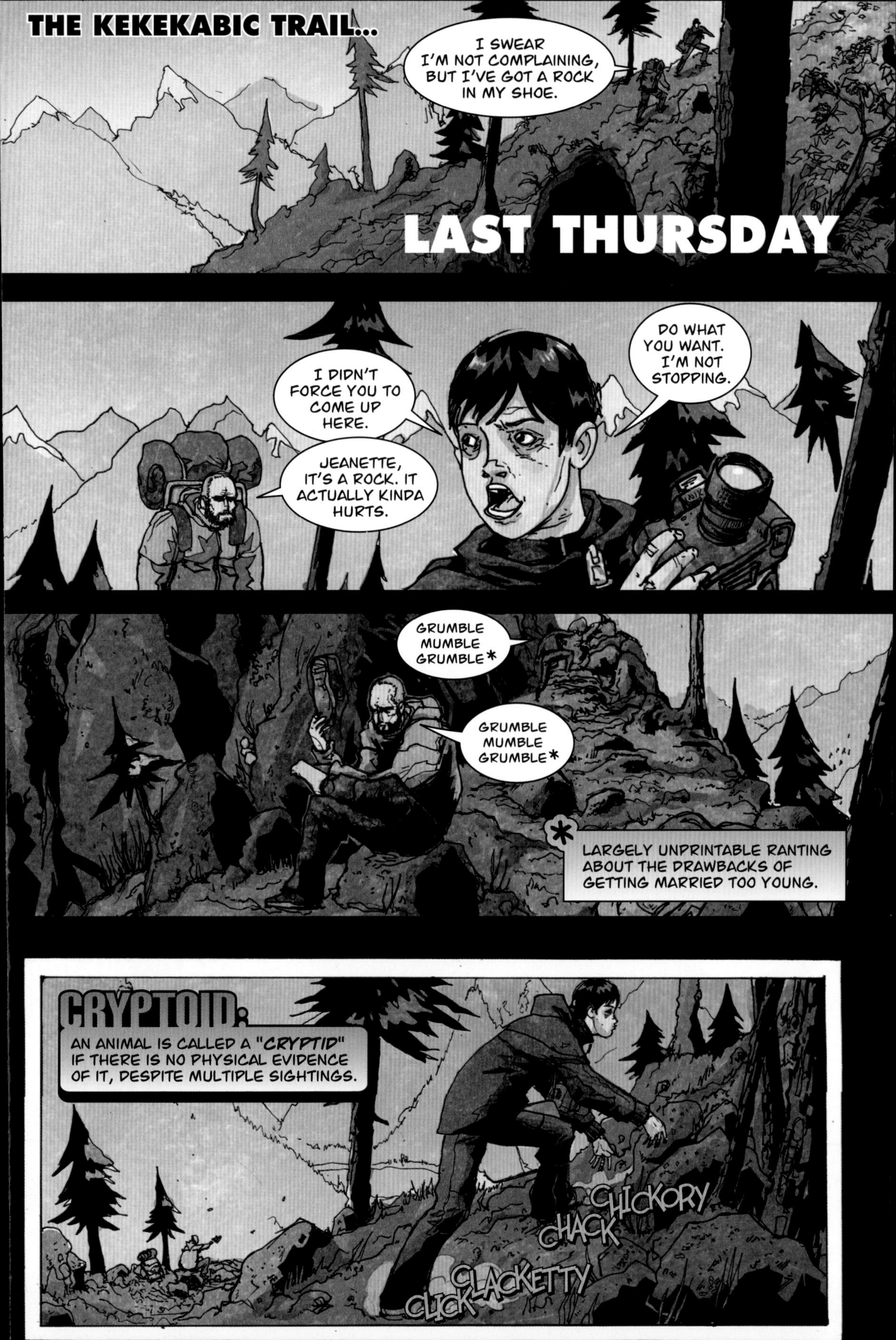
THE KEKEKABIC TRAIL...
I SWEAR I'M NOT COMPLAINING, BUT I'VE GOT A ROCK IN MY SHOE.
LAST THURSDAY
I DIDN'T FORCE YOU TO COME UP HERE.
DO WHAT YOU WANT. I'M NOT STOPPING.
JEANETTE, IT'S A ROCK. IT ACTUALLY KINDA HURTS.
GRUMBLE MUMBLE GRUMBLE*
GRUMBLE MUMBLE GRUMBLE*
* LARGELY UNPRINTABLE RANTING ABOUT THE DRAWBACKS OF GETTING MARRIED TOO YOUNG.
CRYPTOID:
AN ANIMAL IS CALLED A "CRYPTID" IF THERE IS NO PHYSICAL EVIDENCE OF IT, DESPITE MULTIPLE SIGHTINGS.
CHICKORY
CHACK
CLICK-CLACKETTY

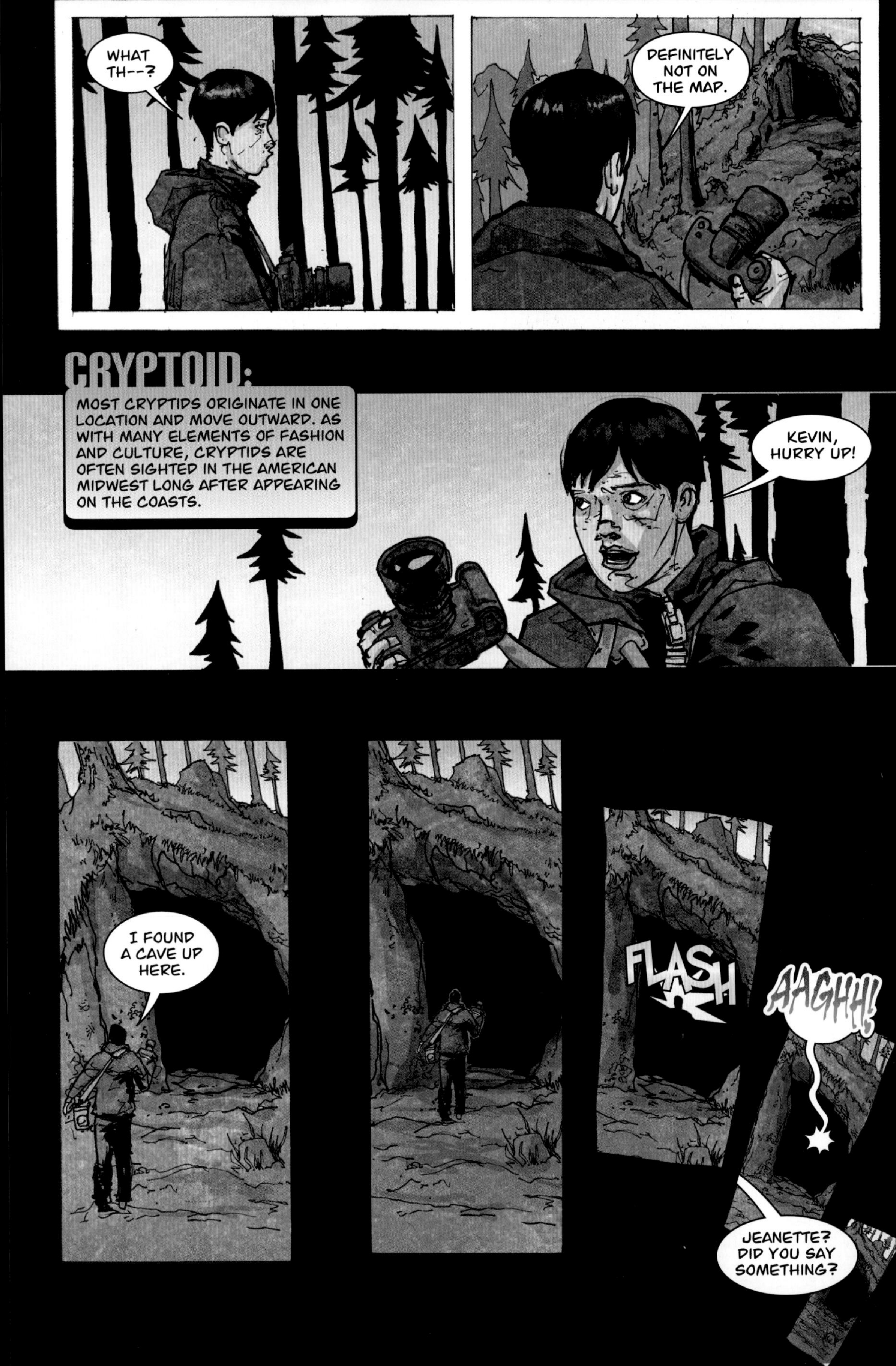
WHAT TH--?
DEFINITELY NOT ON THE MAP.
CRYPTOID:
MOST CRYPTIDS ORIGINATE IN ONE LOCATION AND MOVE OUTWARD. AS WITH MANY ELEMENTS OF FASHION AND CULTURE, CRYPTIDS ARE OFTEN SIGHTED IN THE AMERICAN MIDWEST LONG AFTER APPEARING ON THE COASTS.
KEVIN, HURRY UP!
I FOUND A CAVE UP HERE.
FLASH
AAGHH!
JEANETTE? DID YOU SAY SOMETHING?

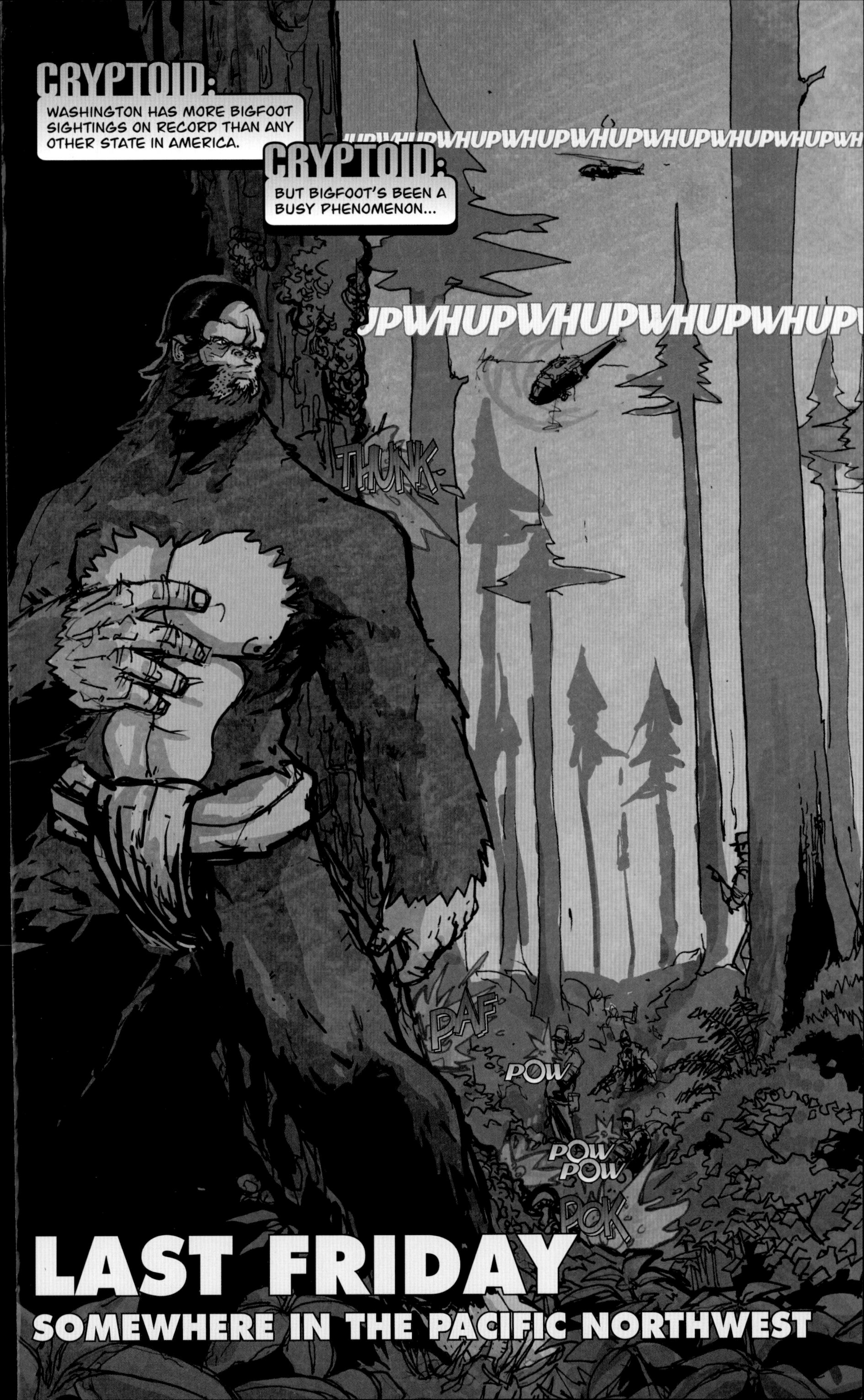
CRYPTOID:
WASHINGTON HAS MORE BIGFOOT SIGHTINGS ON RECORD THAN ANY OTHER STATE IN AMERICA.
WHUPWHUPWHUPWHUPWHUPWHUPWH
CRYPTOID:
BUT BIGFOOT'S BEEN A BUSY PHENOMENON...
PWHUPWHUPWHUPWHUP
THUNK
PAF
POW
POW POW
POK
LAST FRIDAY
SOMEWHERE IN THE PACIFIC NORTHWEST

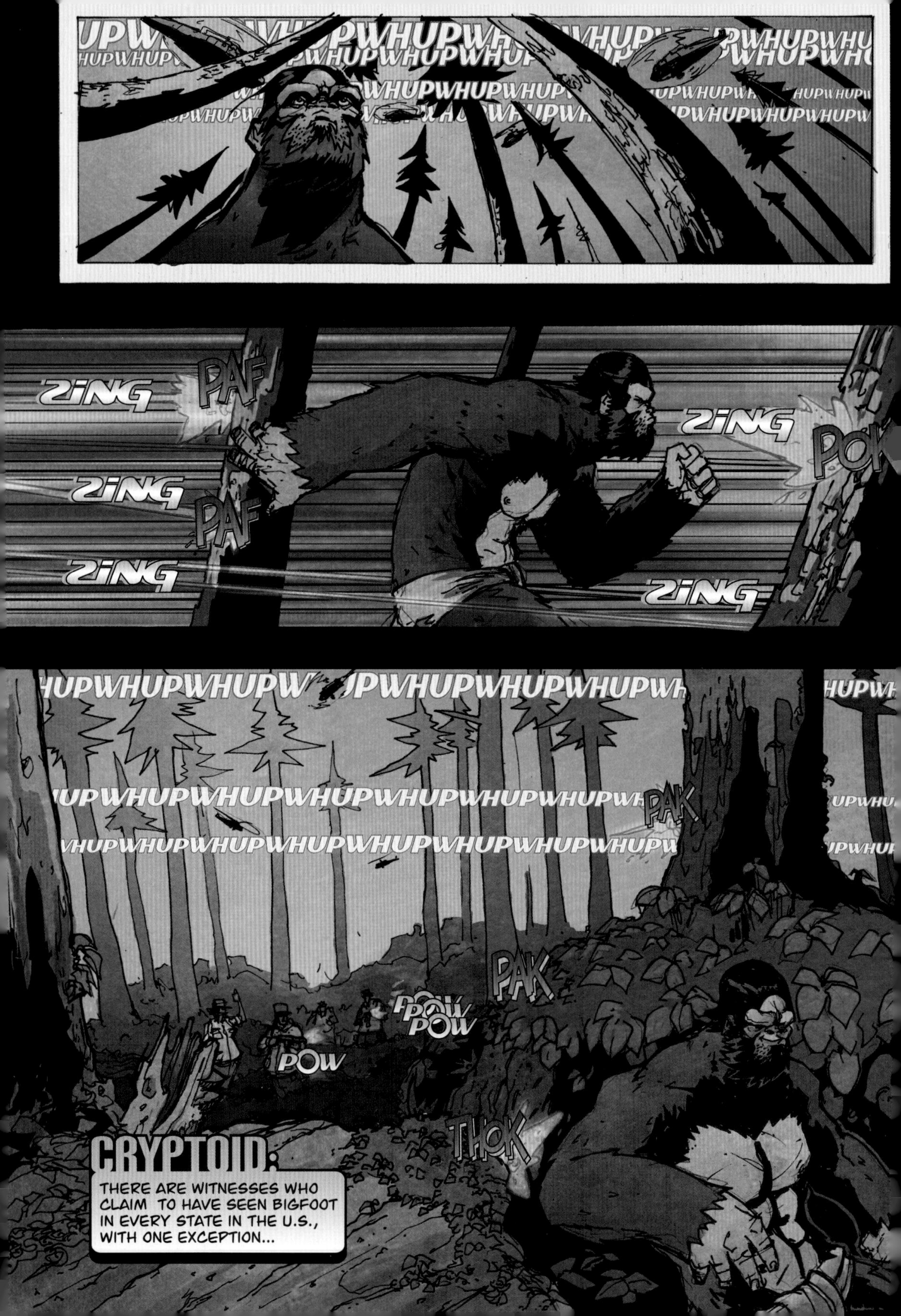
WHUPWHUPWHUPWHUPWHUPWHUPWHUP
ZING
PAF
ZING
PAF
ZING
ZING
POK
ZING
WHUPWHUPWHUPWHUPWHUPWHUP
WHUPWHUPWHUPWHUPWHUPWHUP
PAK
PAK
POW
POW
POW
THOK
CRYPTOID:
THERE ARE WITNESSES WHO CLAIM TO HAVE SEEN BIGFOOT IN EVERY STATE IN THE U.S., WITH ONE EXCEPTION...

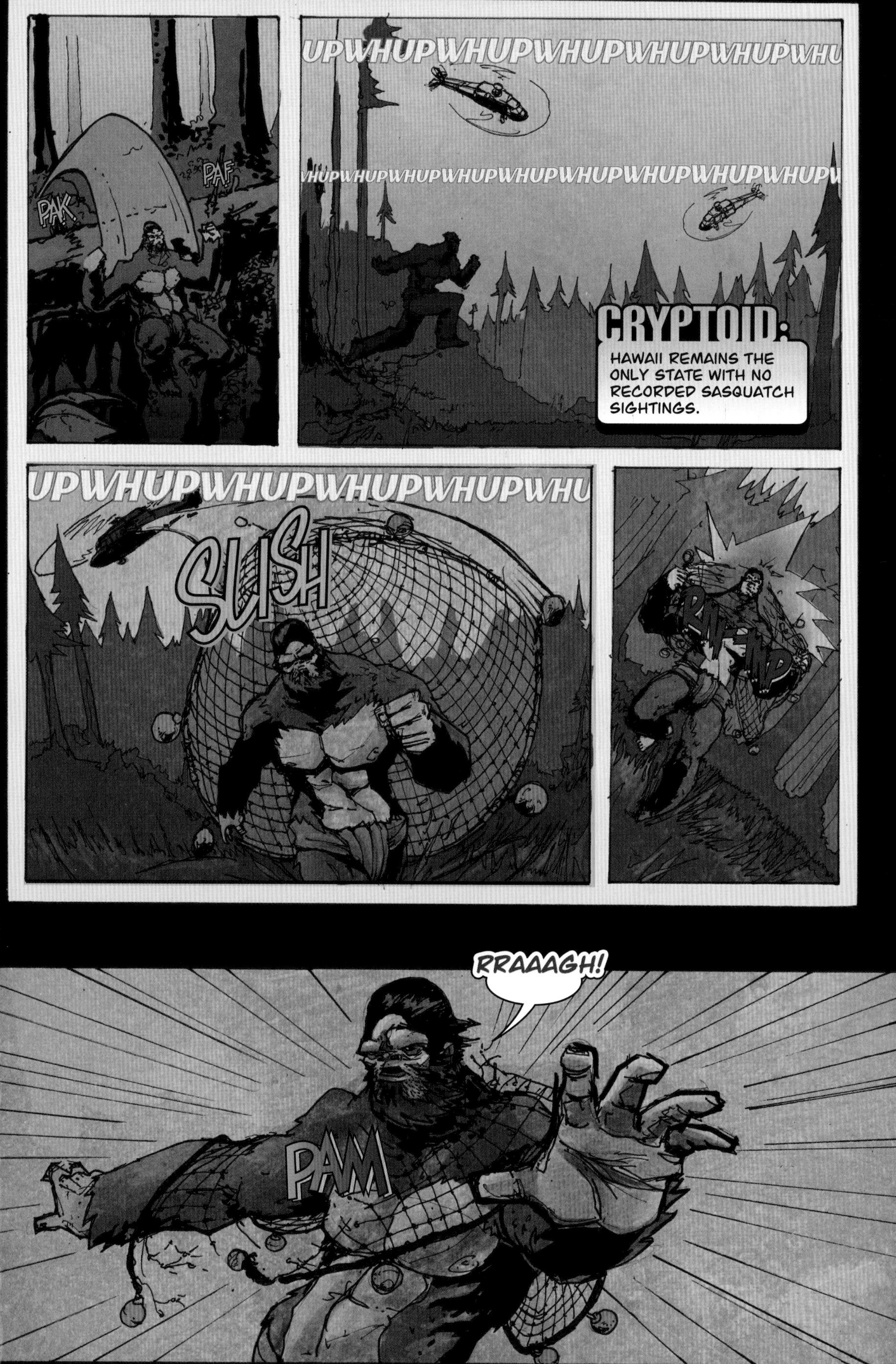
PAK!
PAF!
UPWHUPWHUPWHUPWHUPWHUPWHU
WHUPWHUPWHUPWHUPWHUPWHUPWHUPWHUPWHUPWHUPW
CRYPTOID:
HAWAII REMAINS THE ONLY STATE WITH NO RECORDED SASQUATCH SIGHTINGS.
UPWHUPWHUPWHUPWHUPWHU
SLISH
RRAAAGH!
PAW

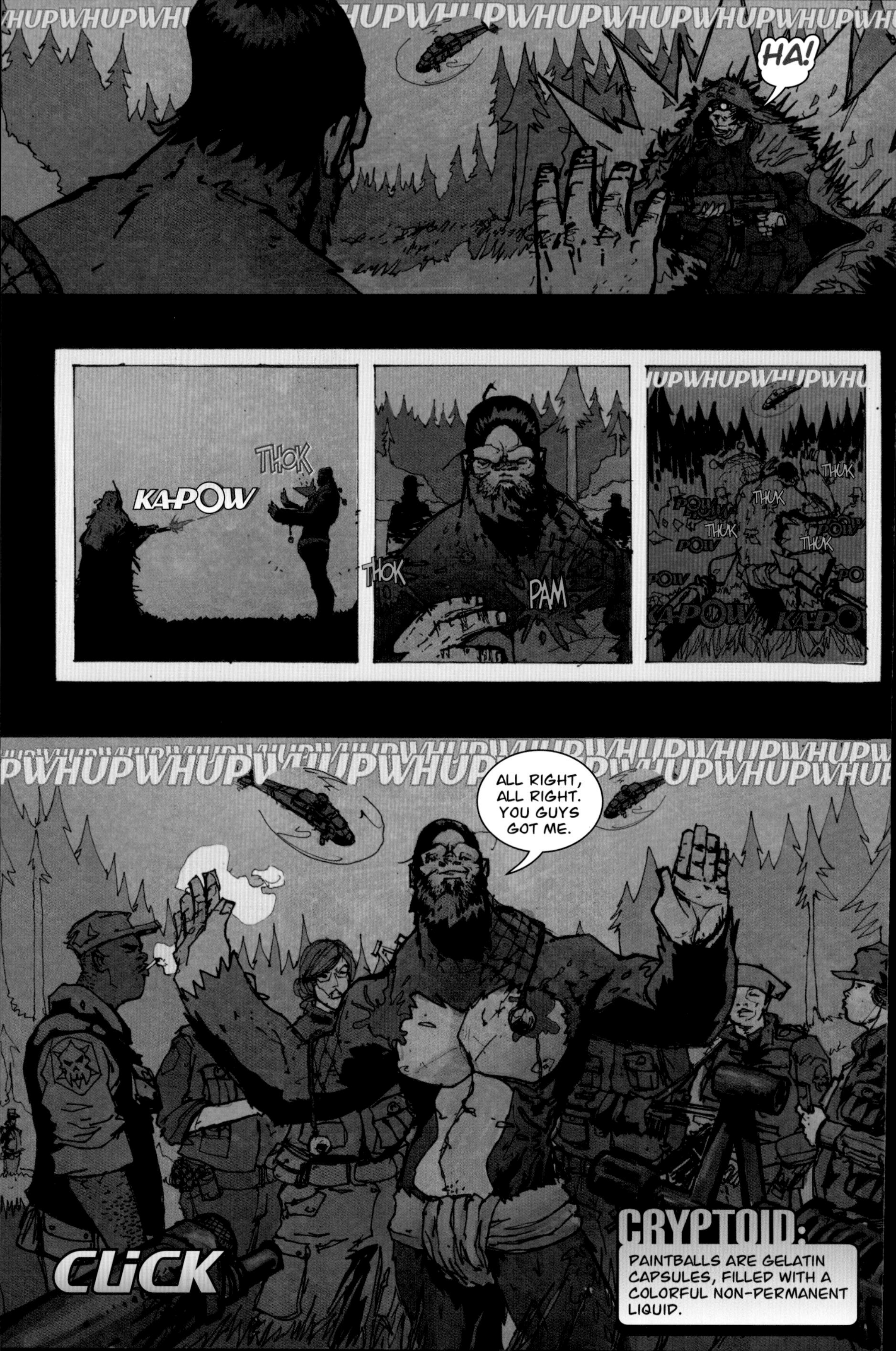
WHUPWHUPWHUPWHUPWHUPWHUPWHUPWHUPWH
HA!
KA-POW
THOK
THOK
PAM
WHUPWHUPWHUPWHU
THUK
POW
THUK
THUK
THUK
POW
POW
THUK
POW
KA-POW
KA-POW
PWHUPWHUPWHUPWHUPWHUPWHUPWHUPWHUPWHU
ALL RIGHT, ALL RIGHT. YOU GUYS GOT ME.
CLICK
CRYPTOID:
PAINTBALLS ARE GELATIN CAPSULES, FILLED WITH A COLORFUL NON-PERMANENT LIQUID.

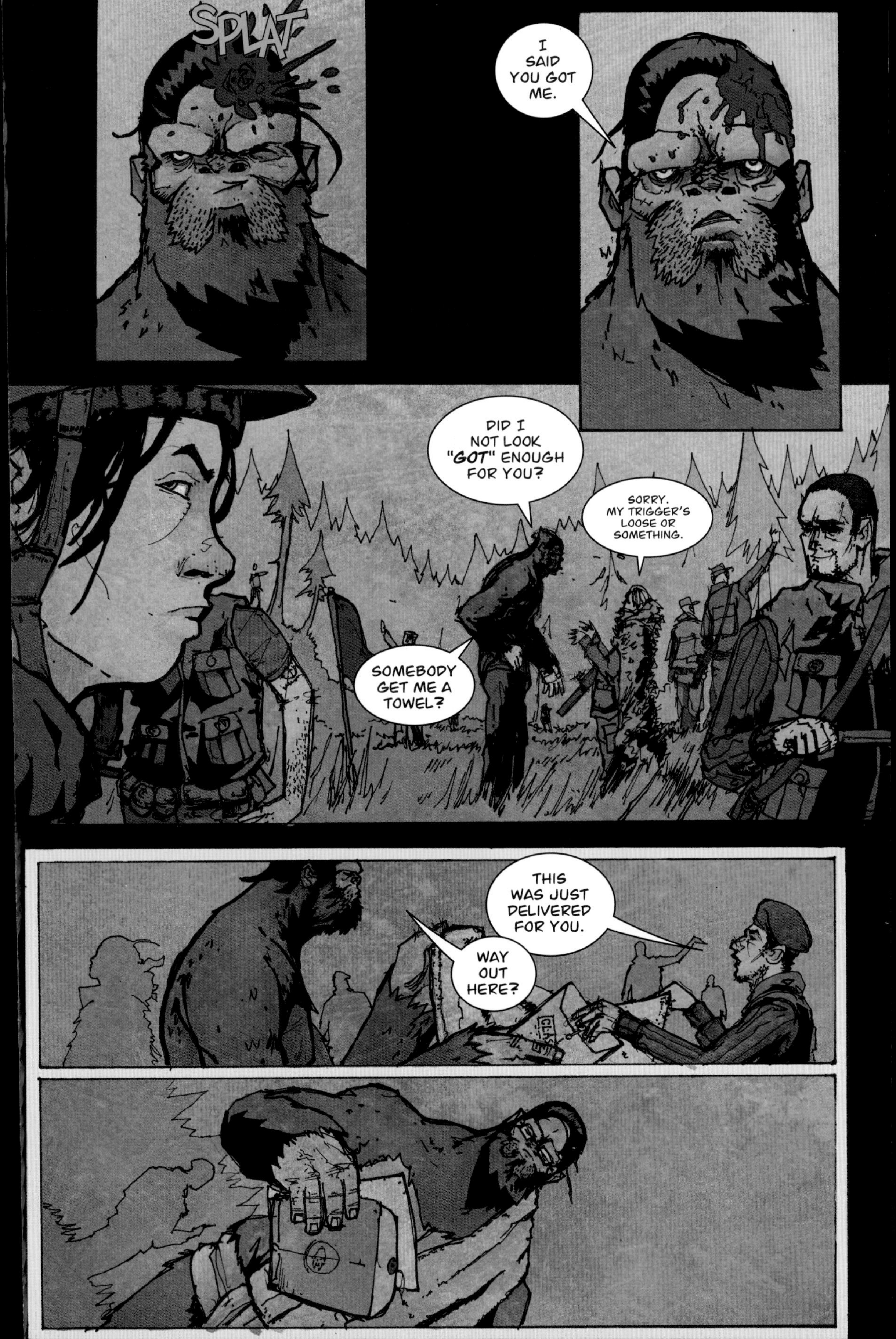

SPLAT
I SAID YOU GOT ME.
DID I NOT LOOK "GOT" ENOUGH FOR YOU?
SORRY. MY TRIGGER'S LOOSE OR SOMETHING.
SOMEBODY GET ME A TOWEL?
THIS WAS JUST DELIVERED FOR YOU.
WAY OUT HERE?

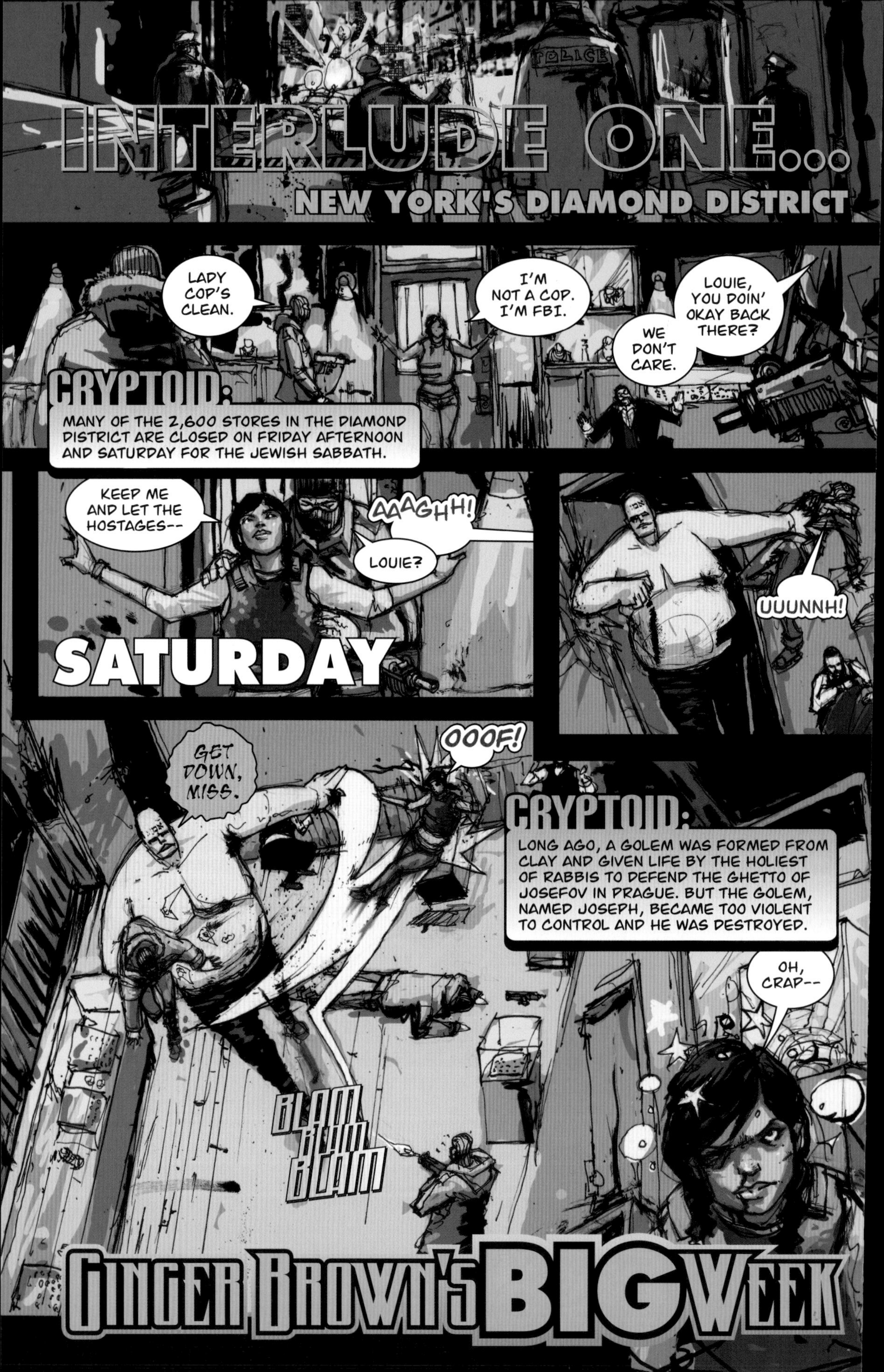

INTERLUDE ONE...
NEW YORK'S DIAMOND DISTRICT
LADY COP'S CLEAN.
I'M NOT A COP. I'M FBI.
WE DON'T CARE.
LOUIE, YOU DOIN' OKAY BACK THERE?
CRYPTOID:
MANY OF THE 2,600 STORES IN THE DIAMOND DISTRICT ARE CLOSED ON FRIDAY AFTERNOON AND SATURDAY FOR THE JEWISH SABBATH.
KEEP ME AND LET THE HOSTAGES--
AAAGHH!
LOUIE?
SATURDAY
UUUNNH!
GET DOWN, MISS.
OOOF!
CRYPTOID:
LONG AGO, A GOLEM WAS FORMED FROM CLAY AND GIVEN LIFE BY THE HOLIEST OF RABBIS TO DEFEND THE GHETTO OF JOSEFOV IN PRAGUE. BUT THE GOLEM, NAMED JOSEPH, BECAME TOO VIOLENT TO CONTROL AND HE WAS DESTROYED.
OH, CRAP--
BLAM BLAM BLAM
GINGER BROWN'S BIG WEEK

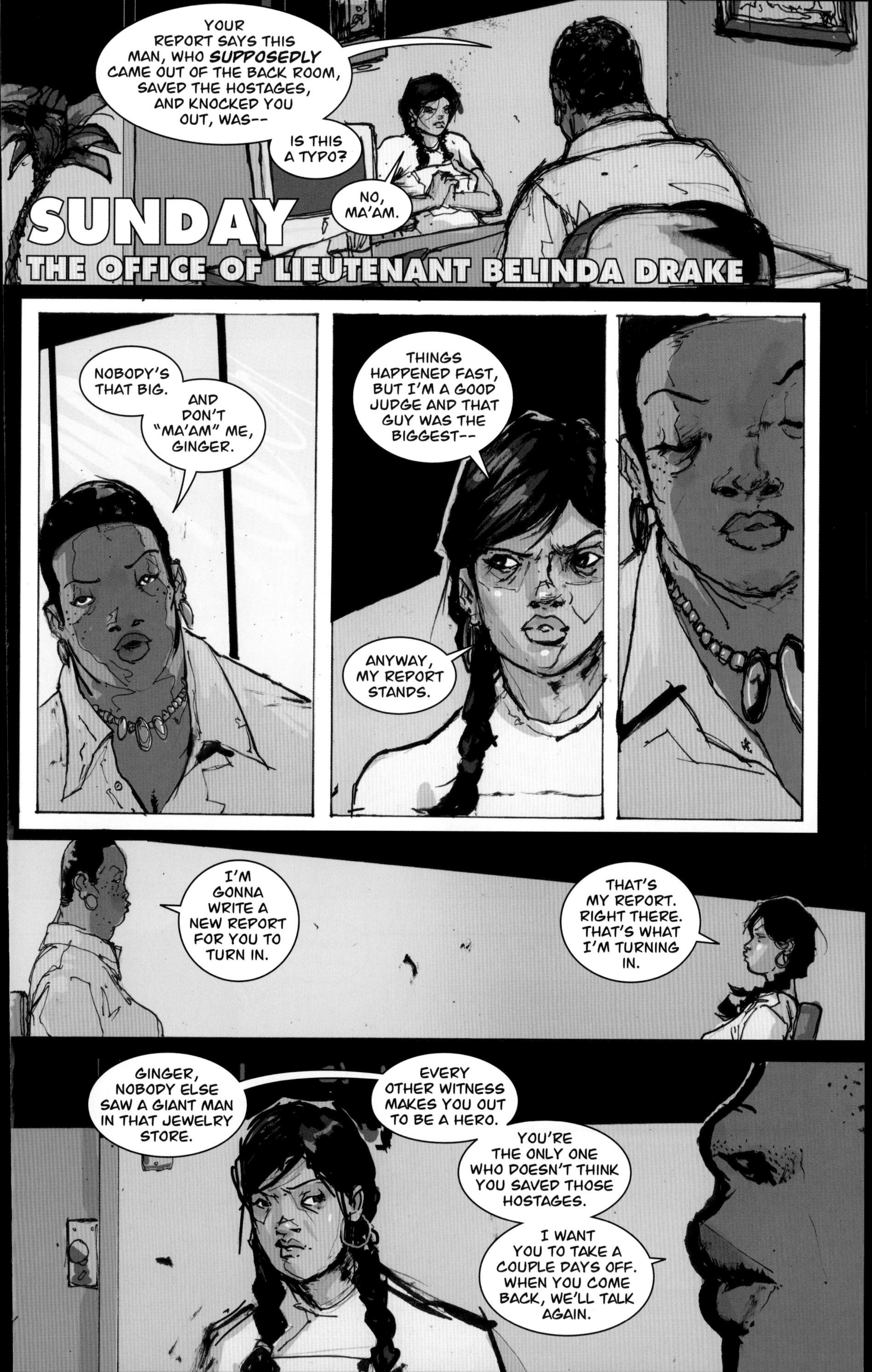
YOUR REPORT SAYS THIS MAN, WHO SUPPOSEDLY CAME OUT OF THE BACK ROOM, SAVED THE HOSTAGES, AND KNOCKED YOU OUT, WAS--
IS THIS A TYPO?
NO, MA'AM.
SUNDAY
THE OFFICE OF LIEUTENANT BELINDA DRAKE
NOBODY'S THAT BIG.
AND DON'T "MA'AM" ME, GINGER.
THINGS HAPPENED FAST, BUT I'M A GOOD JUDGE AND THAT GUY WAS THE BIGGEST--
ANYWAY, MY REPORT STANDS.
I'M GONNA WRITE A NEW REPORT FOR YOU TO TURN IN.
THAT'S MY REPORT. RIGHT THERE. THAT'S WHAT I'M TURNING IN.
GINGER, NOBODY ELSE SAW A GIANT MAN IN THAT JEWELRY STORE.
EVERY OTHER WITNESS MAKES YOU OUT TO BE A HERO.
YOU'RE THE ONLY ONE WHO DOESN'T THINK YOU SAVED THOSE HOSTAGES.
I WANT YOU TO TAKE A COUPLE DAYS OFF. WHEN YOU COME BACK, WE'LL TALK AGAIN.

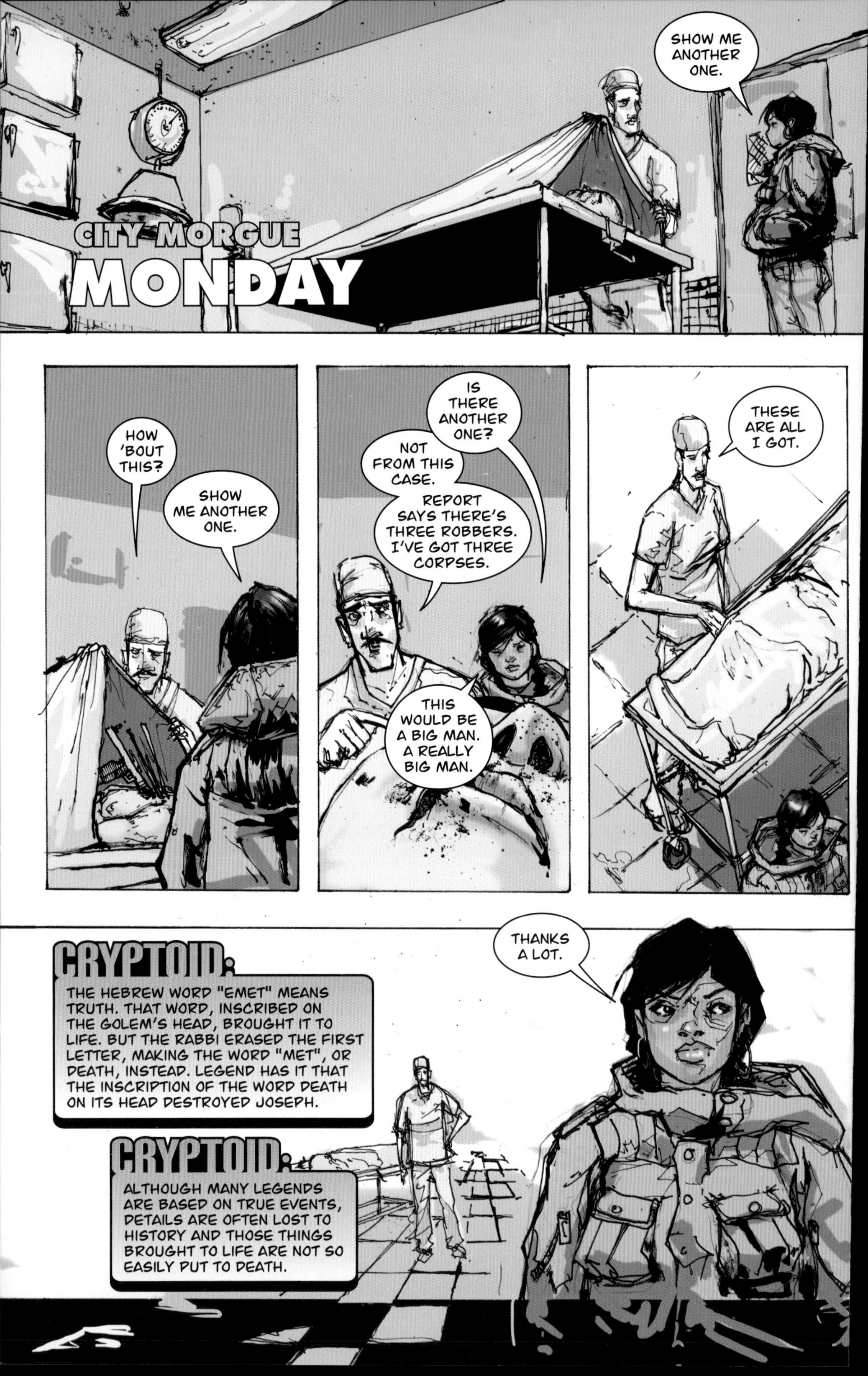
SHOW ME ANOTHER ONE.
CITY MORGUE
MONDAY
HOW 'BOUT THIS?
SHOW ME ANOTHER ONE.
IS THERE ANOTHER ONE?
NOT FROM THIS CASE.
REPORT SAYS THERE'S THREE ROBBERS. I'VE GOT THREE CORPSES.
THIS WOULD BE A BIG MAN. A REALLY BIG MAN.
THESE ARE ALL I GOT.
THANKS A LOT.
CRYPTOID:
THE HEBREW WORD "EMET" MEANS TRUTH. THAT WORD, INSCRIBED ON THE GOLEM'S HEAD, BROUGHT IT TO LIFE. BUT THE RABBI ERASED THE FIRST LETTER, MAKING THE WORD "MET", OR DEATH, INSTEAD. LEGEND HAS IT THAT THE INSCRIPTION OF THE WORD DEATH ON ITS HEAD DESTROYED JOSEPH.
CRYPTOID:
ALTHOUGH MANY LEGENDS ARE BASED ON TRUE EVENTS, DETAILS ARE OFTEN LOST TO HISTORY AND THOSE THINGS BROUGHT TO LIFE ARE NOT SO EASILY PUT TO DEATH.

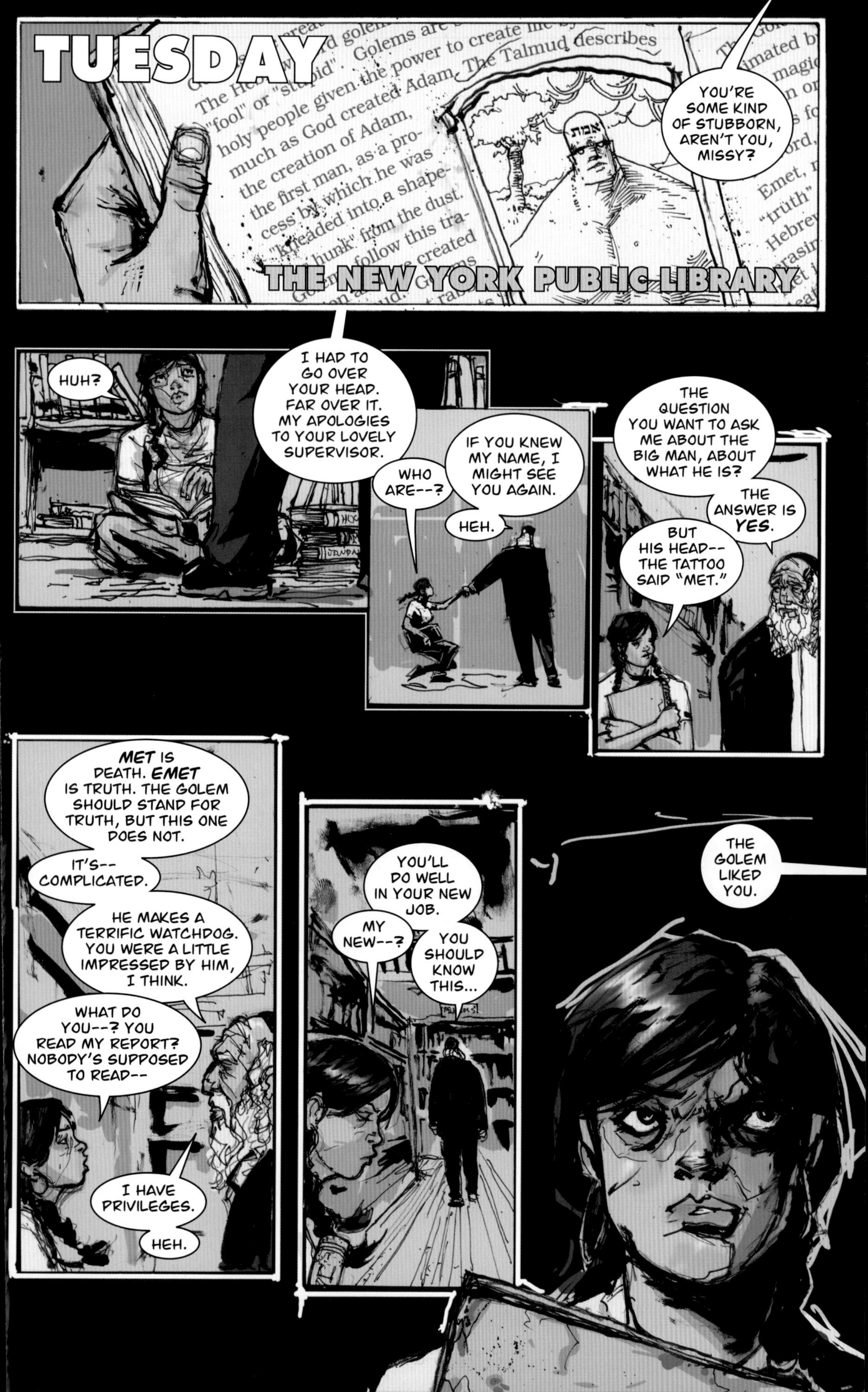
TUESDAY
THE NEW YORK PUBLIC LIBRARY
YOU'RE SOME KIND OF STUBBORN, AREN'T YOU, MISSY?
HUH?
I HAD TO GO OVER YOUR HEAD. FAR OVER IT. MY APOLOGIES TO YOUR LOVELY SUPERVISOR.
WHO ARE--?
IF YOU KNEW MY NAME, I MIGHT SEE YOU AGAIN.
HEH.
THE QUESTION YOU WANT TO ASK ME ABOUT THE BIG MAN, ABOUT WHAT HE IS?
THE ANSWER IS YES.
BUT HIS HEAD-- THE TATTOO SAID "MET."
MET IS DEATH. EMET IS TRUTH. THE GOLEM SHOULD STAND FOR TRUTH, BUT THIS ONE DOES NOT.
IT'S-- COMPLICATED.
HE MAKES A TERRIFIC WATCHDOG. YOU WERE A LITTLE IMPRESSED BY HIM, I THINK.
WHAT DO YOU--? YOU READ MY REPORT? NOBODY'S SUPPOSED TO READ--
I HAVE PRIVILEGES.
HEH.
YOU'LL DO WELL IN YOUR NEW JOB.
MY NEW--?
YOU SHOULD KNOW THIS...
THE GOLEM LIKED YOU.

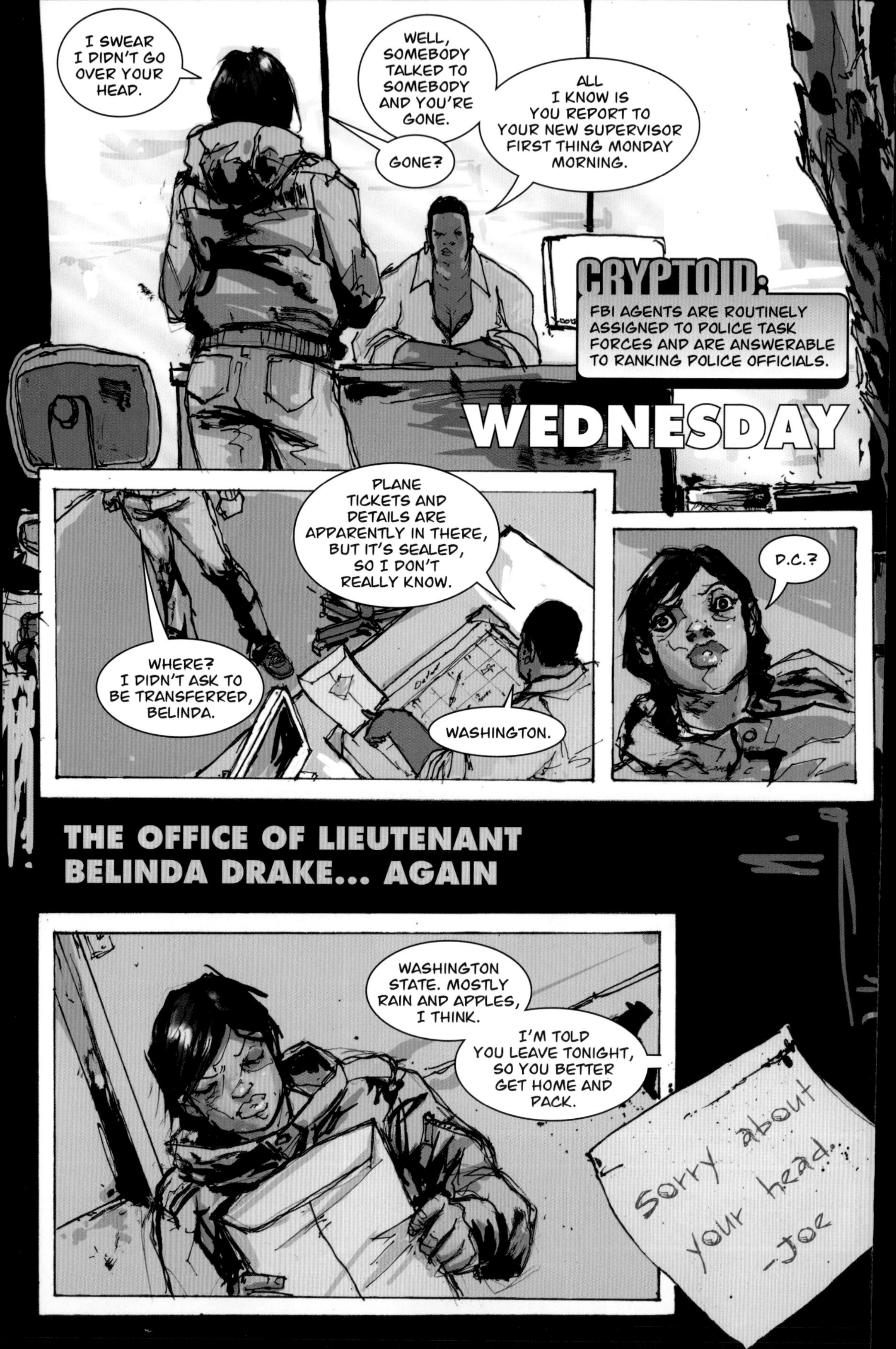
I SWEAR I DIDN'T GO OVER YOUR HEAD.
WELL, SOMEBODY TALKED TO SOMEBODY AND YOU'RE GONE.
GONE?
ALL I KNOW IS YOU REPORT TO YOUR NEW SUPERVISOR FIRST THING MONDAY MORNING.
CRYPTOID:
FBI AGENTS ARE ROUTINELY ASSIGNED TO POLICE TASK FORCES AND ARE ANSWERABLE TO RANKING POLICE OFFICIALS.
WEDNESDAY
PLANE TICKETS AND DETAILS ARE APPARENTLY IN THERE, BUT IT'S SEALED, SO I DON'T REALLY KNOW.
WHERE? I DIDN'T ASK TO BE TRANSFERRED, BELINDA.
WASHINGTON.
D.C.?
THE OFFICE OF LIEUTENANT BELINDA DRAKE... AGAIN
WASHINGTON STATE. MOSTLY RAIN AND APPLES, I THINK.
I'M TOLD YOU LEAVE TONIGHT, SO YOU BETTER GET HOME AND PACK.
Sorry about your head. -Joe

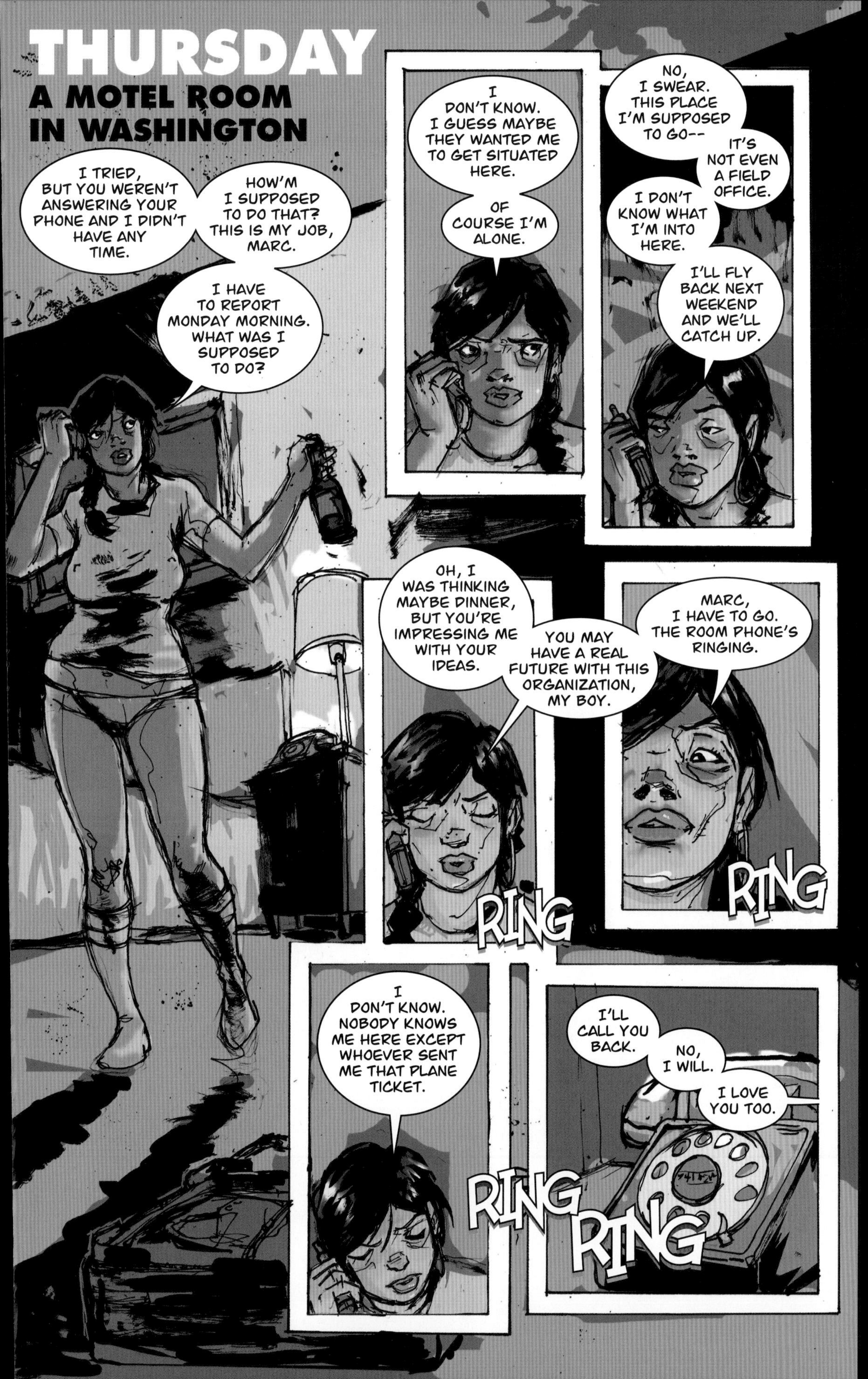
THURSDAY
A MOTEL ROOM IN WASHINGTON
I TRIED, BUT YOU WEREN'T ANSWERING YOUR PHONE AND I DIDN'T HAVE ANY TIME.
HOW'M I SUPPOSED TO DO THAT? THIS IS MY JOB, MARC.
I HAVE TO REPORT MONDAY MORNING. WHAT WAS I SUPPOSED TO DO?
I DON'T KNOW. I GUESS MAYBE THEY WANTED ME TO GET SITUATED HERE.
OF COURSE I'M ALONE.
NO, I SWEAR. THIS PLACE I'M SUPPOSED TO GO--
IT'S NOT EVEN A FIELD OFFICE.
I DON'T KNOW WHAT I'M INTO HERE.
I'LL FLY BACK NEXT WEEKEND AND WE'LL CATCH UP.
OH, I WAS THINKING MAYBE DINNER, BUT YOU'RE IMPRESSING ME WITH YOUR IDEAS.
YOU MAY HAVE A REAL FUTURE WITH THIS ORGANIZATION, MY BOY.
MARC, I HAVE TO GO. THE ROOM PHONE'S RINGING.
RING
RING
I DON'T KNOW. NOBODY KNOWS ME HERE EXCEPT WHOEVER SENT ME THAT PLANE TICKET.
I'LL CALL YOU BACK.
NO, I WILL.
I LOVE YOU TOO.
RING
RING

FRIDAY
THE LODGE

WELCOME TO THE LODGE, AGENT BROWN.

MY NAME IS LEANDER WIGHT.

THE LODGE?

ALL WILL BE REVEALED. WE'RE RUNNING LATE, THOUGH, SO PLEASE BE PATIENT.

I'M AFRAID I'LL HAVE TO ASK YOU FOR THE BULLETS FROM YOUR WEAPON.

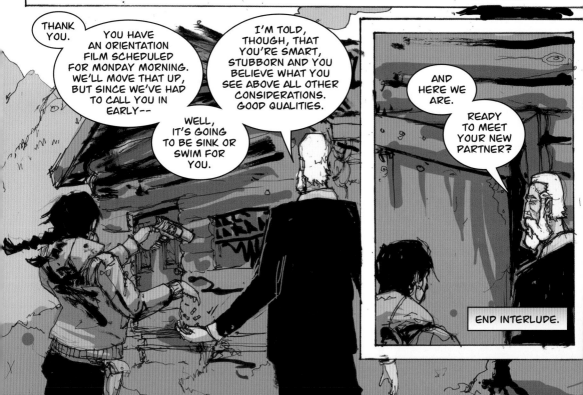

THANK YOU.

YOU HAVE AN ORIENTATION FILM SCHEDULED FOR MONDAY MORNING. WE'LL MOVE THAT UP, BUT SINCE WE'VE HAD TO CALL YOU IN EARLY--

I'M TOLD, THOUGH, THAT YOU'RE SMART, STUBBORN AND YOU BELIEVE WHAT YOU SEE ABOVE ALL OTHER CONSIDERATIONS. GOOD QUALITIES.

WELL, IT'S GOING TO BE SINK OR SWIM FOR YOU.

AND HERE WE ARE.

READY TO MEET YOUR NEW PARTNER?

END INTERLUDE.

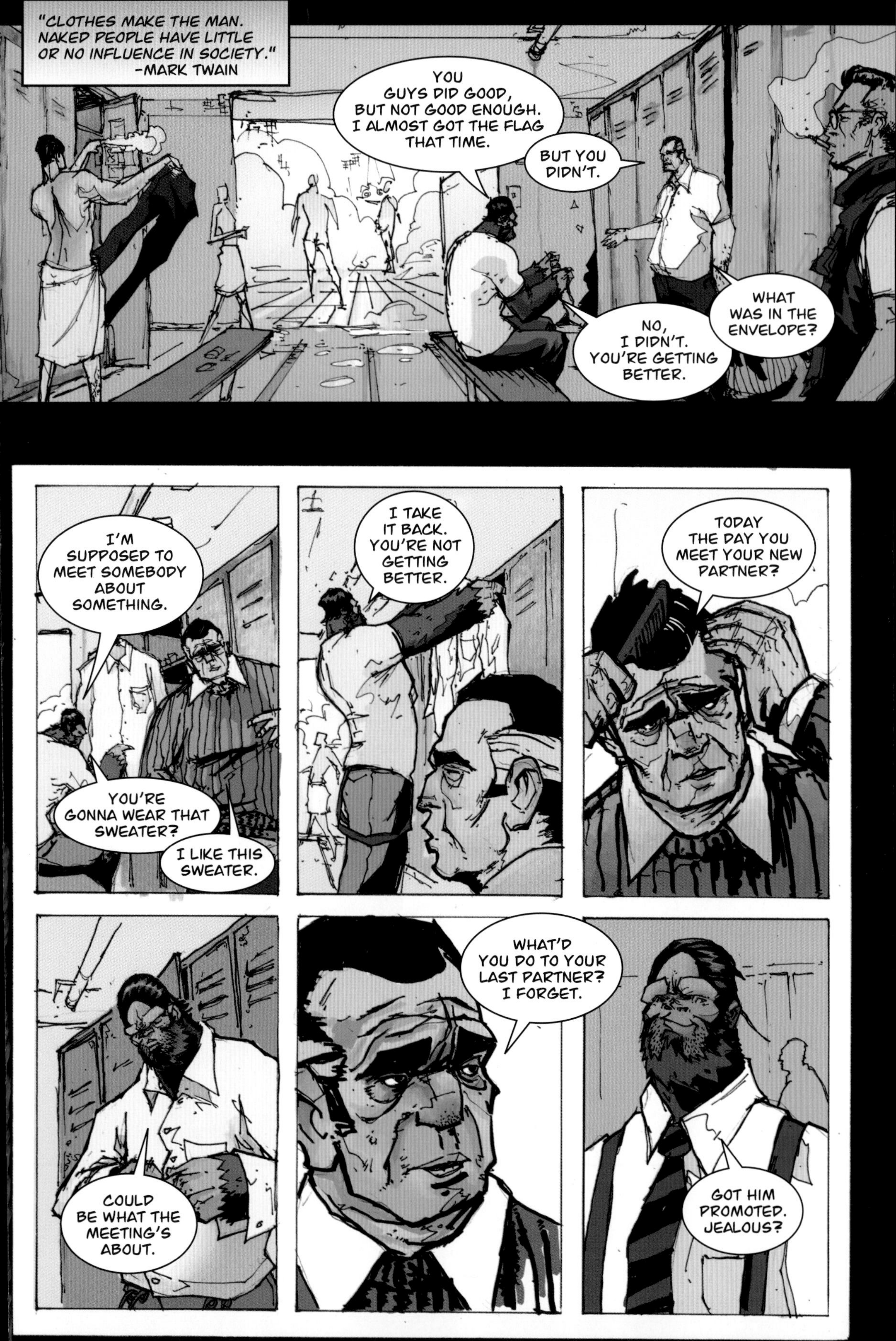
"CLOTHES MAKE THE MAN. NAKED PEOPLE HAVE LITTLE OR NO INFLUENCE IN SOCIETY." -MARK TWAIN
YOU GUYS DID GOOD, BUT NOT GOOD ENOUGH. I ALMOST GOT THE FLAG THAT TIME.
BUT YOU DIDN'T.
NO, I DIDN'T. YOU'RE GETTING BETTER.
WHAT WAS IN THE ENVELOPE?
I'M SUPPOSED TO MEET SOMEBODY ABOUT SOMETHING.
YOU'RE GONNA WEAR THAT SWEATER?
I LIKE THIS SWEATER.
I TAKE IT BACK. YOU'RE NOT GETTING BETTER.
TODAY THE DAY YOU MEET YOUR NEW PARTNER?
COULD BE WHAT THE MEETING'S ABOUT.
WHAT'D YOU DO TO YOUR LAST PARTNER? I FORGET.
GOT HIM PROMOTED. JEALOUS?

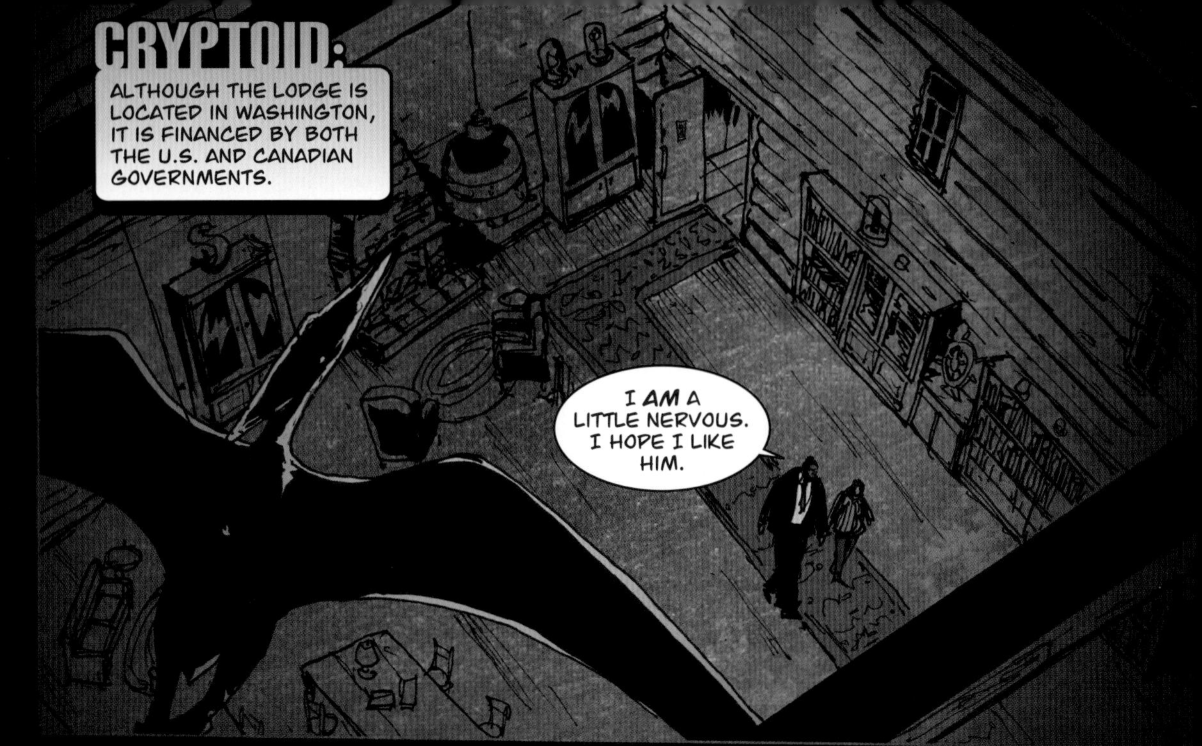
CRYPTOID:
ALTHOUGH THE LODGE IS LOCATED IN WASHINGTON, IT IS FINANCED BY BOTH THE U.S. AND CANADIAN GOVERNMENTS.
I *AM* A LITTLE NERVOUS. I HOPE I LIKE HIM.

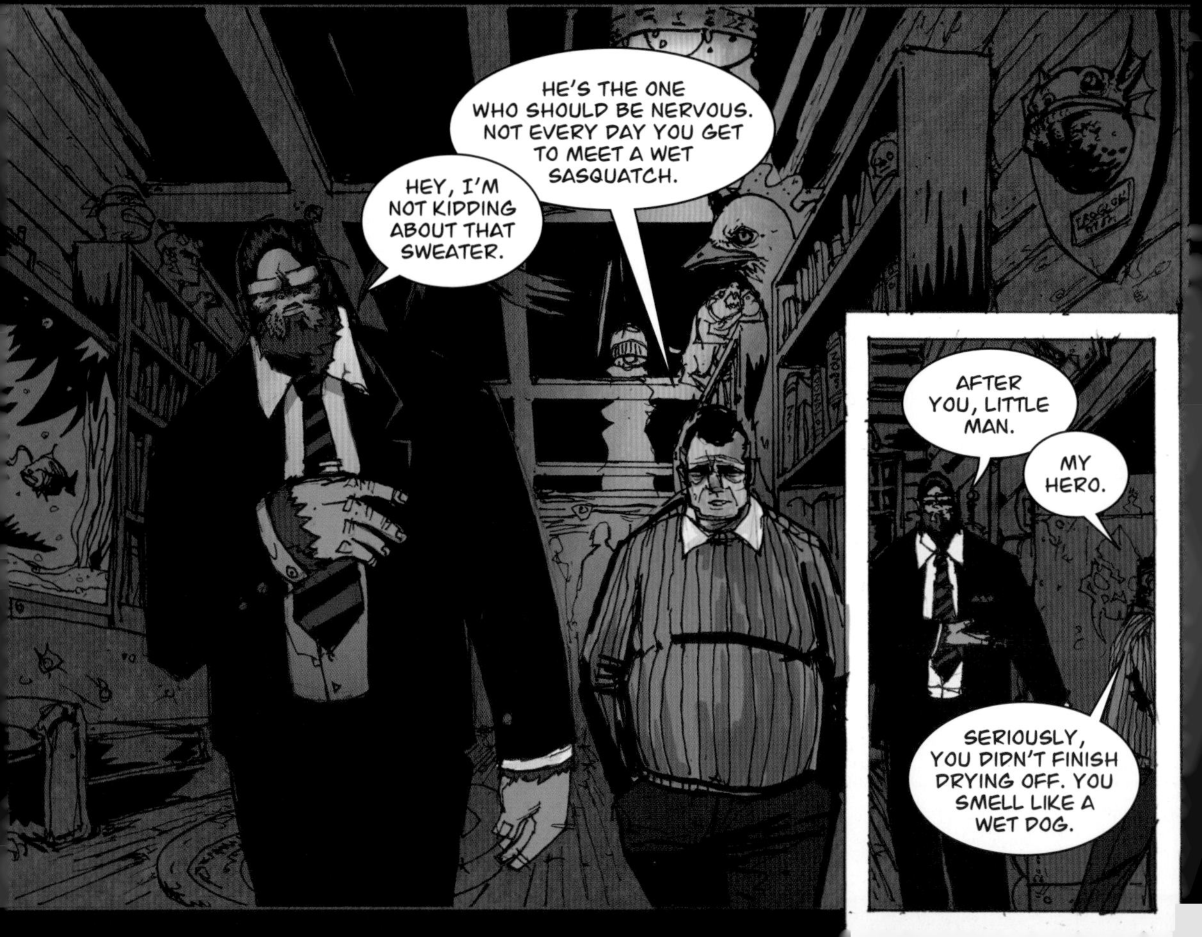
HE'S THE ONE WHO SHOULD BE NERVOUS. NOT EVERY DAY YOU GET TO MEET A WET SASQUATCH.
HEY, I'M NOT KIDDING ABOUT THAT SWEATER.
AFTER YOU, LITTLE MAN.
MY HERO.
SERIOUSLY, YOU DIDN'T FINISH DRYING OFF. YOU SMELL LIKE A WET DOG.

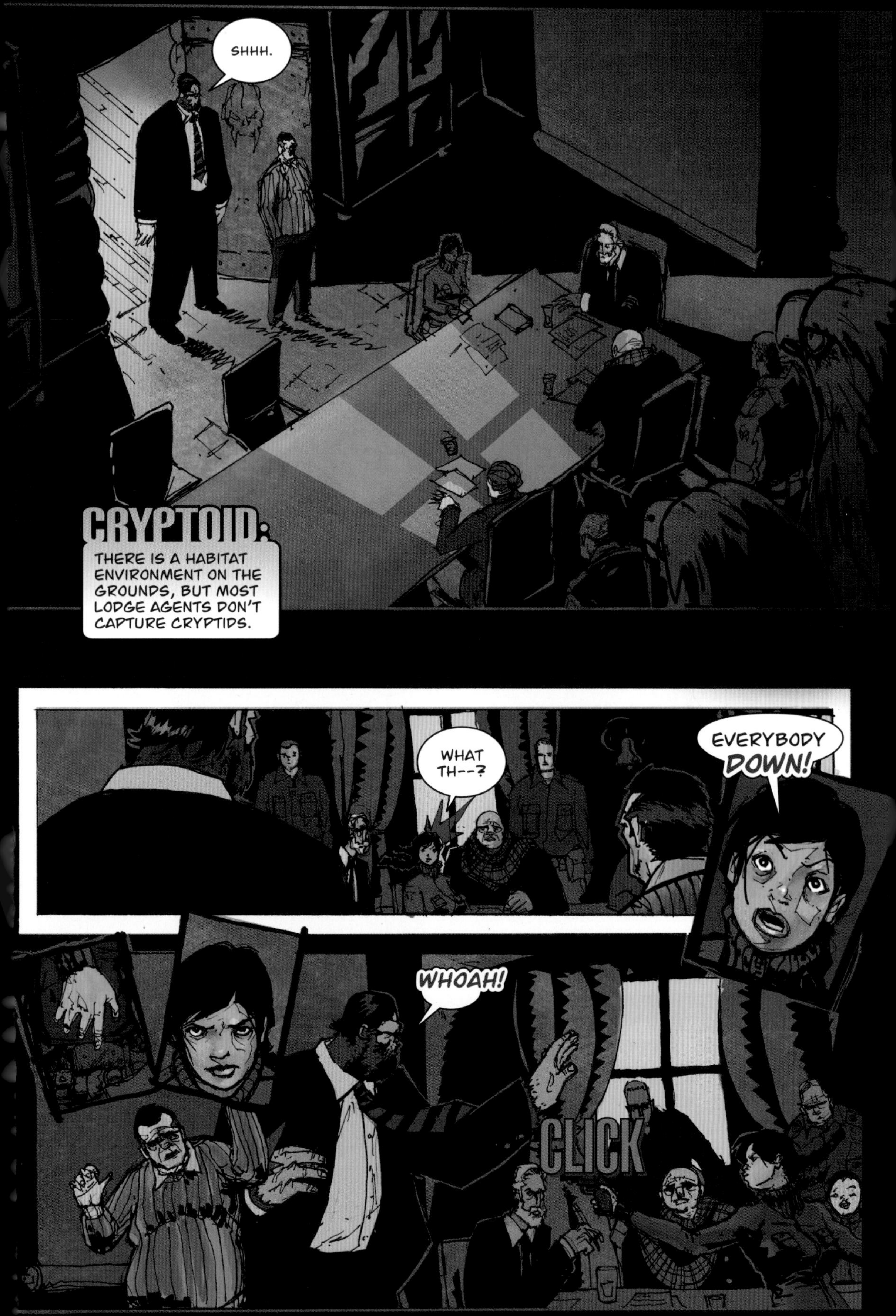
SHHH.
CRYPTOID:
THERE IS A HABITAT ENVIRONMENT ON THE GROUNDS, BUT MOST LODGE AGENTS DON'T CAPTURE CRYPTIDS.
WHAT TH--?
EVERYBODY DOWN!
WHOAH!
CLICK

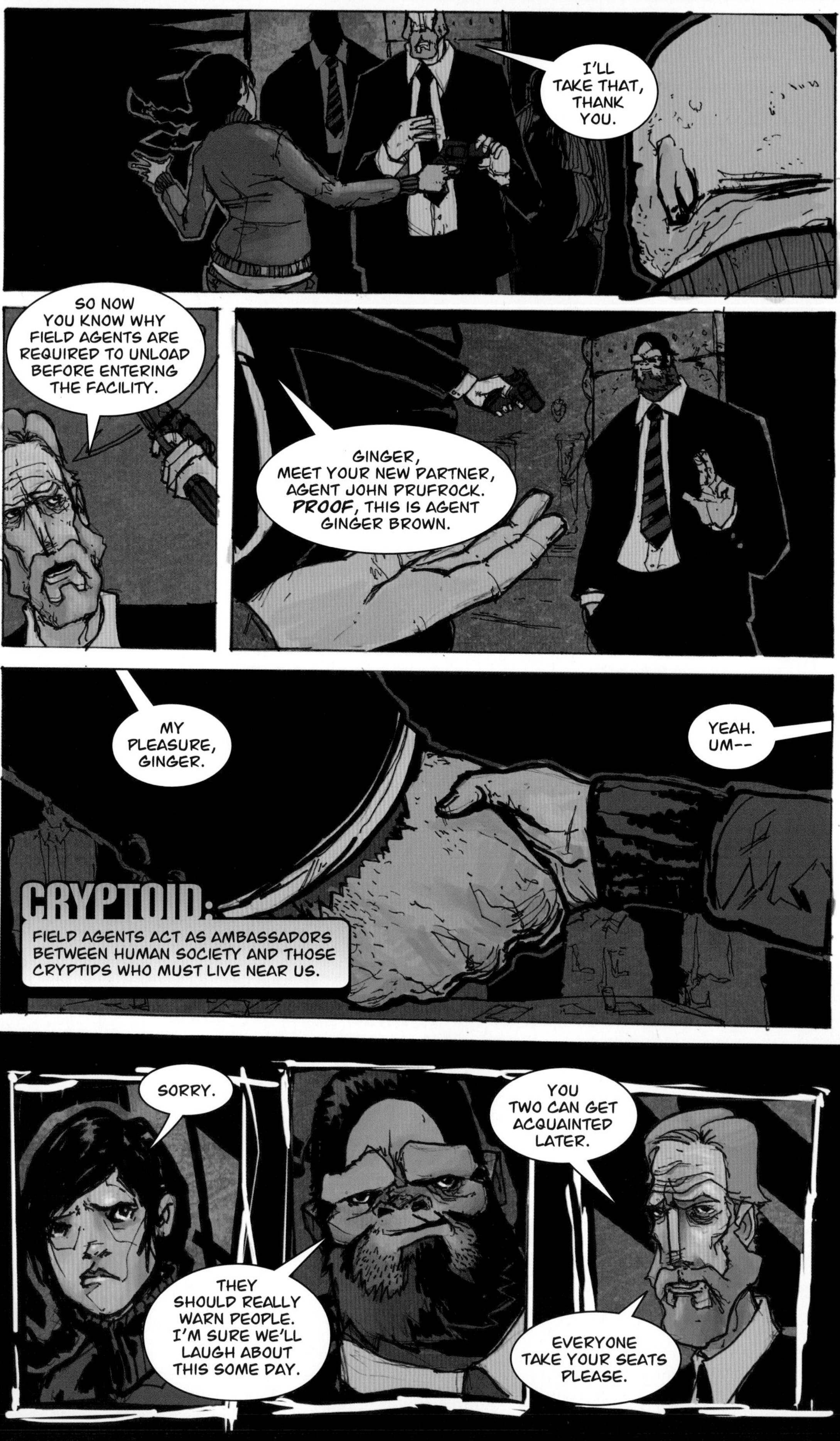
I'LL TAKE THAT, THANK YOU.
SO NOW YOU KNOW WHY FIELD AGENTS ARE REQUIRED TO UNLOAD BEFORE ENTERING THE FACILITY.
GINGER, MEET YOUR NEW PARTNER, AGENT JOHN PRUFROCK. PROOF, THIS IS AGENT GINGER BROWN.
MY PLEASURE, GINGER.
YEAH. UM--
CRYPTOID:
FIELD AGENTS ACT AS AMBASSADORS BETWEEN HUMAN SOCIETY AND THOSE CRYPTIDS WHO MUST LIVE NEAR US.
SORRY.
THEY SHOULD REALLY WARN PEOPLE. I'M SURE WE'LL LAUGH ABOUT THIS SOME DAY.
YOU TWO CAN GET ACQUAINTED LATER.
EVERYONE TAKE YOUR SEATS PLEASE.

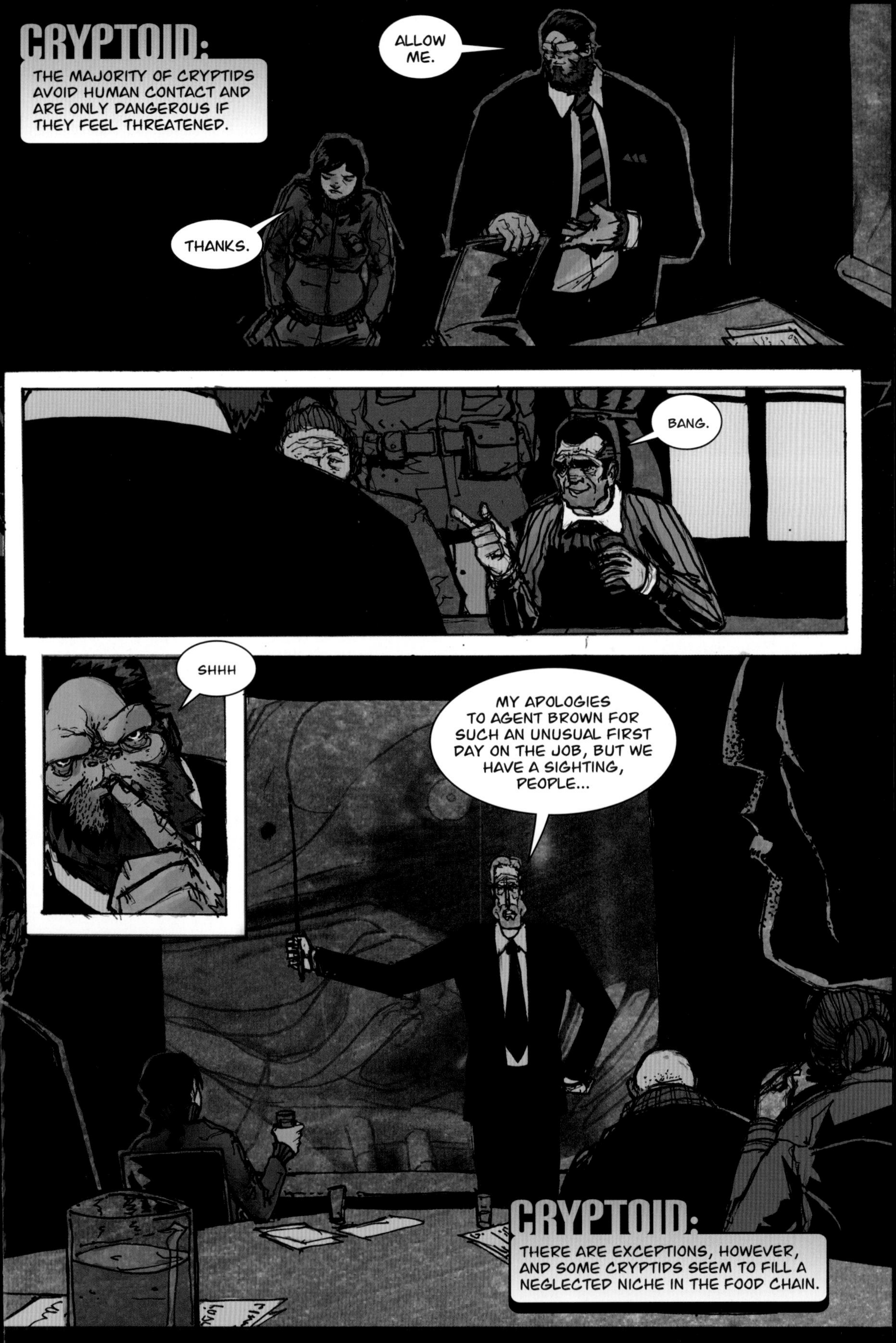
CRYPTOID:
THE MAJORITY OF CRYPTIDS AVOID HUMAN CONTACT AND ARE ONLY DANGEROUS IF THEY FEEL THREATENED.
ALLOW ME.
THANKS.
BANG.
SHHH
MY APOLOGIES TO AGENT BROWN FOR SUCH AN UNUSUAL FIRST DAY ON THE JOB, BUT WE HAVE A SIGHTING, PEOPLE...
CRYPTOID:
THERE ARE EXCEPTIONS, HOWEVER, AND SOME CRYPTIDS SEEM TO FILL A NEGLECTED NICHE IN THE FOOD CHAIN.

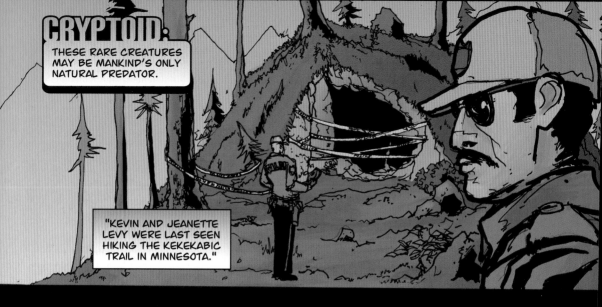

CRYPTOID:

THESE RARE CREATURES MAY BE MANKIND'S ONLY NATURAL PREDATOR.

"KEVIN AND JEANETTE LEVY WERE LAST SEEN HIKING THE KEKEKABIC TRAIL IN MINNESOTA."

"THEY SPLIT OFF FROM THEIR GROUP WITH THE APPARENT INTENTION OF PHOTOGRAPHING THE LOCAL FAUNA."

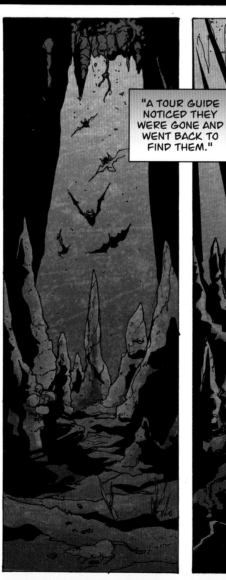

"A TOUR GUIDE NOTICED THEY WERE GONE AND WENT BACK TO FIND THEM."

HMMM ♪
♪ HMM
HMMM ♪

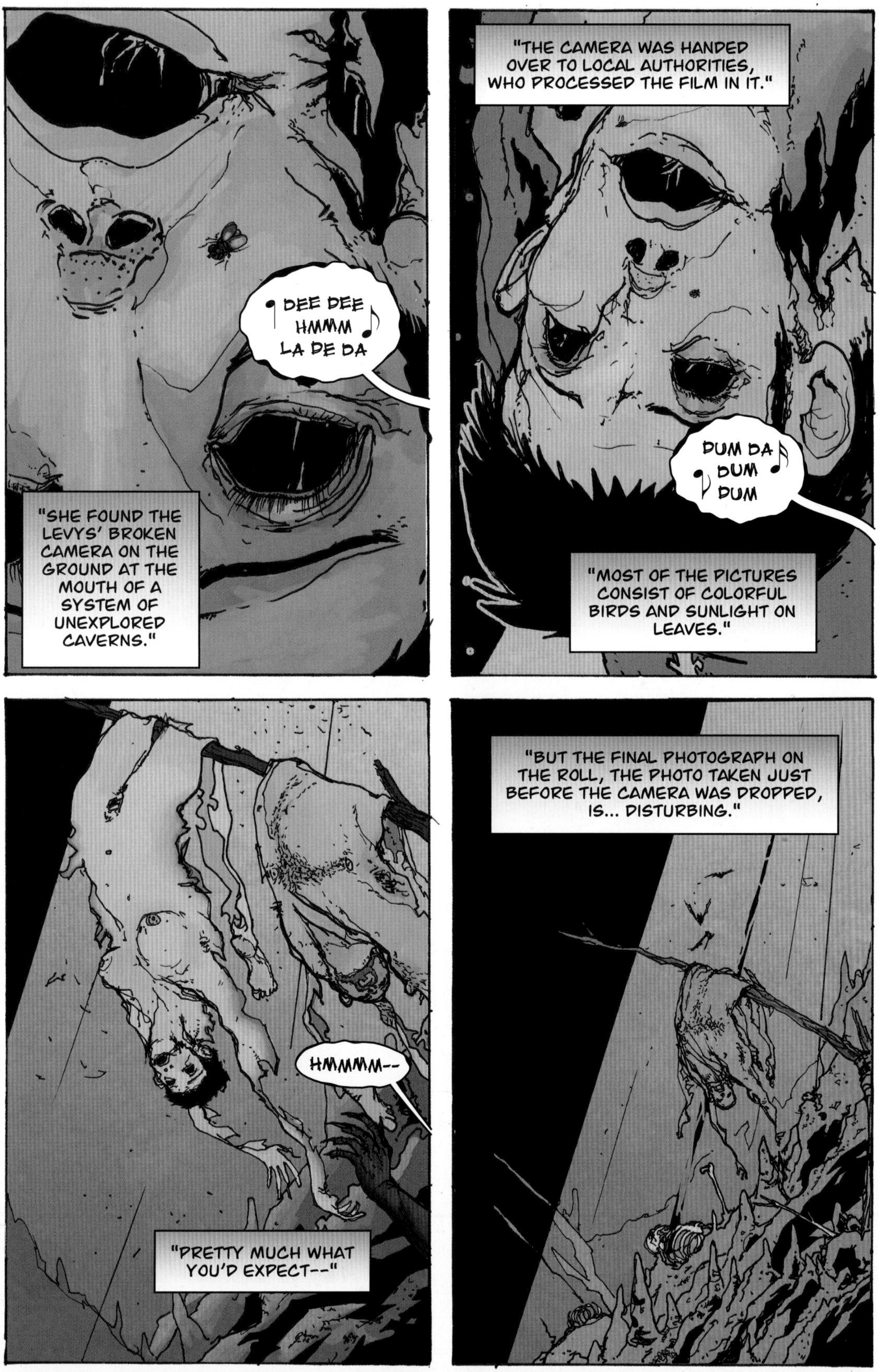
DEE DEE HMMM LA DE DA
"SHE FOUND THE LEVYS' BROKEN CAMERA ON THE GROUND AT THE MOUTH OF A SYSTEM OF UNEXPLORED CAVERNS."
"THE CAMERA WAS HANDED OVER TO LOCAL AUTHORITIES, WHO PROCESSED THE FILM IN IT."
DUM DA DUM DUM
"MOST OF THE PICTURES CONSIST OF COLORFUL BIRDS AND SUNLIGHT ON LEAVES."
HMMMM--
"PRETTY MUCH WHAT YOU'D EXPECT--"
"BUT THE FINAL PHOTOGRAPH ON THE ROLL, THE PHOTO TAKEN JUST BEFORE THE CAMERA WAS DROPPED, IS... DISTURBING."

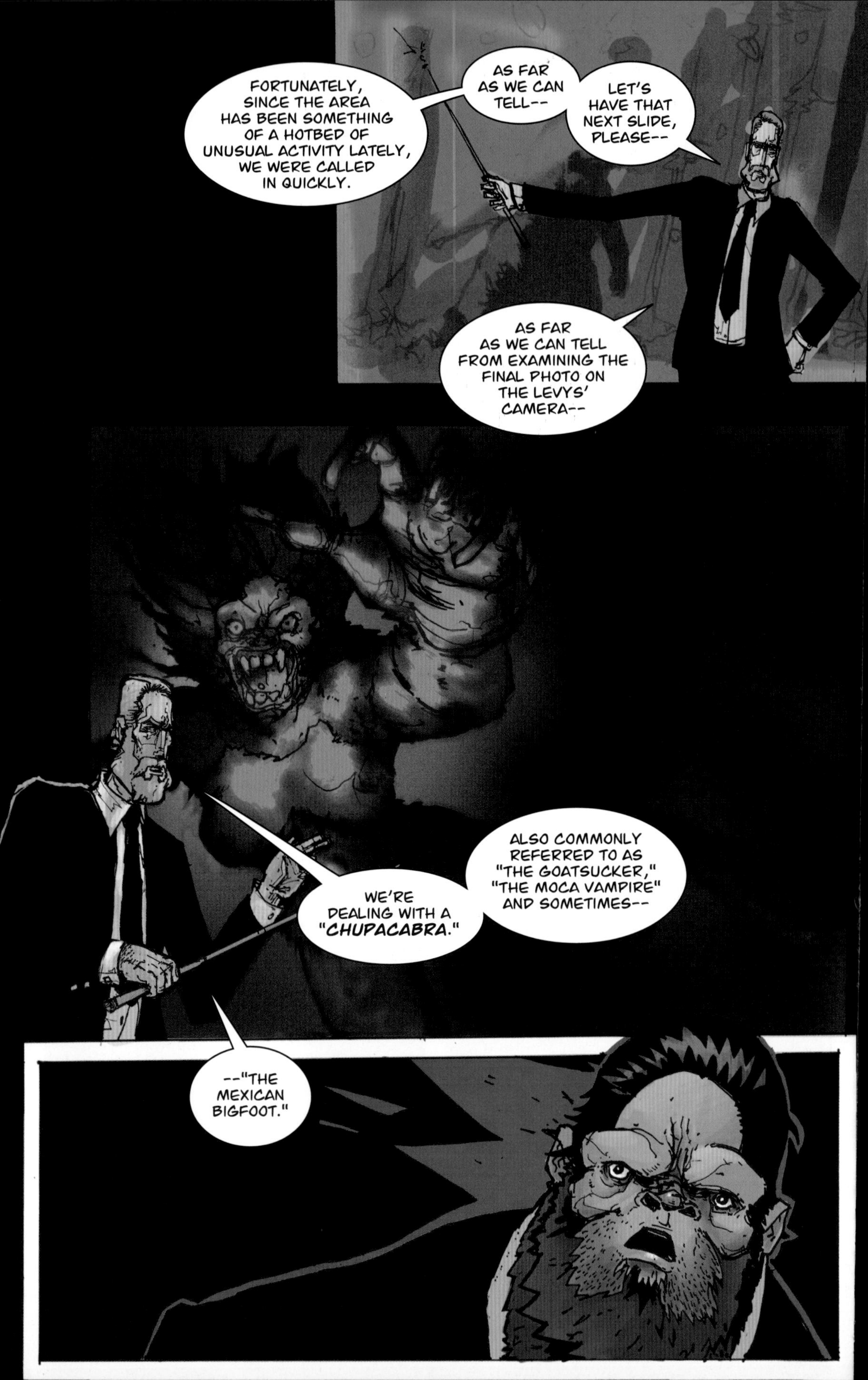
FORTUNATELY, SINCE THE AREA HAS BEEN SOMETHING OF A HOTBED OF UNUSUAL ACTIVITY LATELY, WE WERE CALLED IN QUICKLY.
AS FAR AS WE CAN TELL--
LET'S HAVE THAT NEXT SLIDE, PLEASE--
AS FAR AS WE CAN TELL FROM EXAMINING THE FINAL PHOTO ON THE LEVYS' CAMERA--
WE'RE DEALING WITH A "**CHUPACABRA**."
ALSO COMMONLY REFERRED TO AS "THE GOATSUCKER," "THE MOCA VAMPIRE" AND SOMETIMES--
--"THE MEXICAN BIGFOOT."

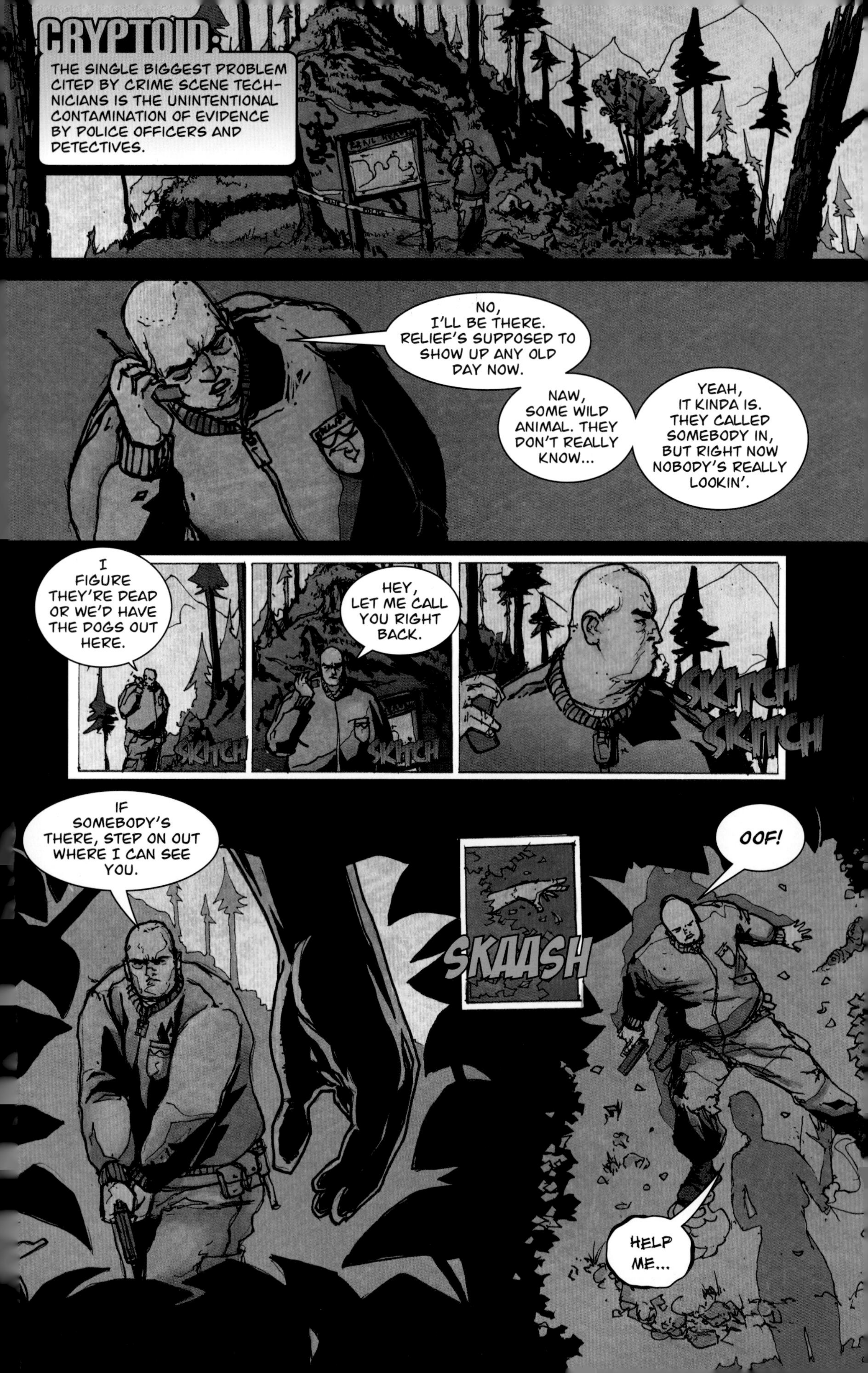
CRYPTOID:
THE SINGLE BIGGEST PROBLEM CITED BY CRIME SCENE TECHNICIANS IS THE UNINTENTIONAL CONTAMINATION OF EVIDENCE BY POLICE OFFICERS AND DETECTIVES.
NO, I'LL BE THERE. RELIEF'S SUPPOSED TO SHOW UP ANY OLD DAY NOW.
NAW, SOME WILD ANIMAL. THEY DON'T REALLY KNOW...
YEAH, IT KINDA IS. THEY CALLED SOMEBODY IN, BUT RIGHT NOW NOBODY'S REALLY LOOKIN'.
I FIGURE THEY'RE DEAD OR WE'D HAVE THE DOGS OUT HERE.
SKITCH
HEY, LET ME CALL YOU RIGHT BACK.
SKITCH
SKITCH SKITCH
IF SOMEBODY'S THERE, STEP ON OUT WHERE I CAN SEE YOU.
SKAASH
OOF!
HELP ME...

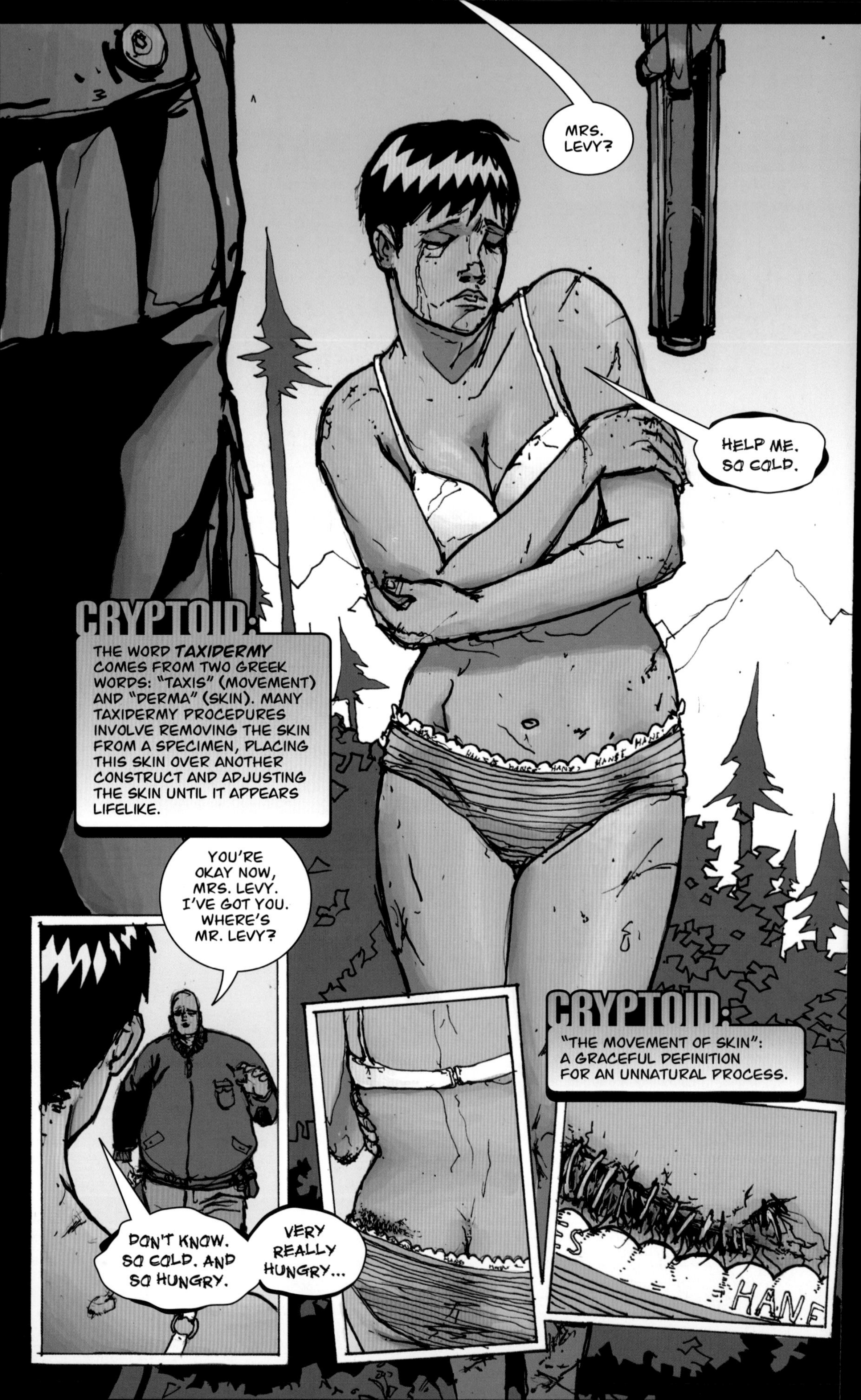
MRS. LEVY?
HELP ME. SO COLD.
CRYPTOID:
THE WORD TAXIDERMY COMES FROM TWO GREEK WORDS: "TAXIS" (MOVEMENT) AND "DERMA" (SKIN). MANY TAXIDERMY PROCEDURES INVOLVE REMOVING THE SKIN FROM A SPECIMEN, PLACING THIS SKIN OVER ANOTHER CONSTRUCT AND ADJUSTING THE SKIN UNTIL IT APPEARS LIFELIKE.
YOU'RE OKAY NOW, MRS. LEVY. I'VE GOT YOU. WHERE'S MR. LEVY?
DON'T KNOW. SO COLD. AND SO HUNGRY.
VERY REALLY HUNGRY...
CRYPTOID:
"THE MOVEMENT OF SKIN": A GRACEFUL DEFINITION FOR AN UNNATURAL PROCESS.

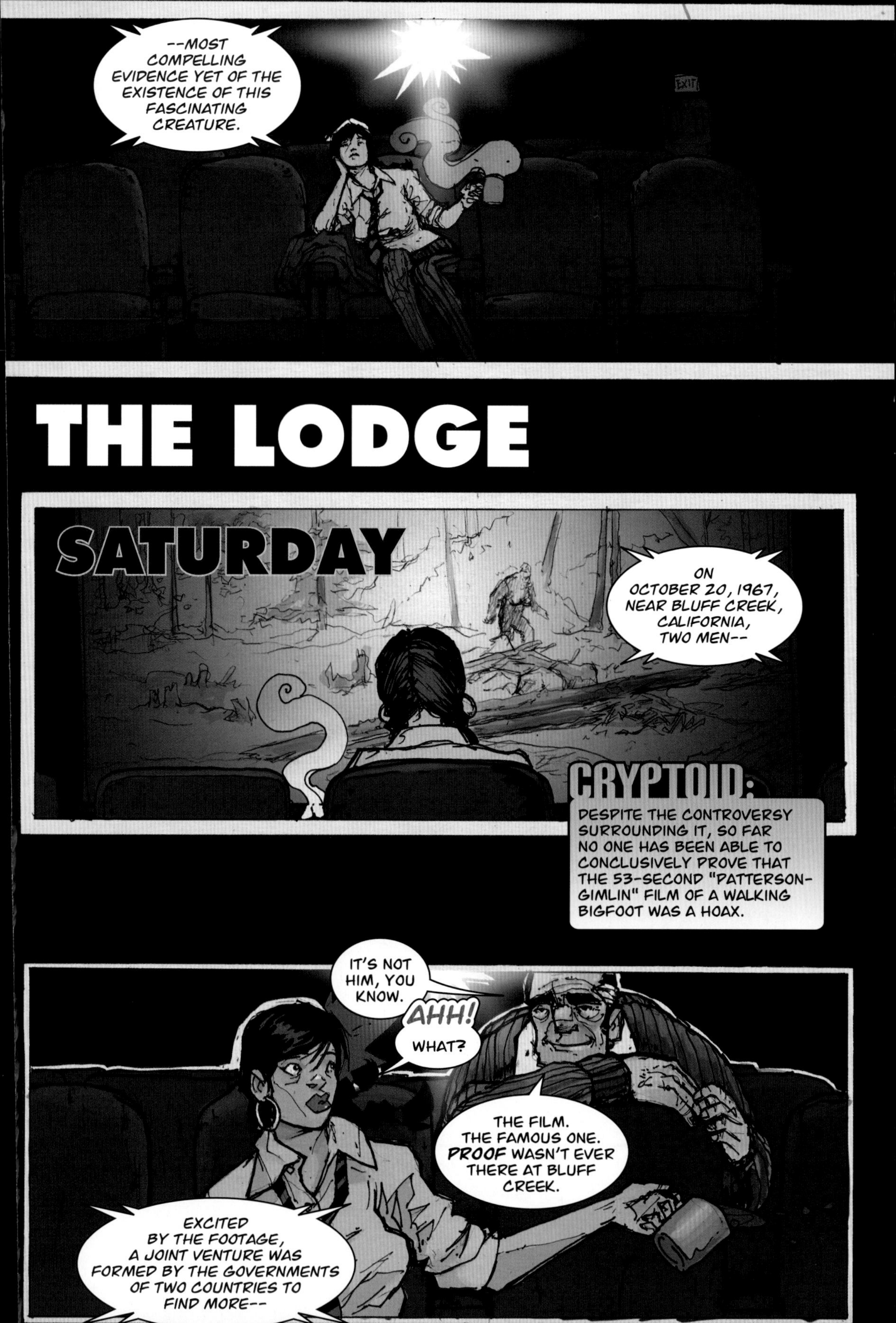

--MOST COMPELLING EVIDENCE YET OF THE EXISTENCE OF THIS FASCINATING CREATURE.
EXIT
THE LODGE
SATURDAY
ON OCTOBER 20, 1967, NEAR BLUFF CREEK, CALIFORNIA, TWO MEN--
CRYPTOID:
DESPITE THE CONTROVERSY SURROUNDING IT, SO FAR NO ONE HAS BEEN ABLE TO CONCLUSIVELY PROVE THAT THE 53-SECOND "PATTERSON-GIMLIN" FILM OF A WALKING BIGFOOT WAS A HOAX.
IT'S NOT HIM, YOU KNOW.
AHH!
WHAT?
THE FILM. THE FAMOUS ONE. PROOF WASN'T EVER THERE AT BLUFF CREEK.
EXCITED BY THE FOOTAGE, A JOINT VENTURE WAS FORMED BY THE GOVERNMENTS OF TWO COUNTRIES TO FIND MORE--

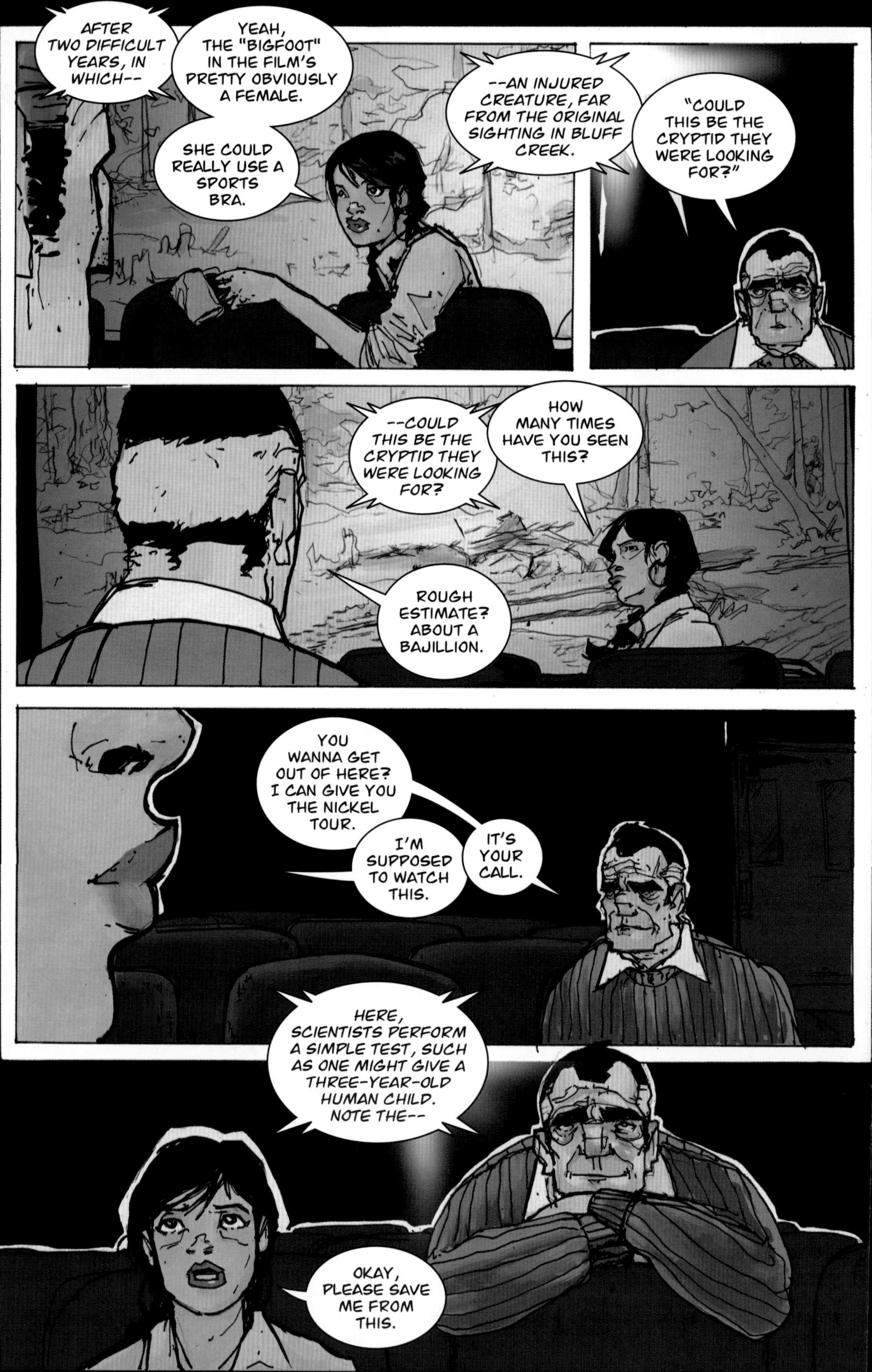
AFTER TWO DIFFICULT YEARS, IN WHICH--
YEAH, THE "BIGFOOT" IN THE FILM'S PRETTY OBVIOUSLY A FEMALE.
SHE COULD REALLY USE A SPORTS BRA.
--AN INJURED CREATURE, FAR FROM THE ORIGINAL SIGHTING IN BLUFF CREEK.
"COULD THIS BE THE CRYPTID THEY WERE LOOKING FOR?"
--COULD THIS BE THE CRYPTID THEY WERE LOOKING FOR?
HOW MANY TIMES HAVE YOU SEEN THIS?
ROUGH ESTIMATE? ABOUT A BAJILLION.
YOU WANNA GET OUT OF HERE? I CAN GIVE YOU THE NICKEL TOUR.
I'M SUPPOSED TO WATCH THIS.
IT'S YOUR CALL.
HERE, SCIENTISTS PERFORM A SIMPLE TEST, SUCH AS ONE MIGHT GIVE A THREE-YEAR-OLD HUMAN CHILD. NOTE THE--
OKAY, PLEASE SAVE ME FROM THIS.

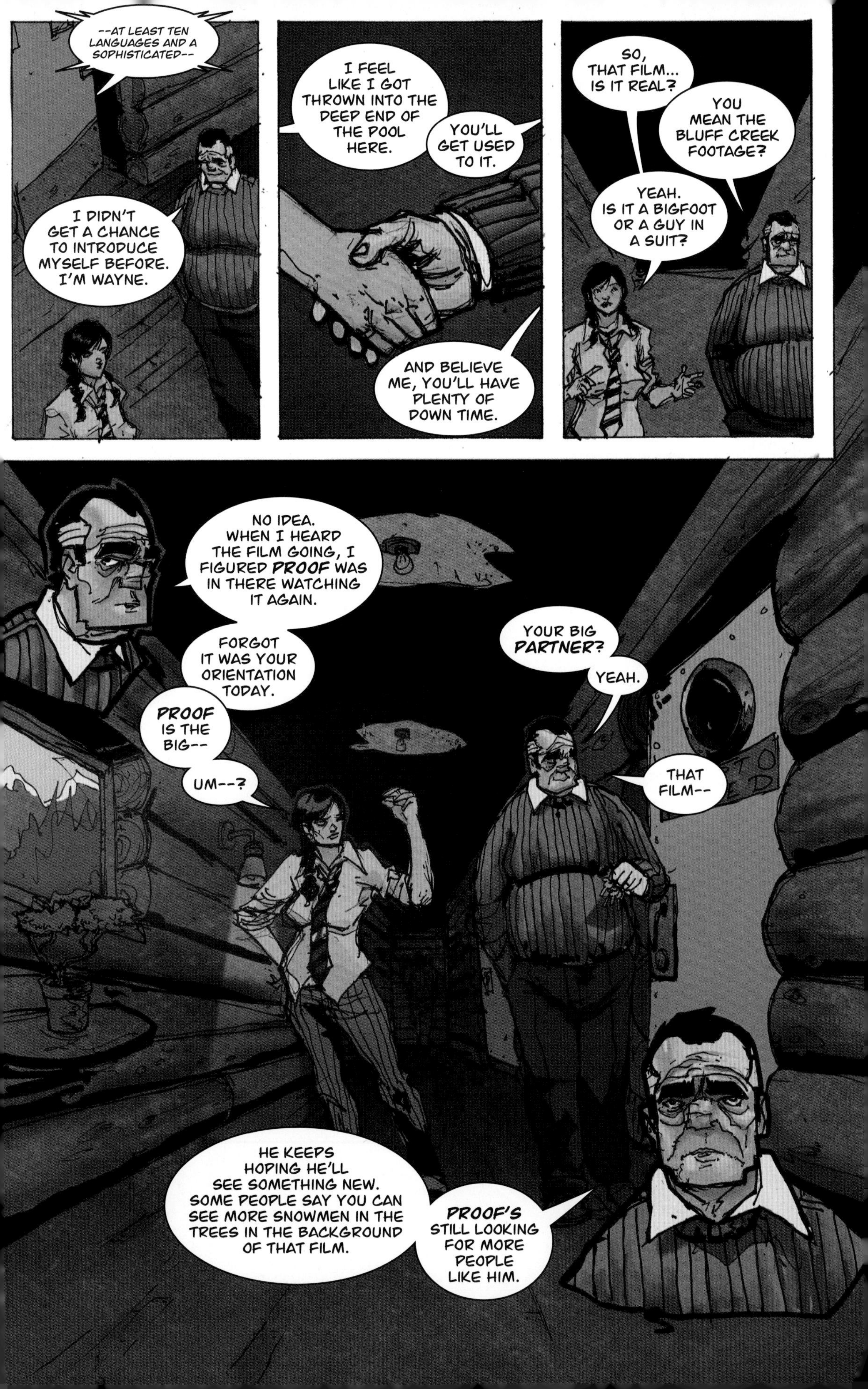
--AT LEAST TEN LANGUAGES AND A SOPHISTICATED--
I DIDN'T GET A CHANCE TO INTRODUCE MYSELF BEFORE. I'M WAYNE.
I FEEL LIKE I GOT THROWN INTO THE DEEP END OF THE POOL HERE.
YOU'LL GET USED TO IT.
AND BELIEVE ME, YOU'LL HAVE PLENTY OF DOWN TIME.
SO, THAT FILM... IS IT REAL?
YOU MEAN THE BLUFF CREEK FOOTAGE?
YEAH. IS IT A BIGFOOT OR A GUY IN A SUIT?
NO IDEA. WHEN I HEARD THE FILM GOING, I FIGURED PROOF WAS IN THERE WATCHING IT AGAIN.
FORGOT IT WAS YOUR ORIENTATION TODAY.
PROOF IS THE BIG--
UM--?
YOUR BIG PARTNER?
YEAH.
THAT FILM--
HE KEEPS HOPING HE'LL SEE SOMETHING NEW. SOME PEOPLE SAY YOU CAN SEE MORE SNOWMEN IN THE TREES IN THE BACKGROUND OF THAT FILM.
PROOF'S STILL LOOKING FOR MORE PEOPLE LIKE HIM.

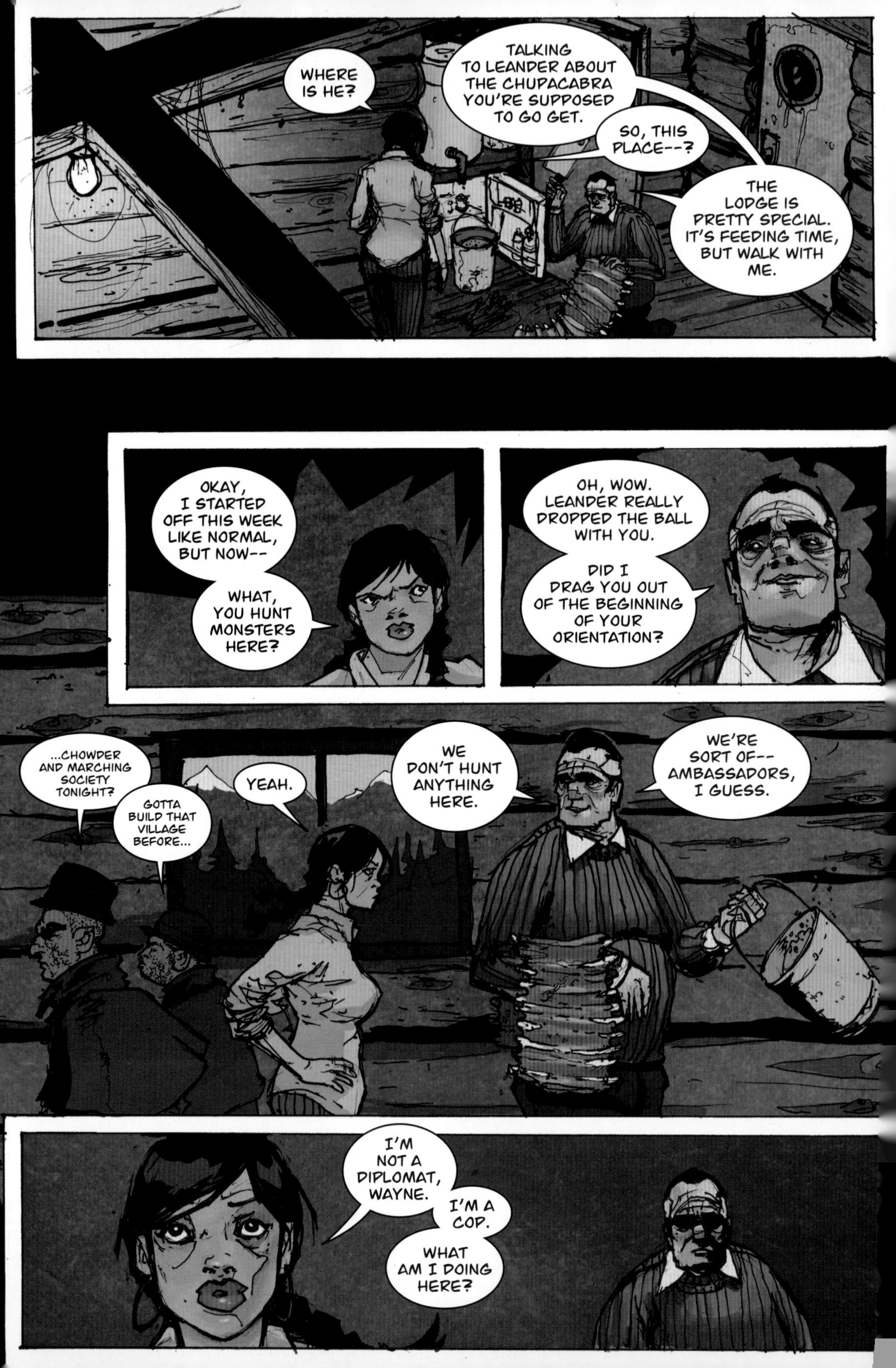
WHERE IS HE?
TALKING TO LEANDER ABOUT THE CHUPACABRA YOU'RE SUPPOSED TO GO GET.
SO, THIS PLACE--?
THE LODGE IS PRETTY SPECIAL. IT'S FEEDING TIME, BUT WALK WITH ME.
OKAY, I STARTED OFF THIS WEEK LIKE NORMAL, BUT NOW--
WHAT, YOU HUNT MONSTERS HERE?
OH, WOW. LEANDER REALLY DROPPED THE BALL WITH YOU.
DID I DRAG YOU OUT OF THE BEGINNING OF YOUR ORIENTATION?
...CHOWDER AND MARCHING SOCIETY TONIGHT?
GOTTA BUILD THAT VILLAGE BEFORE...
YEAH.
WE DON'T HUNT ANYTHING HERE.
WE'RE SORT OF-- AMBASSADORS, I GUESS.
I'M NOT A DIPLOMAT, WAYNE.
I'M A COP.
WHAT AM I DOING HERE?

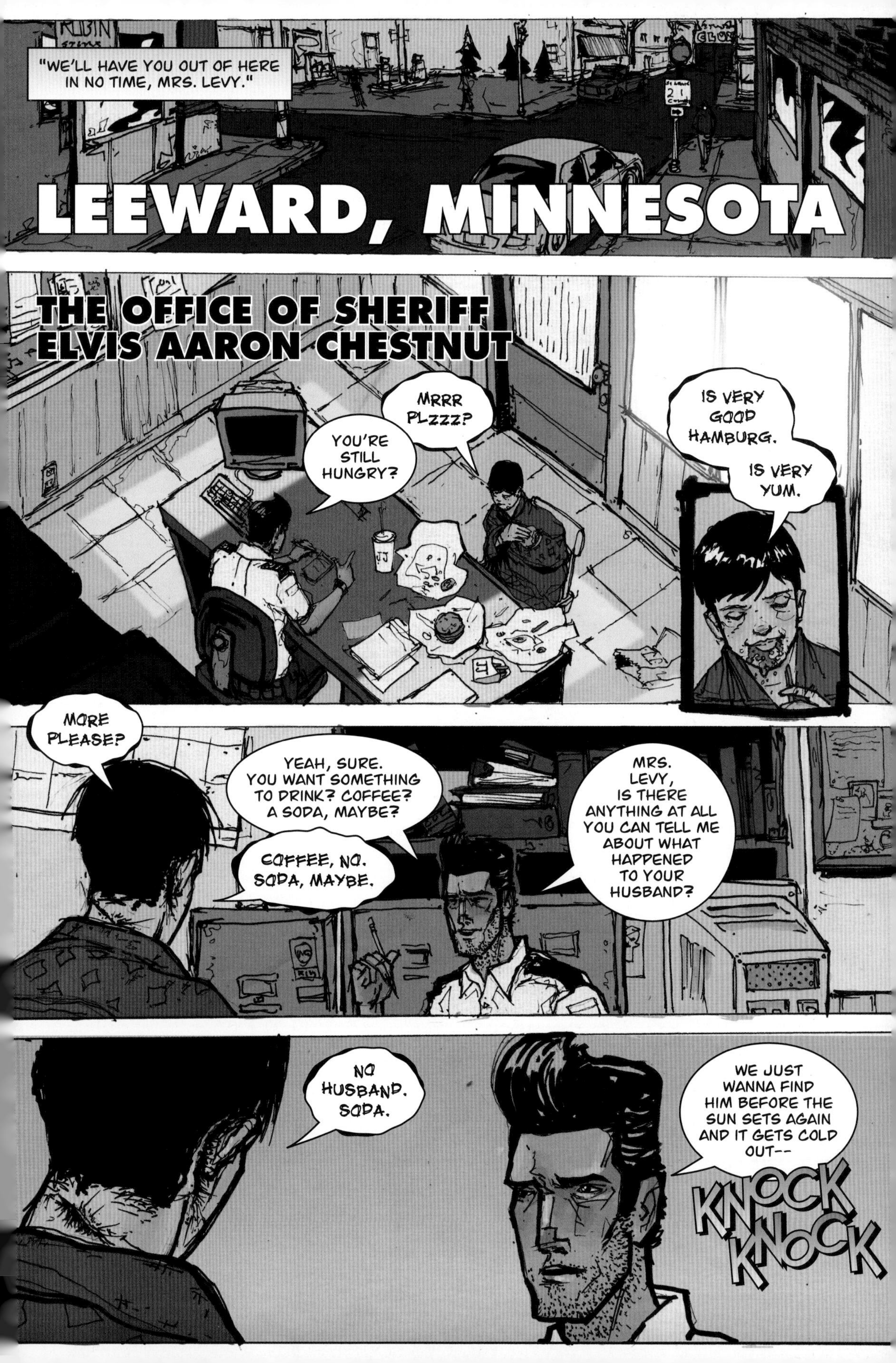
"WE'LL HAVE YOU OUT OF HERE IN NO TIME, MRS. LEVY."
LEEWARD, MINNESOTA
THE OFFICE OF SHERIFF ELVIS AARON CHESTNUT
YOU'RE STILL HUNGRY?
MRRR PLZZZ?
IS VERY GOOD HAMBURG.
IS VERY YUM.
MORE PLEASE?
YEAH, SURE. YOU WANT SOMETHING TO DRINK? COFFEE? A SODA, MAYBE?
COFFEE, NO. SODA, MAYBE.
MRS. LEVY, IS THERE ANYTHING AT ALL YOU CAN TELL ME ABOUT WHAT HAPPENED TO YOUR HUSBAND?
NO HUSBAND. SODA.
WE JUST WANNA FIND HIM BEFORE THE SUN SETS AGAIN AND IT GETS COLD OUT--
KNOCK KNOCK

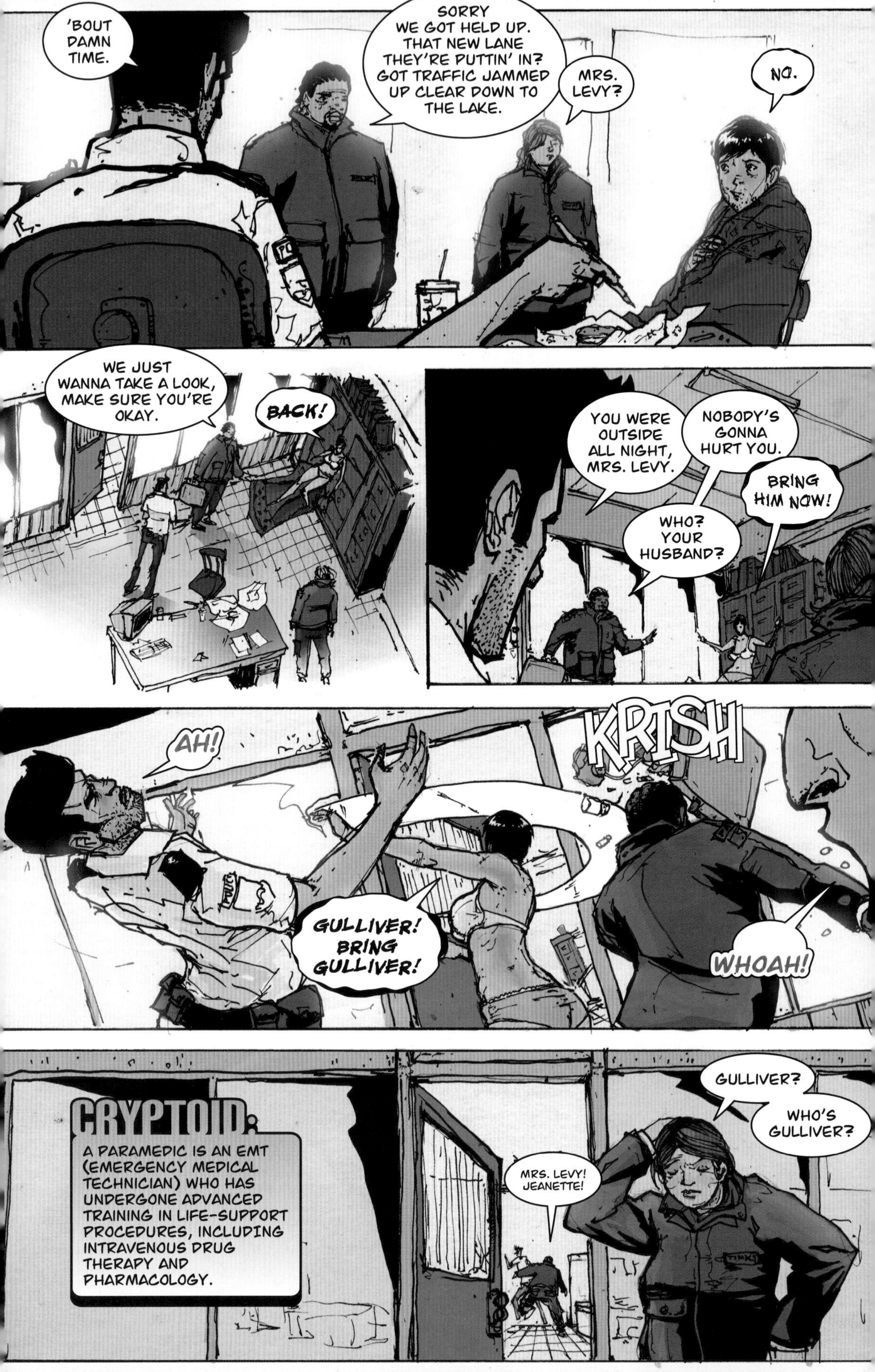
'BOUT DAMN TIME.
SORRY WE GOT HELD UP. THAT NEW LANE THEY'RE PUTTIN' IN? GOT TRAFFIC JAMMED UP CLEAR DOWN TO THE LAKE.
MRS. LEVY?
NO.
WE JUST WANNA TAKE A LOOK, MAKE SURE YOU'RE OKAY.
BACK!
YOU WERE OUTSIDE ALL NIGHT, MRS. LEVY.
NOBODY'S GONNA HURT YOU.
BRING HIM NOW!
WHO? YOUR HUSBAND?
AH!
KRISH
GULLIVER! BRING GULLIVER!
WHOAH!
CRYPTOID:
A PARAMEDIC IS AN EMT (EMERGENCY MEDICAL TECHNICIAN) WHO HAS UNDERGONE ADVANCED TRAINING IN LIFE-SUPPORT PROCEDURES, INCLUDING INTRAVENOUS DRUG THERAPY AND PHARMACOLOGY.
GULLIVER?
WHO'S GULLIVER?
MRS. LEVY! JEANETTE!

THE LODGE

THANKS.

WHAT IS THIS?

THIS IS MY HOME AWAY FROM WORK.

THE *GARDEN*. IT'S A HABITAT FOR SOME OF THEM.

"THEM" WHO?

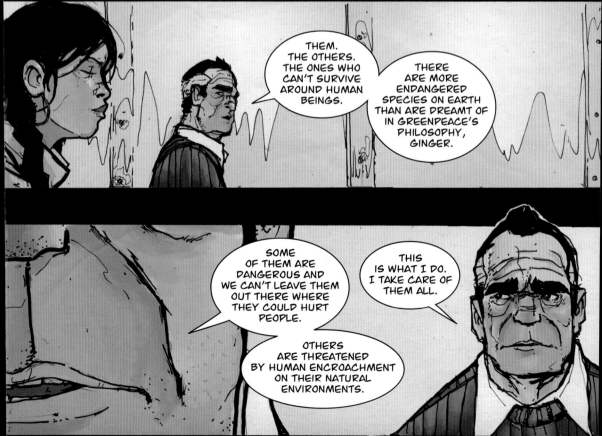

THEM. THE OTHERS. THE ONES WHO CAN'T SURVIVE AROUND HUMAN BEINGS.

THERE ARE MORE ENDANGERED SPECIES ON EARTH THAN ARE DREAMT OF IN GREENPEACE'S PHILOSOPHY, GINGER.

SOME OF THEM ARE DANGEROUS AND WE CAN'T LEAVE THEM OUT THERE WHERE THEY COULD HURT PEOPLE.

THIS IS WHAT I DO. I TAKE CARE OF THEM ALL.

OTHERS ARE THREATENED BY HUMAN ENCROACHMENT ON THEIR NATURAL ENVIRONMENTS.

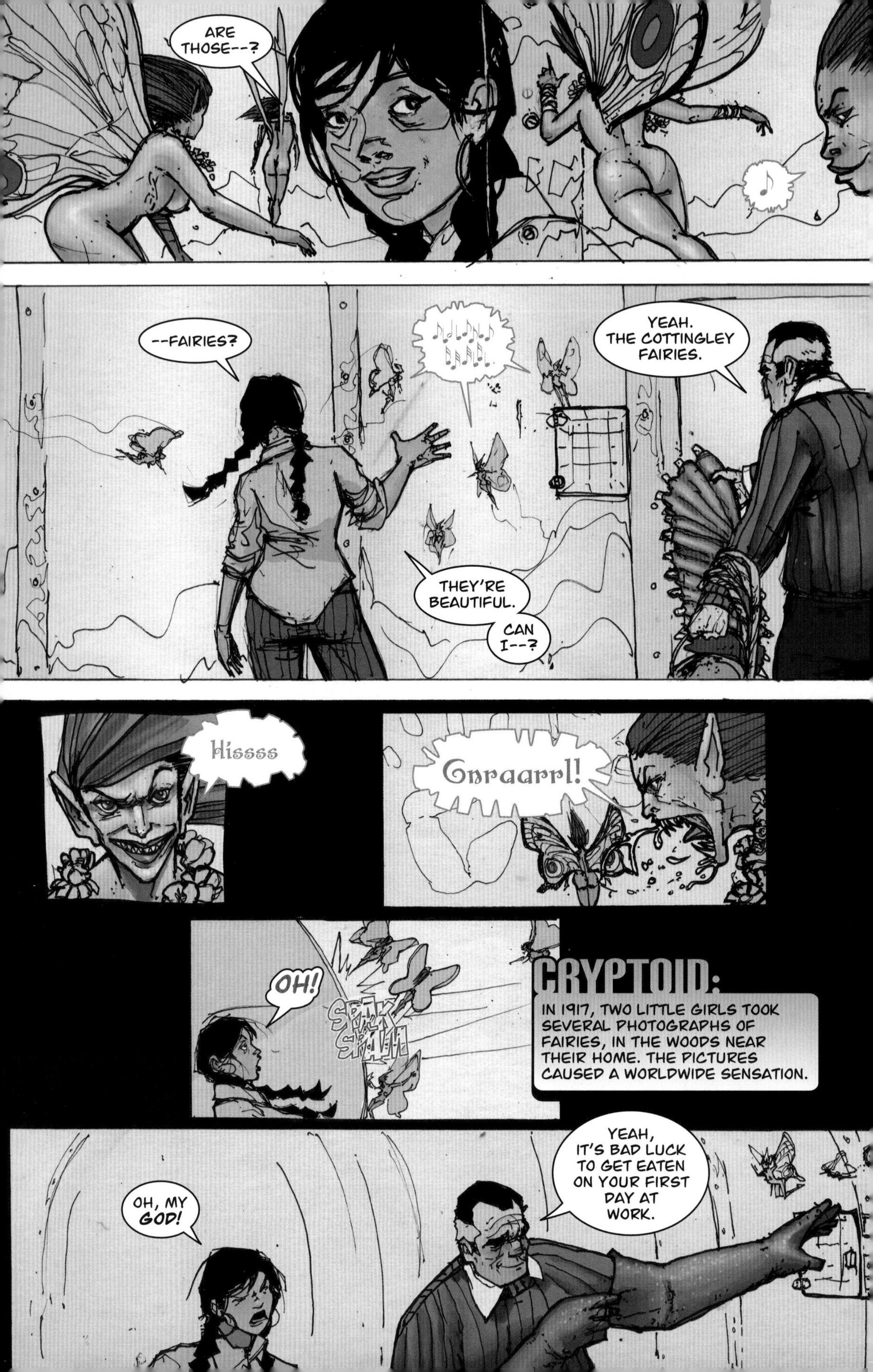
ARE THOSE--?
--FAIRIES?
YEAH. THE COTTINGLEY FAIRIES.
THEY'RE BEAUTIFUL.
CAN I--?
Hissss
Gnraarrl!
OH!
SPAK SPAM
CRYPTOID:
IN 1917, TWO LITTLE GIRLS TOOK SEVERAL PHOTOGRAPHS OF FAIRIES, IN THE WOODS NEAR THEIR HOME. THE PICTURES CAUSED A WORLDWIDE SENSATION.
OH, MY GOD!
YEAH, IT'S BAD LUCK TO GET EATEN ON YOUR FIRST DAY AT WORK.

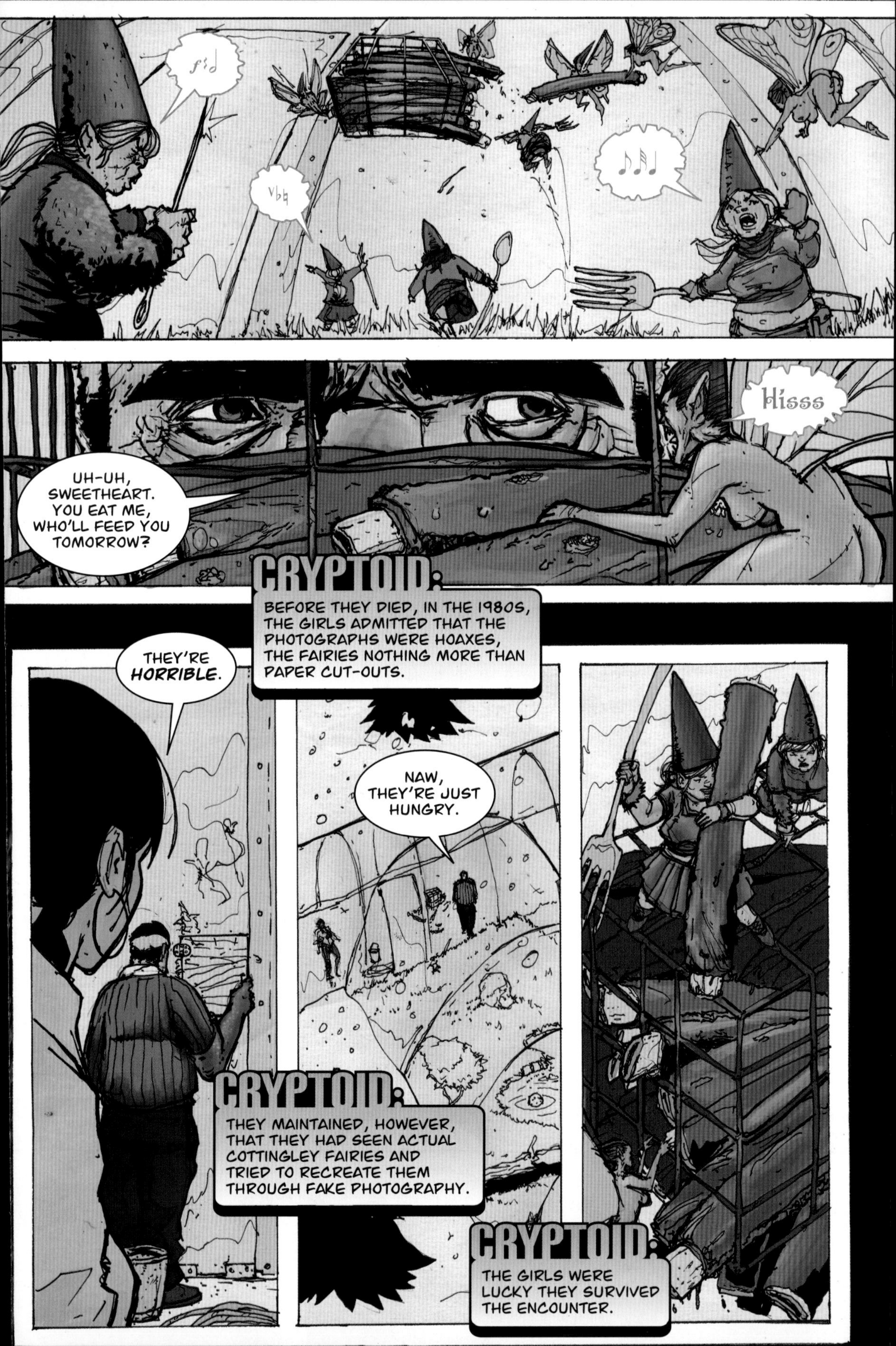
Hisss
UH-UH, SWEETHEART. YOU EAT ME, WHO'LL FEED YOU TOMORROW?
CRYPTOID:
BEFORE THEY DIED, IN THE 1980S, THE GIRLS ADMITTED THAT THE PHOTOGRAPHS WERE HOAXES, THE FAIRIES NOTHING MORE THAN PAPER CUT-OUTS.
THEY'RE HORRIBLE.
NAW, THEY'RE JUST HUNGRY.
CRYPTOID:
THEY MAINTAINED, HOWEVER, THAT THEY HAD SEEN ACTUAL COTTINGLEY FAIRIES AND TRIED TO RECREATE THEM THROUGH FAKE PHOTOGRAPHY.
CRYPTOID:
THE GIRLS WERE LUCKY THEY SURVIVED THE ENCOUNTER.

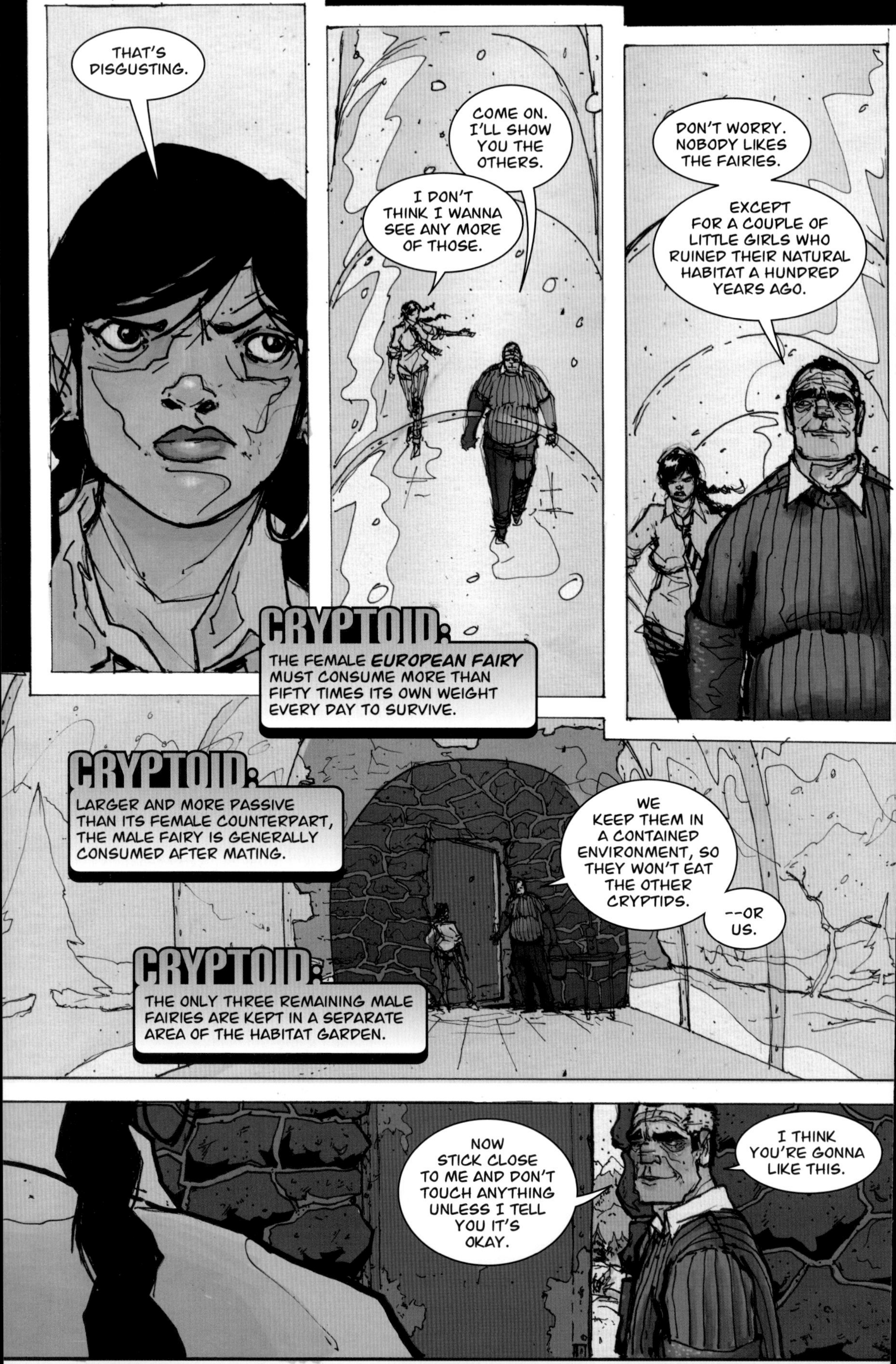
THAT'S DISGUSTING.
COME ON. I'LL SHOW YOU THE OTHERS.
I DON'T THINK I WANNA SEE ANY MORE OF THOSE.
DON'T WORRY. NOBODY LIKES THE FAIRIES.
EXCEPT FOR A COUPLE OF LITTLE GIRLS WHO RUINED THEIR NATURAL HABITAT A HUNDRED YEARS AGO.
CRYPTOID:
THE FEMALE EUROPEAN FAIRY MUST CONSUME MORE THAN FIFTY TIMES ITS OWN WEIGHT EVERY DAY TO SURVIVE.
CRYPTOID:
LARGER AND MORE PASSIVE THAN ITS FEMALE COUNTERPART, THE MALE FAIRY IS GENERALLY CONSUMED AFTER MATING.
WE KEEP THEM IN A CONTAINED ENVIRONMENT, SO THEY WON'T EAT THE OTHER CRYPTIDS.
--OR US.
CRYPTOID:
THE ONLY THREE REMAINING MALE FAIRIES ARE KEPT IN A SEPARATE AREA OF THE HABITAT GARDEN.
NOW STICK CLOSE TO ME AND DON'T TOUCH ANYTHING UNLESS I TELL YOU IT'S OKAY.
I THINK YOU'RE GONNA LIKE THIS.

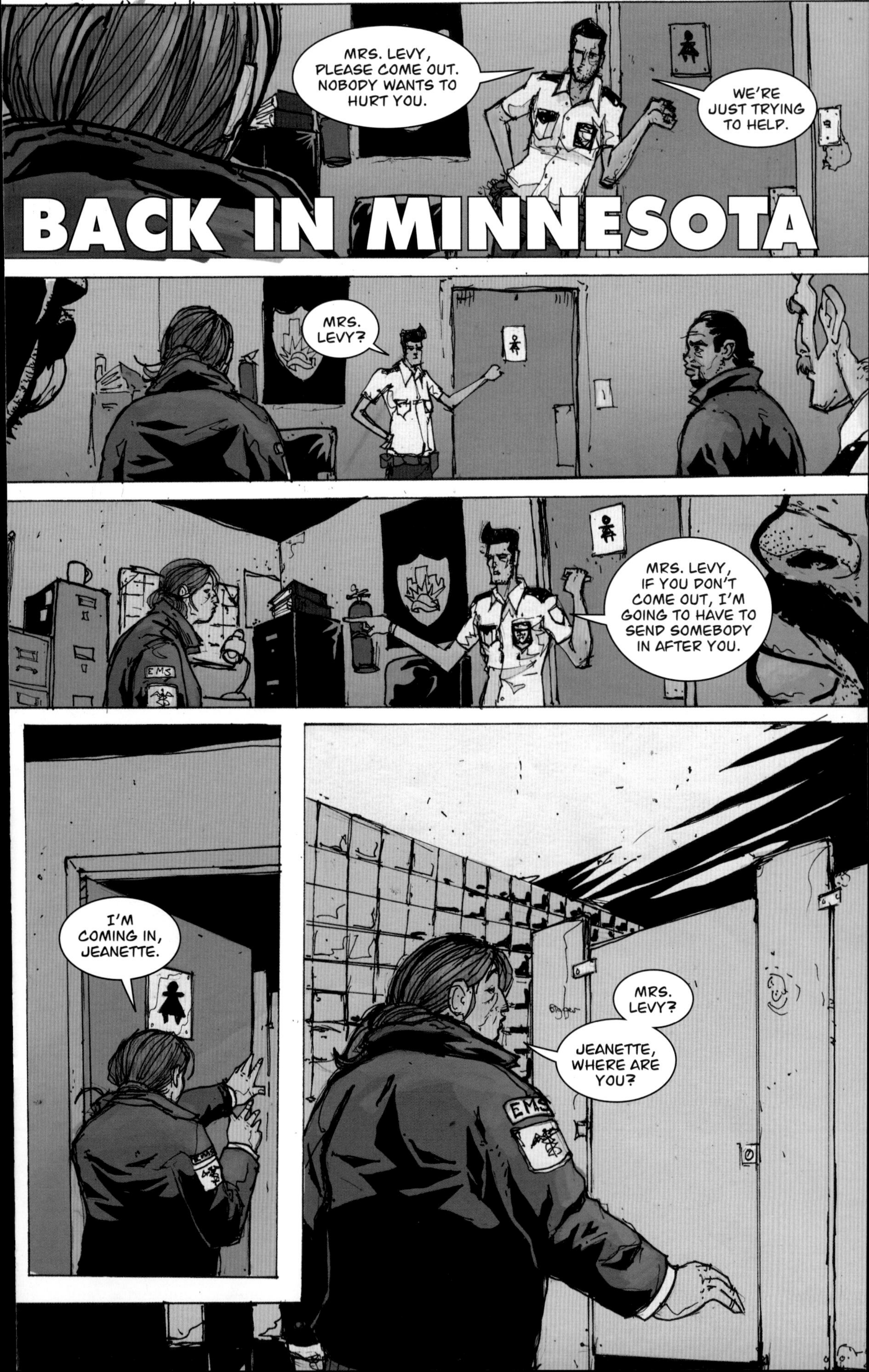
MRS. LEVY, PLEASE COME OUT. NOBODY WANTS TO HURT YOU.
WE'RE JUST TRYING TO HELP.
BACK IN MINNESOTA
MRS. LEVY?
MRS. LEVY, IF YOU DON'T COME OUT, I'M GOING TO HAVE TO SEND SOMEBODY IN AFTER YOU.
EMS
I'M COMING IN, JEANETTE.
MRS. LEVY?
JEANETTE, WHERE ARE YOU?
EMS

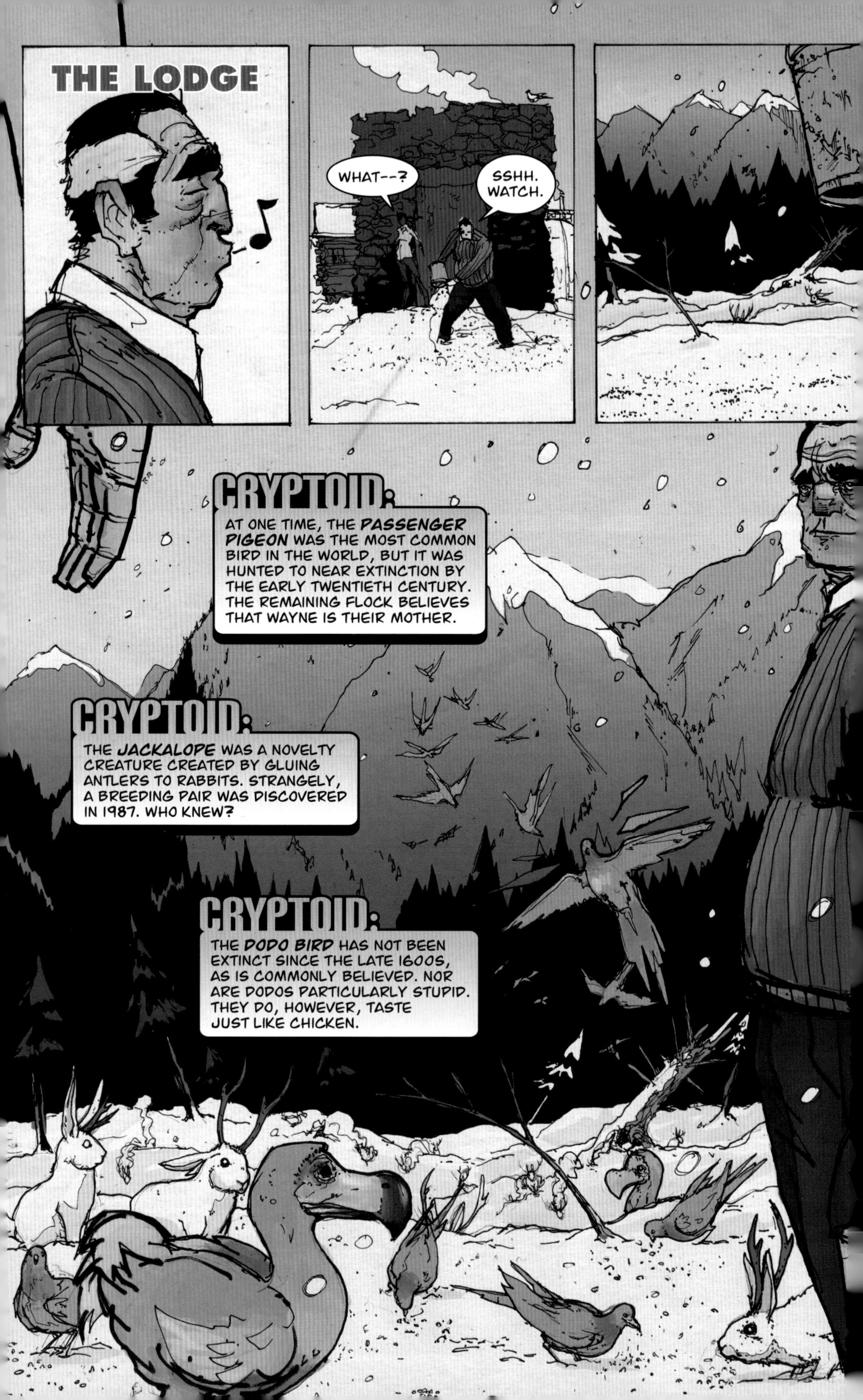

THE LODGE
WHAT--?
SSHH. WATCH.
CRYPTOID:
AT ONE TIME, THE PASSENGER PIGEON WAS THE MOST COMMON BIRD IN THE WORLD, BUT IT WAS HUNTED TO NEAR EXTINCTION BY THE EARLY TWENTIETH CENTURY. THE REMAINING FLOCK BELIEVES THAT WAYNE IS THEIR MOTHER.
CRYPTOID:
THE JACKALOPE WAS A NOVELTY CREATURE CREATED BY GLUING ANTLERS TO RABBITS. STRANGELY, A BREEDING PAIR WAS DISCOVERED IN 1987. WHO KNEW?
CRYPTOID:
THE DODO BIRD HAS NOT BEEN EXTINCT SINCE THE LATE 1600S, AS IS COMMONLY BELIEVED. NOR ARE DODOS PARTICULARLY STUPID. THEY DO, HOWEVER, TASTE JUST LIKE CHICKEN.

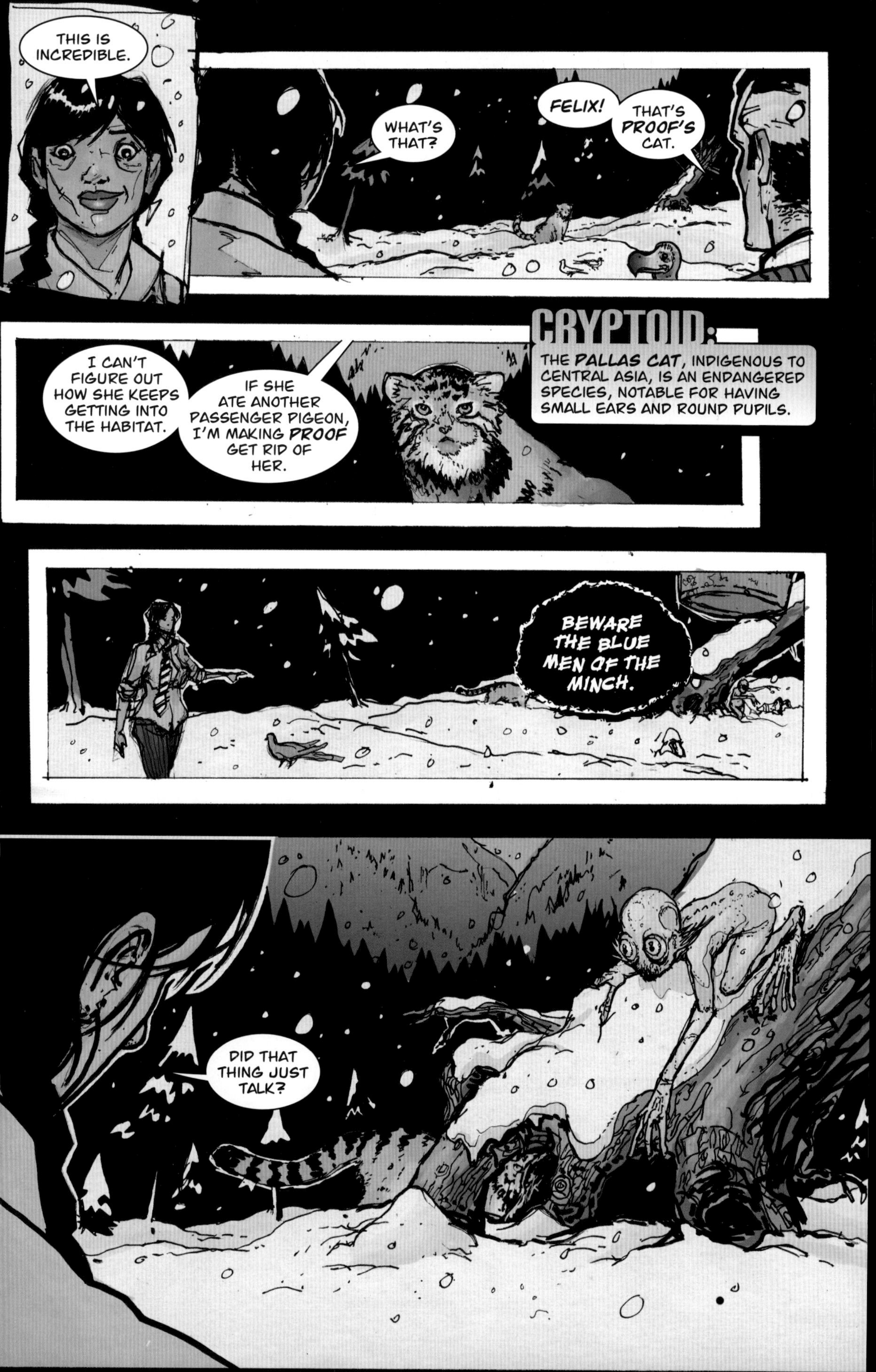
THIS IS INCREDIBLE.
WHAT'S THAT?
FELIX!
THAT'S PROOF'S CAT.
I CAN'T FIGURE OUT HOW SHE KEEPS GETTING INTO THE HABITAT.
IF SHE ATE ANOTHER PASSENGER PIGEON, I'M MAKING PROOF GET RID OF HER.
CRYPTOID:
THE PALLAS CAT, INDIGENOUS TO CENTRAL ASIA, IS AN ENDANGERED SPECIES, NOTABLE FOR HAVING SMALL EARS AND ROUND PUPILS.
BEWARE THE BLUE MEN OF THE MINCH.
DID THAT THING JUST TALK?

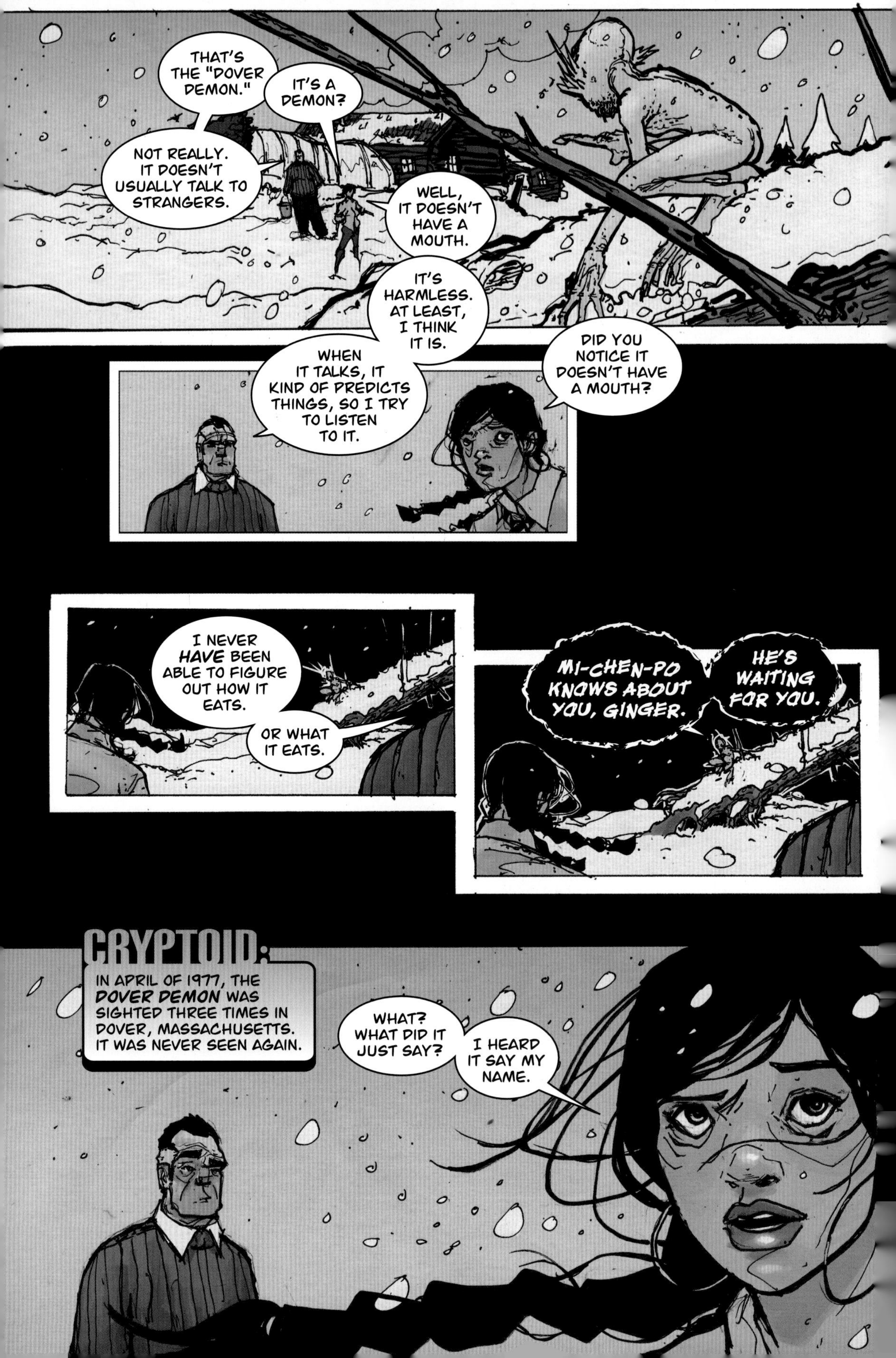
THAT'S THE "DOVER DEMON."
IT'S A DEMON?
NOT REALLY. IT DOESN'T USUALLY TALK TO STRANGERS.
WELL, IT DOESN'T HAVE A MOUTH.
IT'S HARMLESS. AT LEAST, I THINK IT IS.
WHEN IT TALKS, IT KIND OF PREDICTS THINGS, SO I TRY TO LISTEN TO IT.
DID YOU NOTICE IT DOESN'T HAVE A MOUTH?
I NEVER HAVE BEEN ABLE TO FIGURE OUT HOW IT EATS.
OR WHAT IT EATS.
MI-CHEN-PO KNOWS ABOUT YOU, GINGER.
HE'S WAITING FOR YOU.
CRYPTOID:
IN APRIL OF 1977, THE DOVER DEMON WAS SIGHTED THREE TIMES IN DOVER, MASSACHUSETTS. IT WAS NEVER SEEN AGAIN.
WHAT? WHAT DID IT JUST SAY?
I HEARD IT SAY MY NAME.

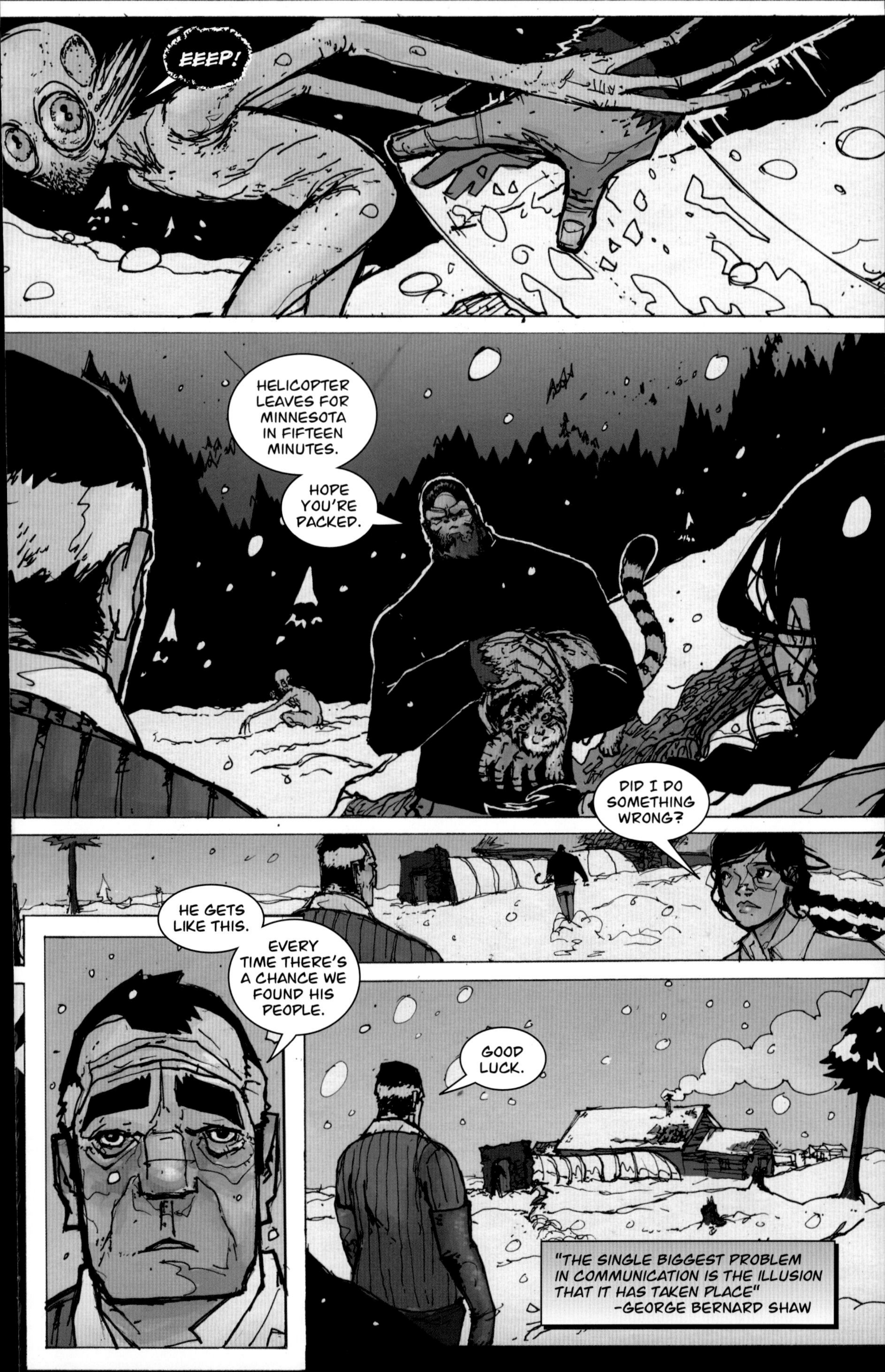
EEEP!
HELICOPTER LEAVES FOR MINNESOTA IN FIFTEEN MINUTES.
HOPE YOU'RE PACKED.
DID I DO SOMETHING WRONG?
HE GETS LIKE THIS.
EVERY TIME THERE'S A CHANCE WE FOUND HIS PEOPLE.
GOOD LUCK.
"THE SINGLE BIGGEST PROBLEM IN COMMUNICATION IS THE ILLUSION THAT IT HAS TAKEN PLACE"
-GEORGE BERNARD SHAW

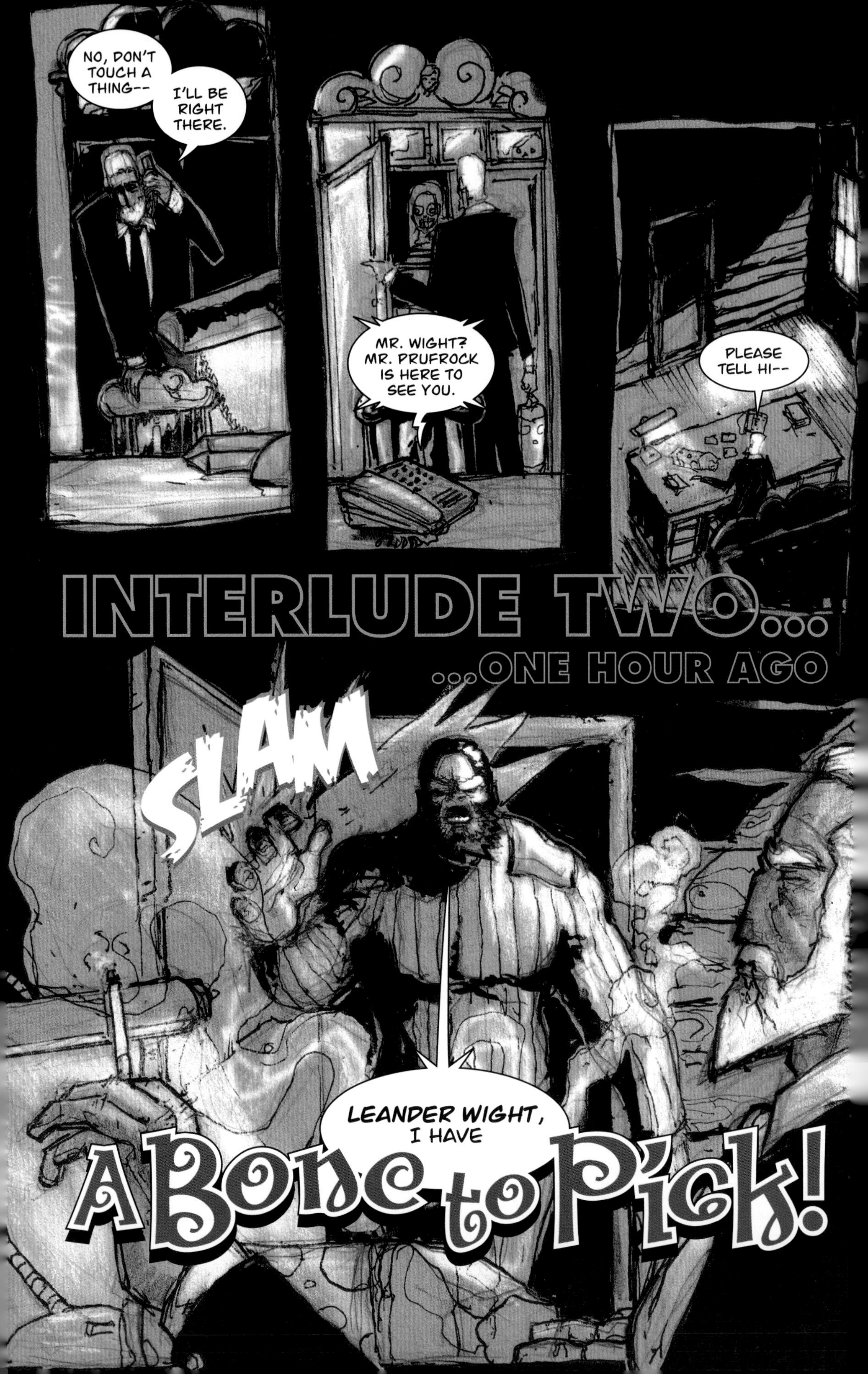
NO, DON'T TOUCH A THING--
I'LL BE RIGHT THERE.
MR. WIGHT? MR. PRUFROCK IS HERE TO SEE YOU.
PLEASE TELL HI--
INTERLUDE TWO...
...ONE HOUR AGO
SLAM
LEANDER WIGHT, I HAVE
A Bone to Pick!

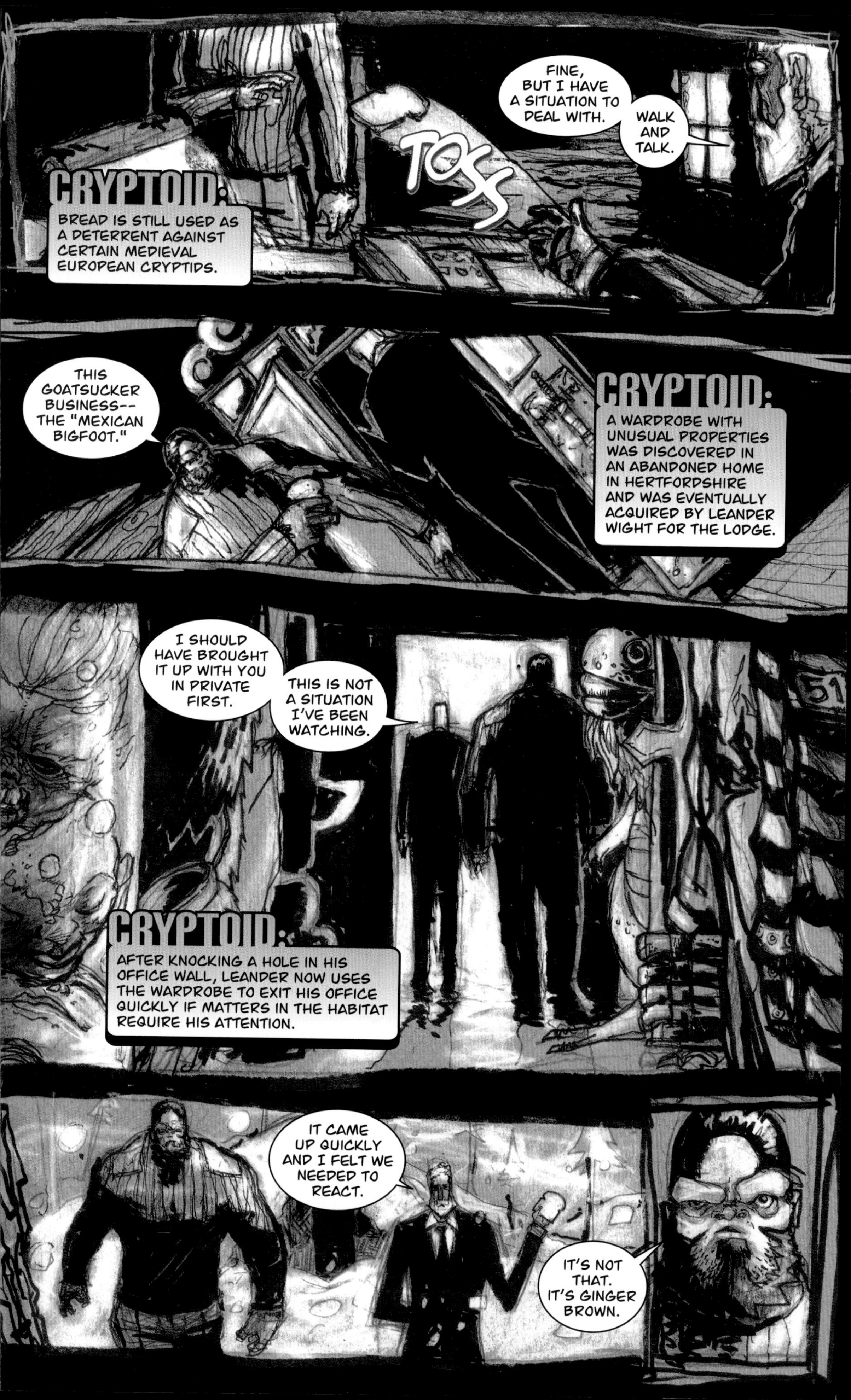
FINE, BUT I HAVE A SITUATION TO DEAL WITH.
WALK AND TALK.
TOSS
CRYPTOID:
BREAD IS STILL USED AS A DETERRENT AGAINST CERTAIN MEDIEVAL EUROPEAN CRYPTIDS.
THIS GOATSUCKER BUSINESS-- THE "MEXICAN BIGFOOT."
CRYPTOID:
A WARDROBE WITH UNUSUAL PROPERTIES WAS DISCOVERED IN AN ABANDONED HOME IN HERTFORDSHIRE AND WAS EVENTUALLY ACQUIRED BY LEANDER WIGHT FOR THE LODGE.
I SHOULD HAVE BROUGHT IT UP WITH YOU IN PRIVATE FIRST.
THIS IS NOT A SITUATION I'VE BEEN WATCHING.
CRYPTOID:
AFTER KNOCKING A HOLE IN HIS OFFICE WALL, LEANDER NOW USES THE WARDROBE TO EXIT HIS OFFICE QUICKLY IF MATTERS IN THE HABITAT REQUIRE HIS ATTENTION.
IT CAME UP QUICKLY AND I FELT WE NEEDED TO REACT.
IT'S NOT THAT. IT'S GINGER BROWN.

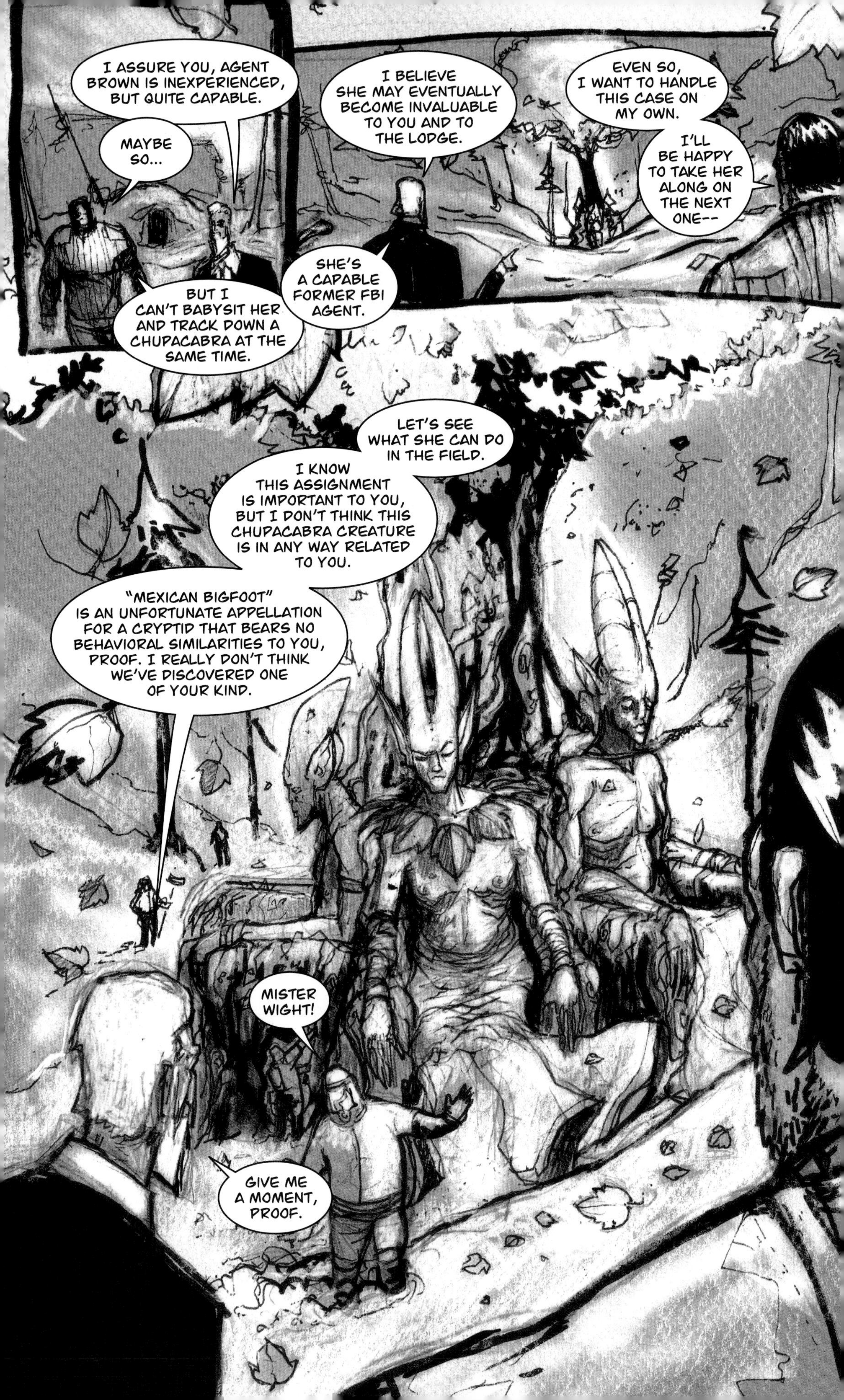
I ASSURE YOU, AGENT BROWN IS INEXPERIENCED, BUT QUITE CAPABLE.
MAYBE SO...
BUT I CAN'T BABYSIT HER AND TRACK DOWN A CHUPACABRA AT THE SAME TIME.
I BELIEVE SHE MAY EVENTUALLY BECOME INVALUABLE TO YOU AND TO THE LODGE.
SHE'S A CAPABLE FORMER FBI AGENT.
EVEN SO, I WANT TO HANDLE THIS CASE ON MY OWN.
I'LL BE HAPPY TO TAKE HER ALONG ON THE NEXT ONE--
LET'S SEE WHAT SHE CAN DO IN THE FIELD.
I KNOW THIS ASSIGNMENT IS IMPORTANT TO YOU, BUT I DON'T THINK THIS CHUPACABRA CREATURE IS IN ANY WAY RELATED TO YOU.
"MEXICAN BIGFOOT" IS AN UNFORTUNATE APPELLATION FOR A CRYPTID THAT BEARS NO BEHAVIORAL SIMILARITIES TO YOU, PROOF. I REALLY DON'T THINK WE'VE DISCOVERED ONE OF YOUR KIND.
MISTER WIGHT!
GIVE ME A MOMENT, PROOF.

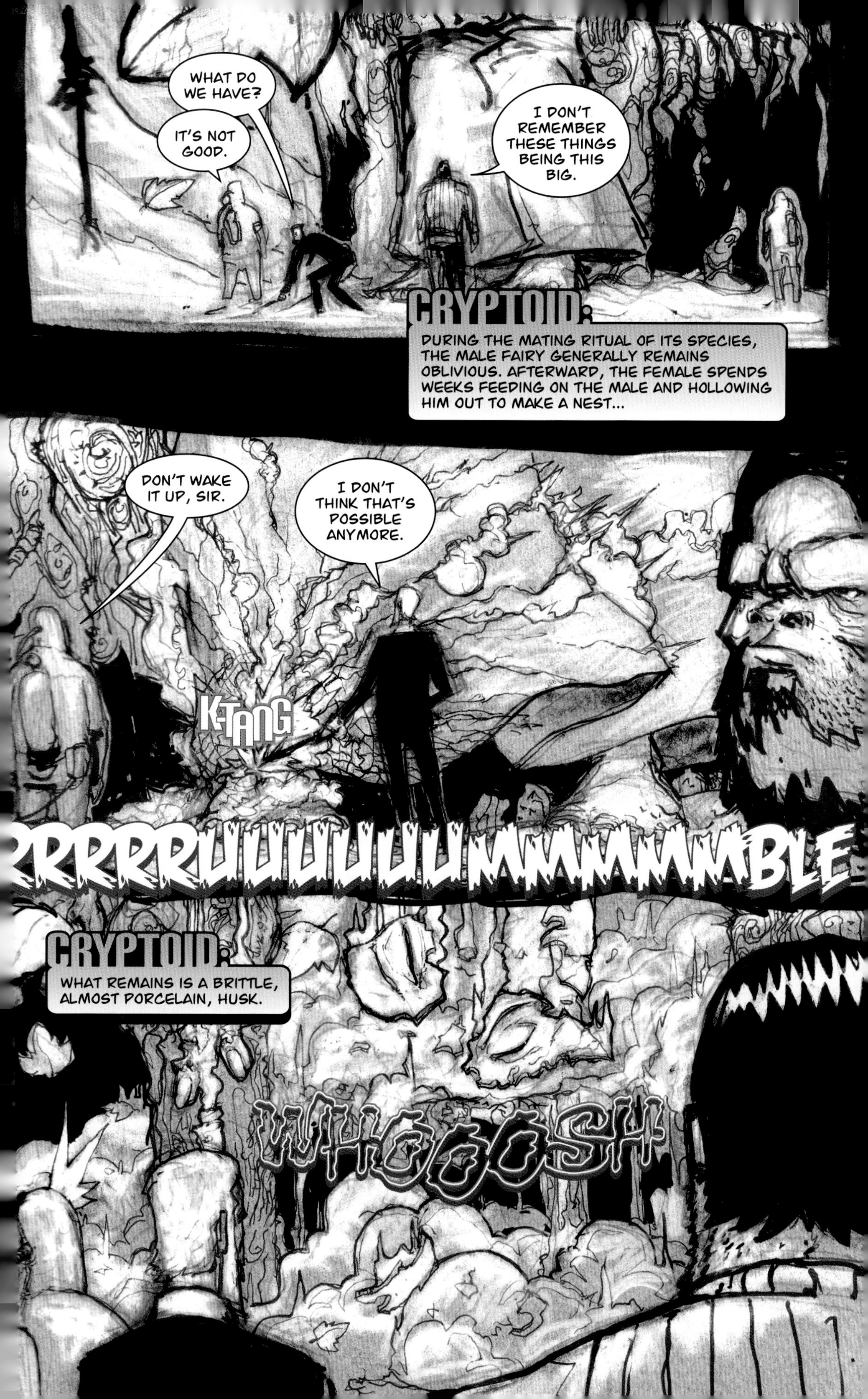

WHAT DO WE HAVE?
IT'S NOT GOOD.
I DON'T REMEMBER THESE THINGS BEING THIS BIG.
CRYPTOID:
DURING THE MATING RITUAL OF ITS SPECIES, THE MALE FAIRY GENERALLY REMAINS OBLIVIOUS. AFTERWARD, THE FEMALE SPENDS WEEKS FEEDING ON THE MALE AND HOLLOWING HIM OUT TO MAKE A NEST...
DON'T WAKE IT UP, SIR.
I DON'T THINK THAT'S POSSIBLE ANYMORE.
K-TANG
RRRRRUUUUUUUMMMMMMBLE
CRYPTOID:
WHAT REMAINS IS A BRITTLE, ALMOST PORCELAIN, HUSK.
WHOOOSH

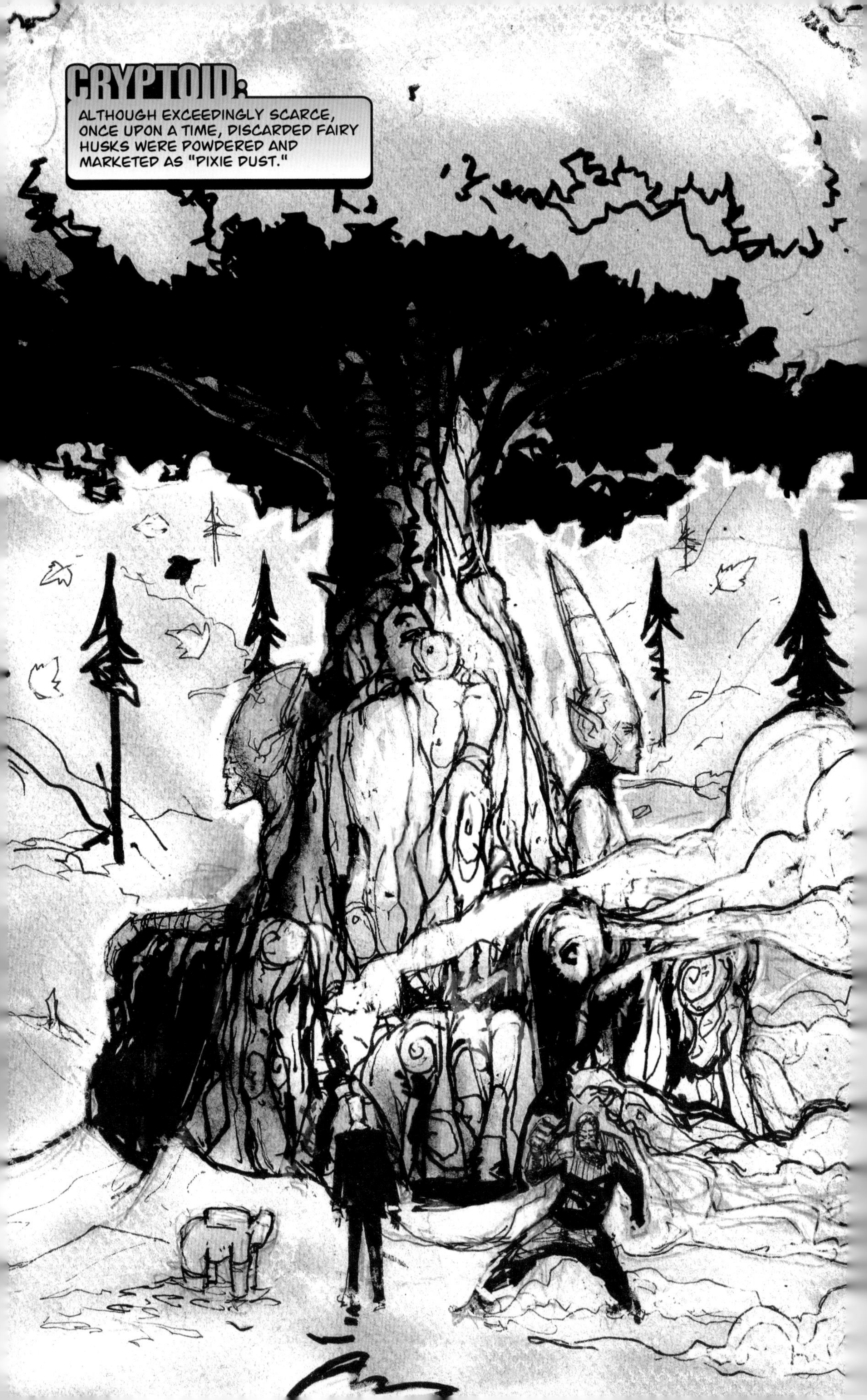
CRYPTOID:
ALTHOUGH EXCEEDINGLY SCARCE, ONCE UPON A TIME, DISCARDED FAIRY HUSKS WERE POWDERED AND MARKETED AS "PIXIE DUST."

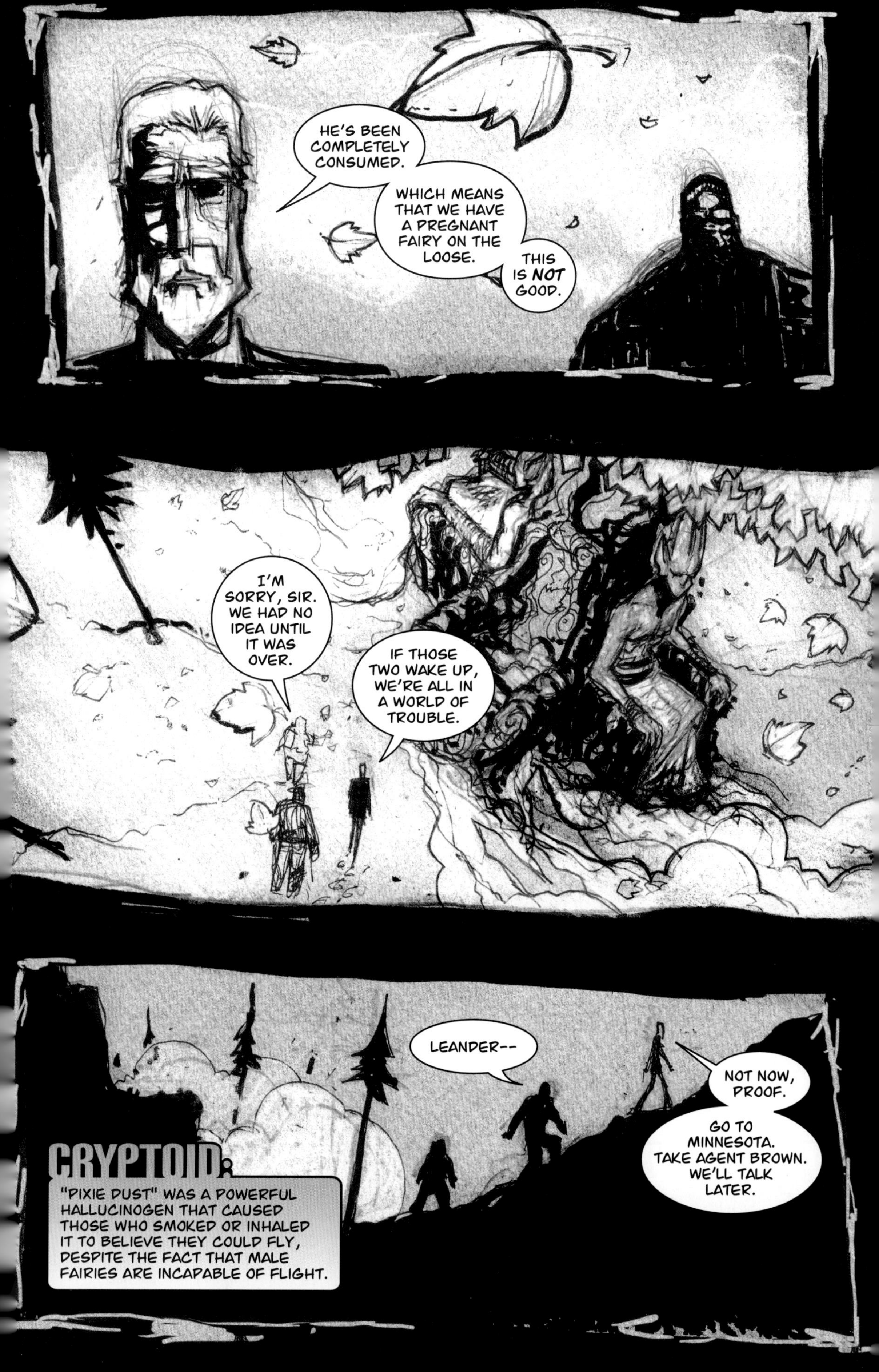
HE'S BEEN COMPLETELY CONSUMED.
WHICH MEANS THAT WE HAVE A PREGNANT FAIRY ON THE LOOSE.
THIS IS **NOT** GOOD.
I'M SORRY, SIR. WE HAD NO IDEA UNTIL IT WAS OVER.
IF THOSE TWO WAKE UP, WE'RE ALL IN A WORLD OF TROUBLE.
LEANDER--
NOT NOW, PROOF.
GO TO MINNESOTA. TAKE AGENT BROWN. WE'LL TALK LATER.
CRYPTOID:
"PIXIE DUST" WAS A POWERFUL HALLUCINOGEN THAT CAUSED THOSE WHO SMOKED OR INHALED IT TO BELIEVE THEY COULD FLY, DESPITE THE FACT THAT MALE FAIRIES ARE INCAPABLE OF FLIGHT.

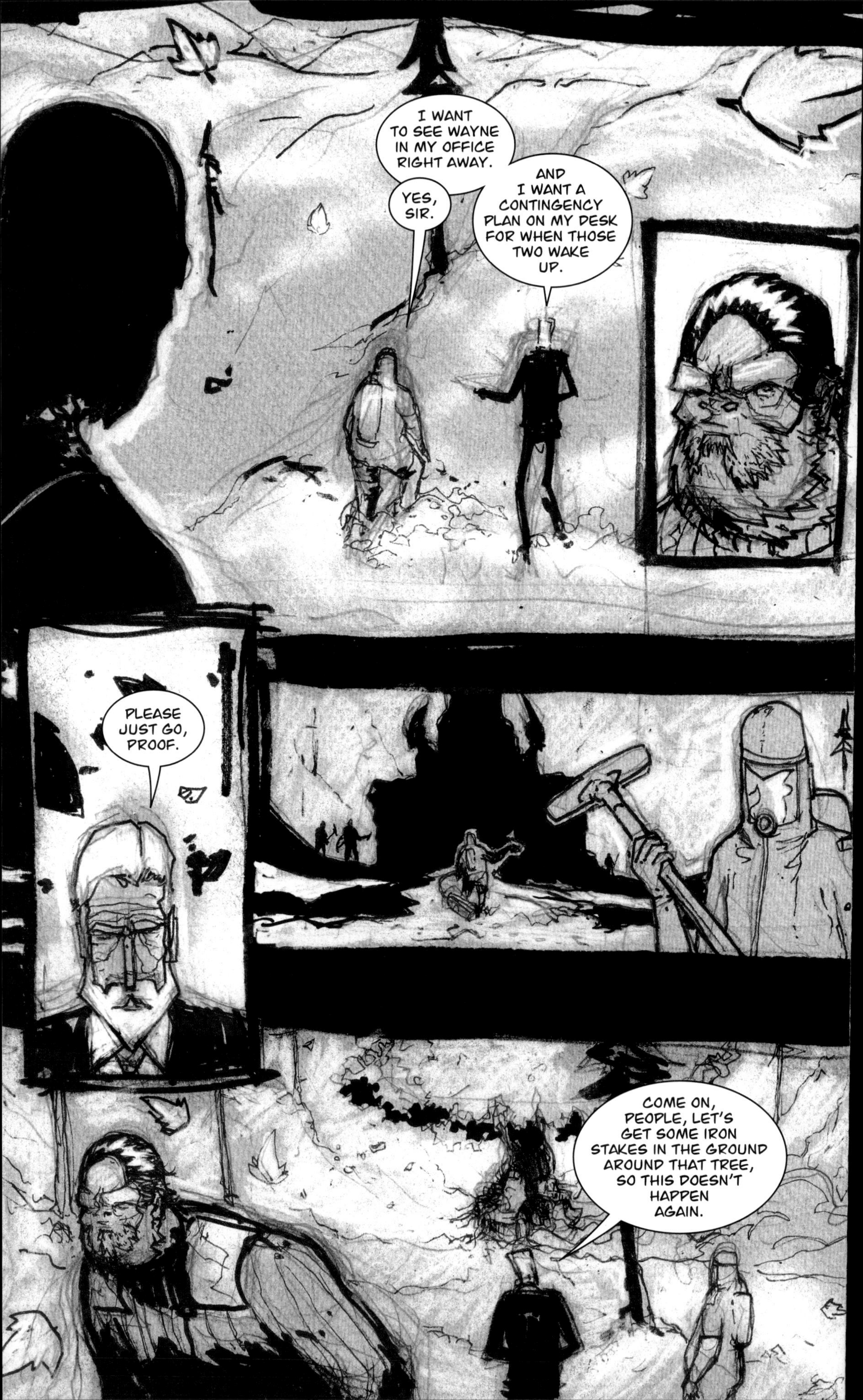
I WANT TO SEE WAYNE IN MY OFFICE RIGHT AWAY.
YES, SIR.
AND I WANT A CONTINGENCY PLAN ON MY DESK FOR WHEN THOSE TWO WAKE UP.
PLEASE JUST GO, PROOF.
COME ON, PEOPLE, LET'S GET SOME IRON STAKES IN THE GROUND AROUND THAT TREE, SO THIS DOESN'T HAPPEN AGAIN.

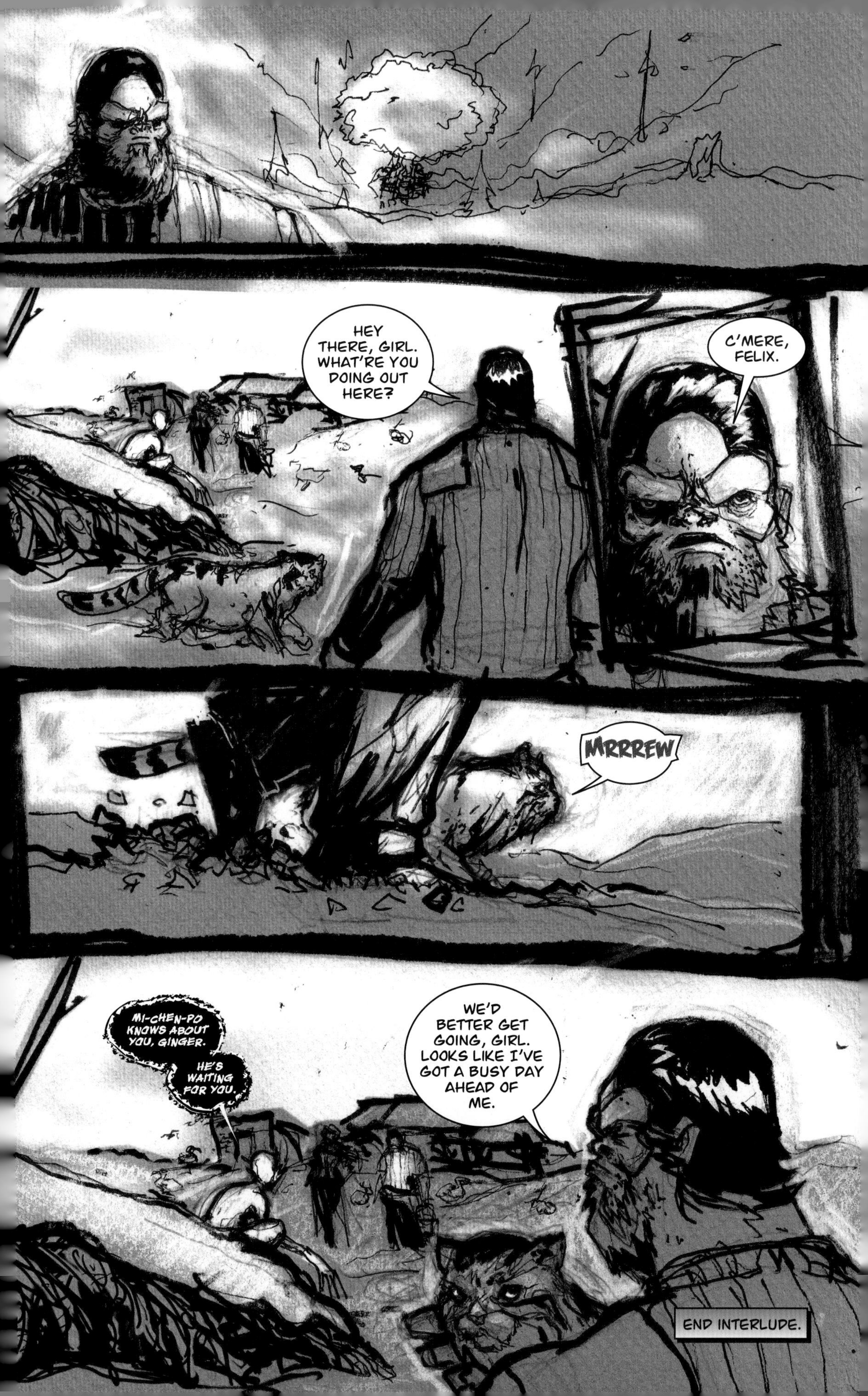
HEY THERE, GIRL. WHAT'RE YOU DOING OUT HERE?
C'MERE, FELIX.
MRRREW
MI-CHEN-PO KNOWS ABOUT YOU, GINGER.
HE'S WAITING FOR YOU.
WE'D BETTER GET GOING, GIRL. LOOKS LIKE I'VE GOT A BUSY DAY AHEAD OF ME.
END INTERLUDE.

LEEWARD, MINNESOTA

WELL?
NOT IN THERE. GONE OUT THROUGH THE WINDOW, MAYBE.
OH, CRAP!
WE GOT A RUNNER, PEOPLE!
LARRY, GET TO THE ALLEY AND SEE IF YOU CAN HEAD HER OFF.
BOB, YOU COME WITH ME.

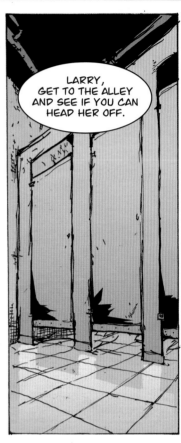

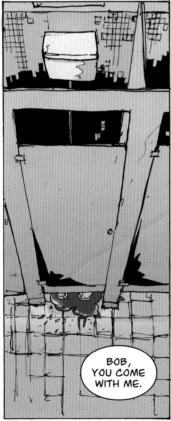

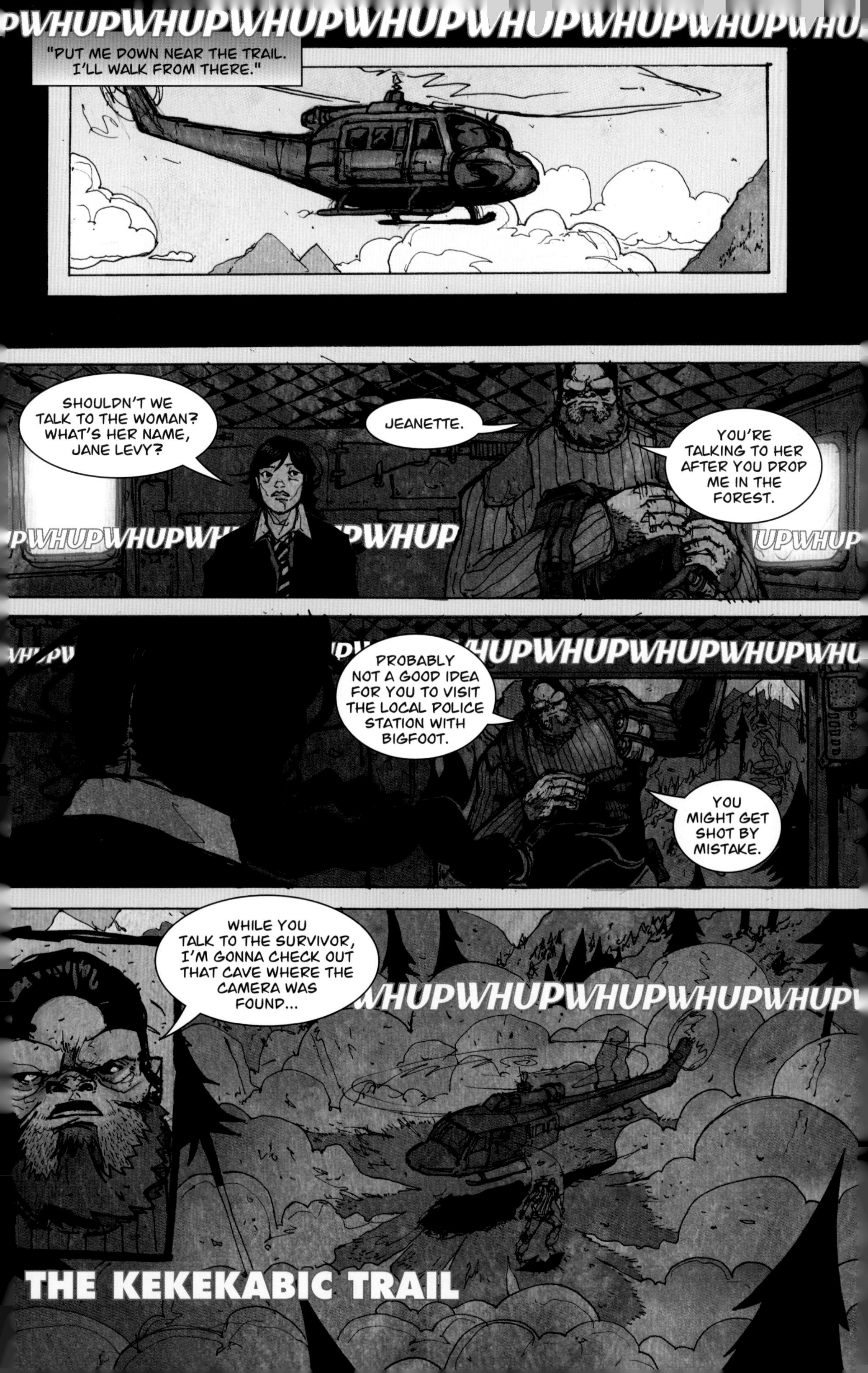
WHUPWHUPWHUPWHUPWHUPWHUPWHUP
"PUT ME DOWN NEAR THE TRAIL. I'LL WALK FROM THERE."
SHOULDN'T WE TALK TO THE WOMAN? WHAT'S HER NAME, JANE LEVY?
JEANETTE.
YOU'RE TALKING TO HER AFTER YOU DROP ME IN THE FOREST.
WHUPWHUPWHUPWHUP
PROBABLY NOT A GOOD IDEA FOR YOU TO VISIT THE LOCAL POLICE STATION WITH BIGFOOT.
YOU MIGHT GET SHOT BY MISTAKE.
WHUPWHUPWHUPWHU
WHILE YOU TALK TO THE SURVIVOR, I'M GONNA CHECK OUT THAT CAVE WHERE THE CAMERA WAS FOUND...
WHUPWHUPWHUPWHUP
THE KEKEKABIC TRAIL

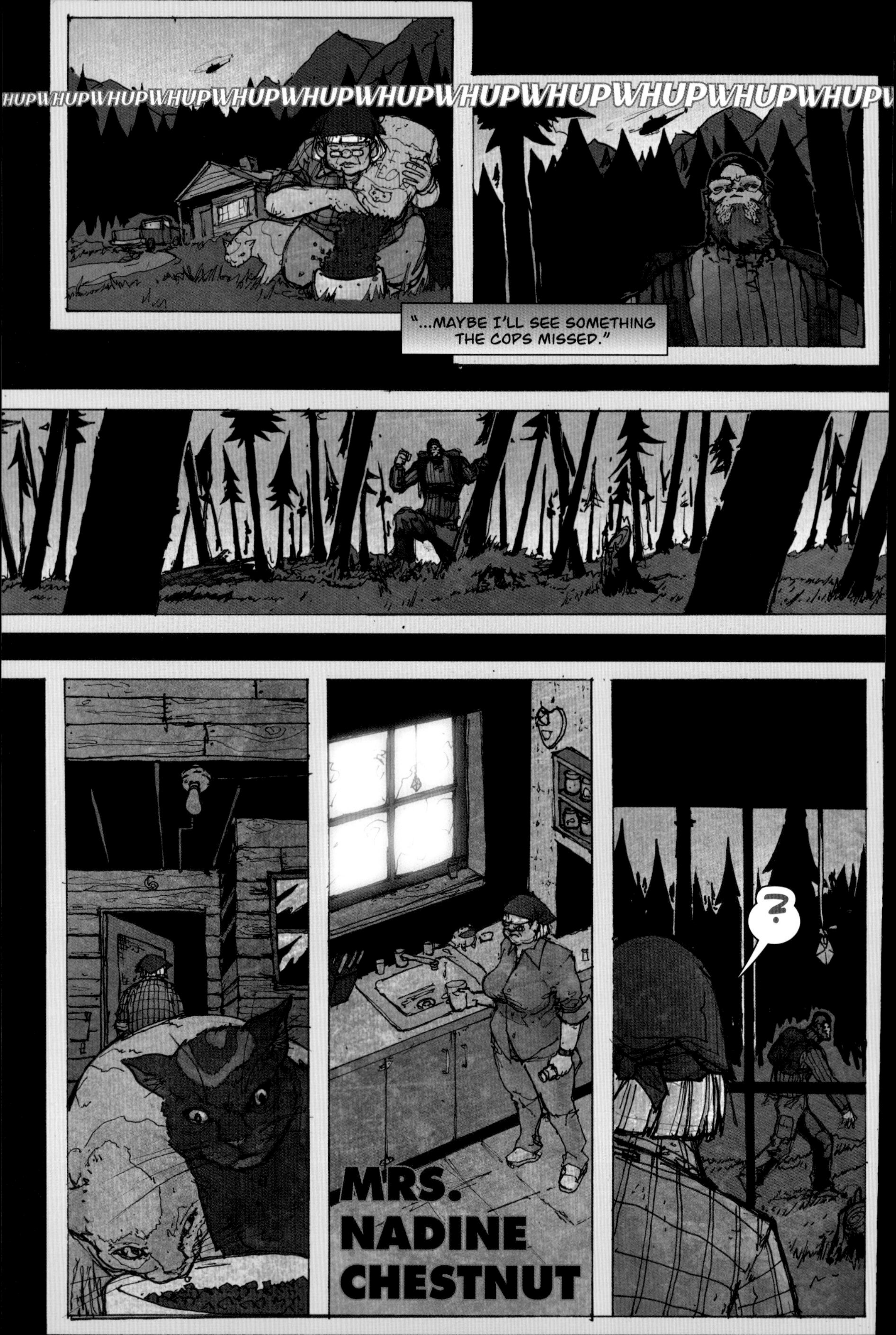

HUPWHUPWHUPWHUPWHUPWHUPWHUPWHUPWHUPWHUPWHUPWHUPWHUPWHUPWHUPW
"...MAYBE I'LL SEE SOMETHING THE COPS MISSED."
MRS. NADINE CHESTNUT
?

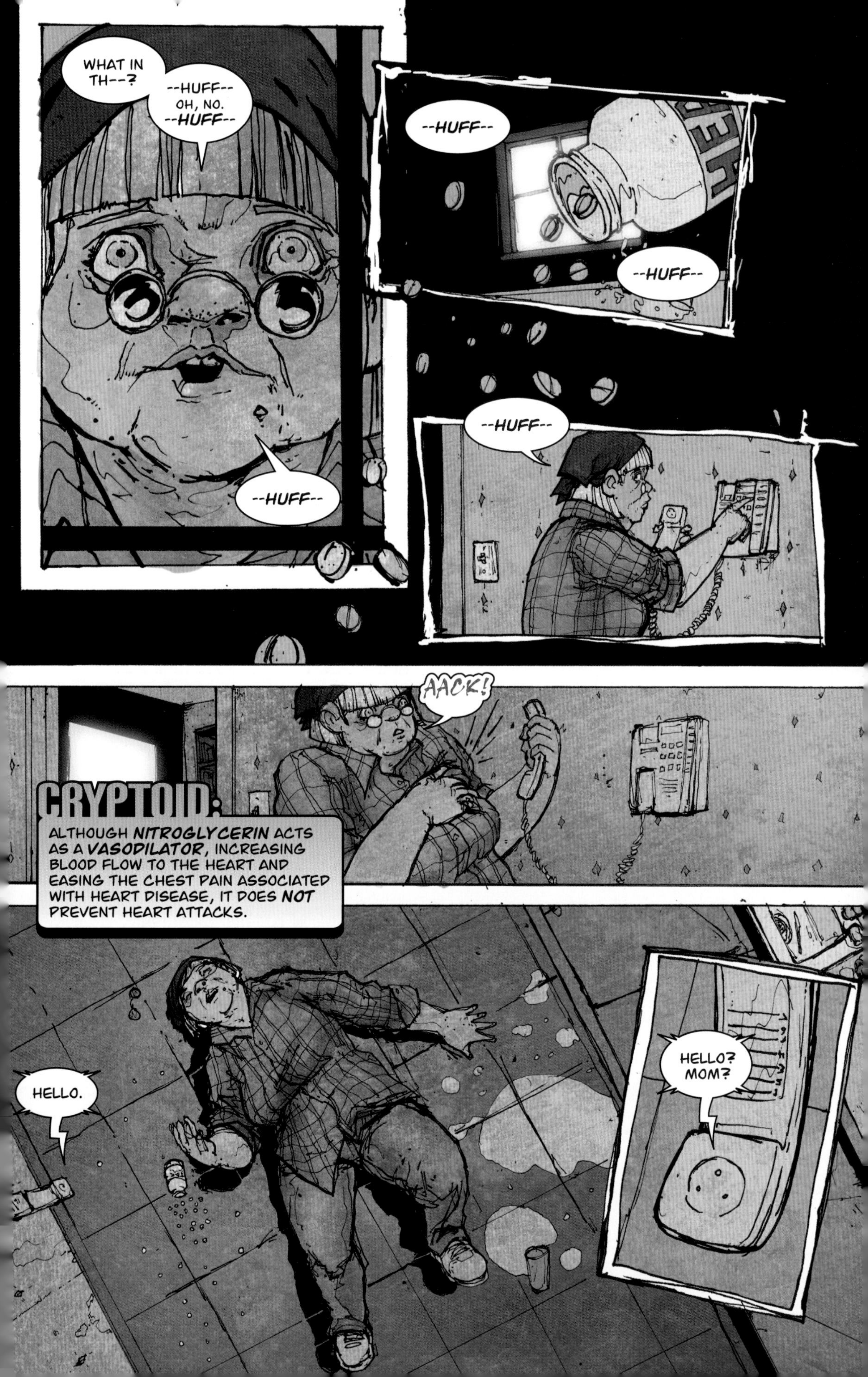
WHAT IN TH--?
--HUFF-- OH, NO. --HUFF--
--HUFF--
--HUFF--
--HUFF--
--HUFF--
AACK!
CRYPTOID:
ALTHOUGH NITROGLYCERIN ACTS AS A VASODILATOR, INCREASING BLOOD FLOW TO THE HEART AND EASING THE CHEST PAIN ASSOCIATED WITH HEART DISEASE, IT DOES NOT PREVENT HEART ATTACKS.
HELLO.
HELLO? MOM?

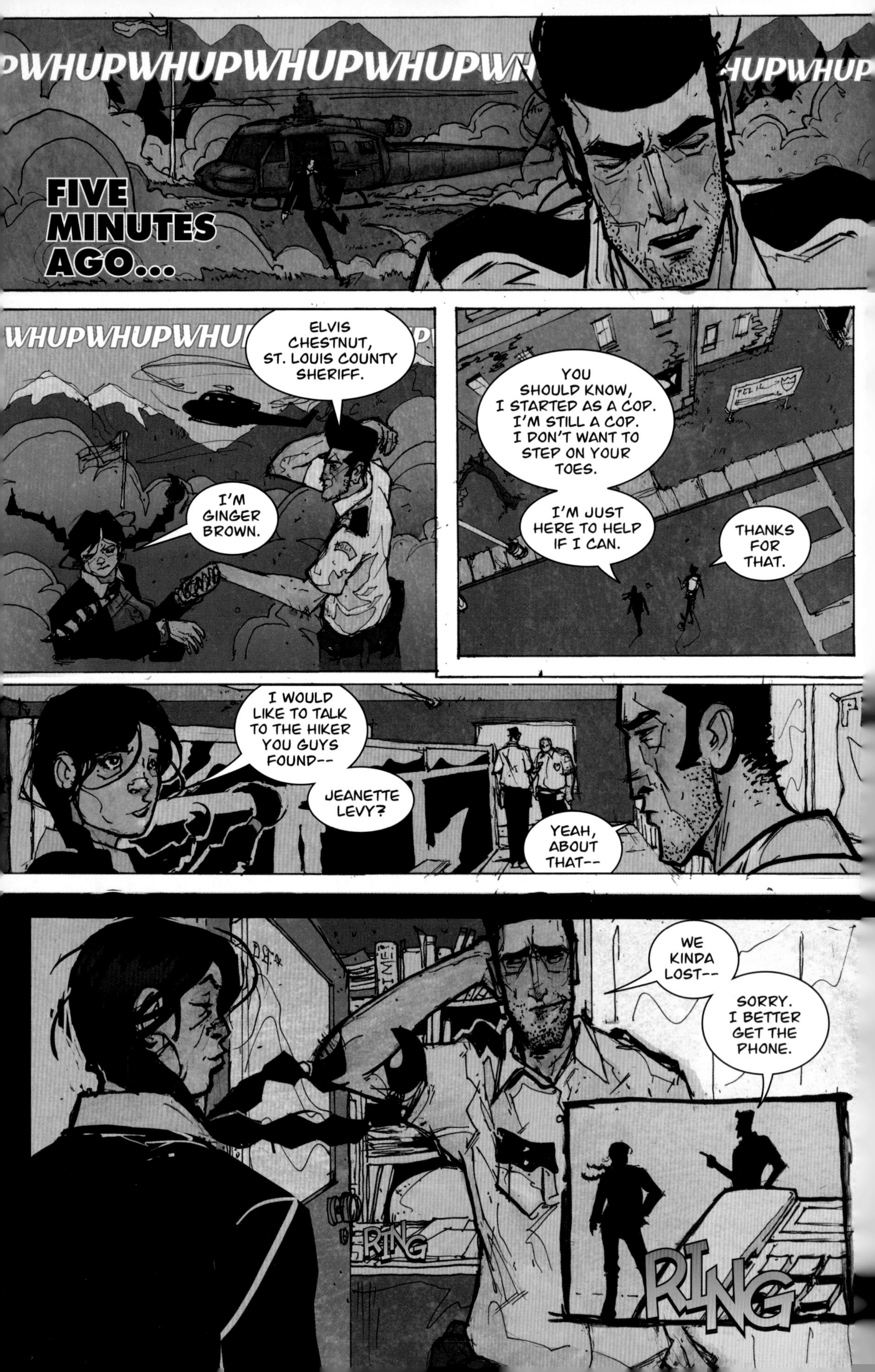
WHUPWHUPWHUPWHUPWH
HUPWHUP
FIVE MINUTES AGO...
WHUPWHUPWHU
ELVIS CHESTNUT, ST. LOUIS COUNTY SHERIFF.
I'M GINGER BROWN.
YOU SHOULD KNOW, I STARTED AS A COP. I'M STILL A COP. I DON'T WANT TO STEP ON YOUR TOES.
I'M JUST HERE TO HELP IF I CAN.
THANKS FOR THAT.
I WOULD LIKE TO TALK TO THE HIKER YOU GUYS FOUND--
JEANETTE LEVY?
YEAH, ABOUT THAT--
WE KINDA LOST--
SORRY. I BETTER GET THE PHONE.
RING
RING

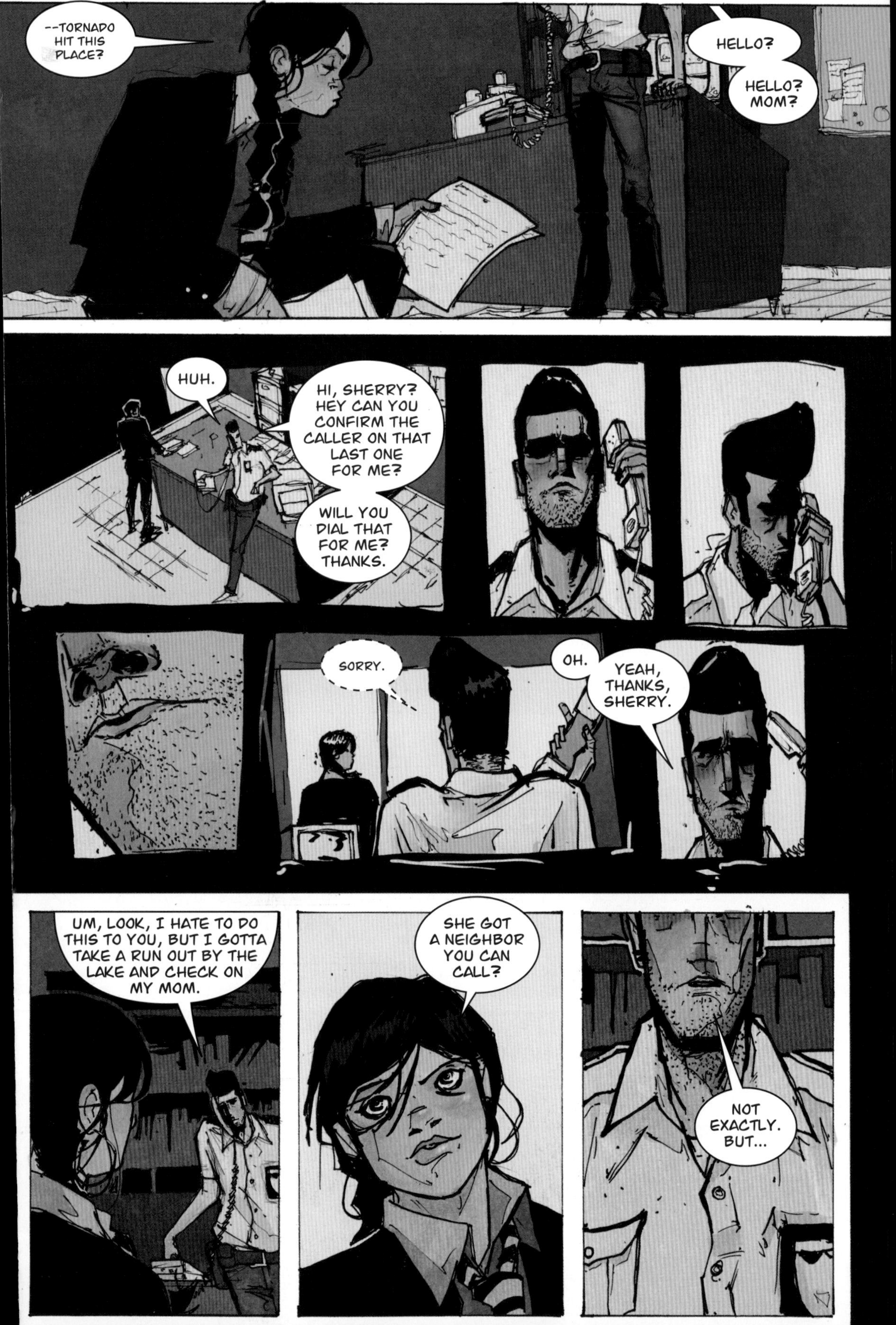
--TORNADO HIT THIS PLACE?
HELLO?
HELLO? MOM?
HUH.
HI, SHERRY? HEY CAN YOU CONFIRM THE CALLER ON THAT LAST ONE FOR ME?
WILL YOU DIAL THAT FOR ME? THANKS.
SORRY.
OH.
YEAH, THANKS, SHERRY.
UM, LOOK, I HATE TO DO THIS TO YOU, BUT I GOTTA TAKE A RUN OUT BY THE LAKE AND CHECK ON MY MOM.
SHE GOT A NEIGHBOR YOU CAN CALL?
NOT EXACTLY. BUT...

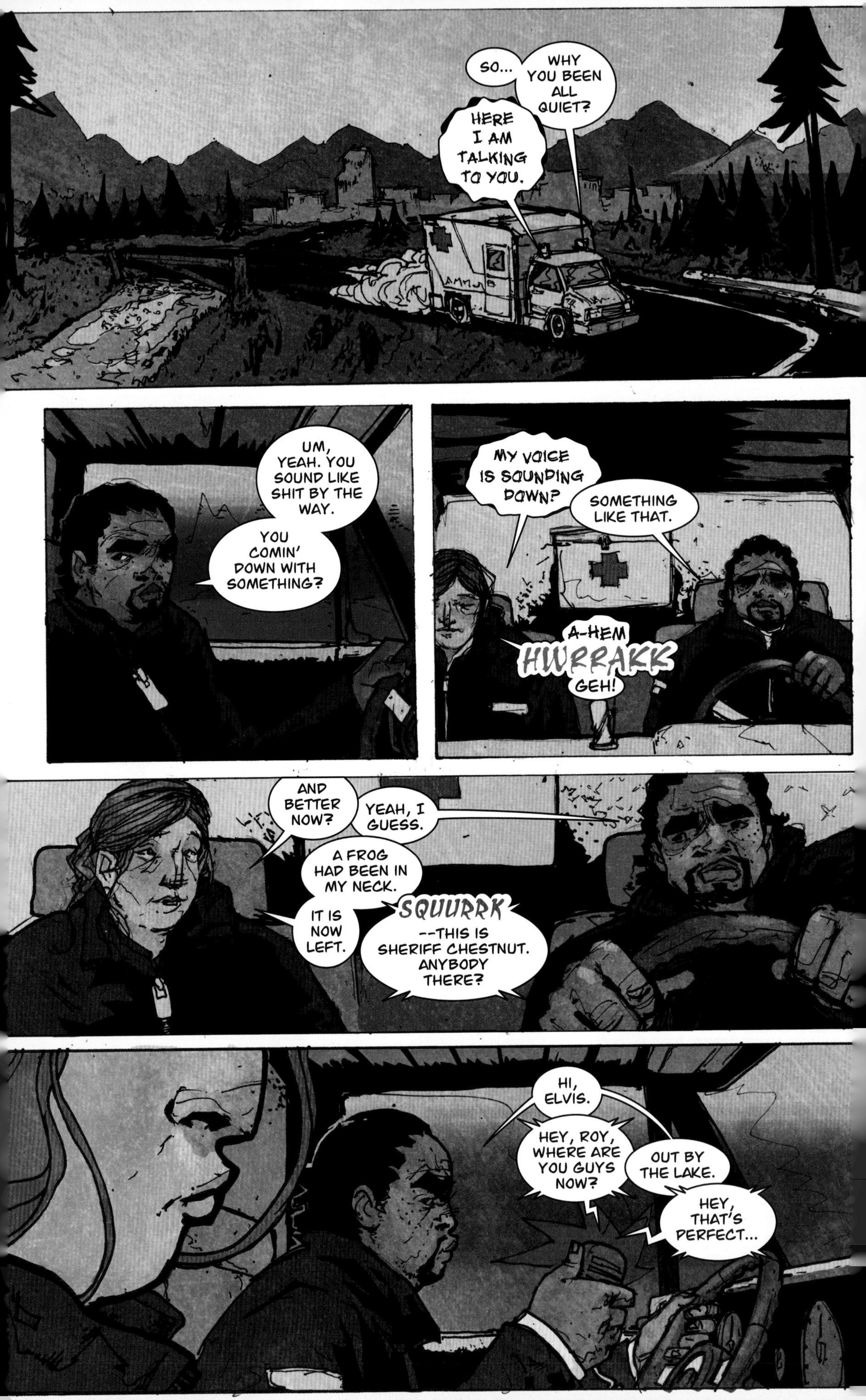
SO...
WHY YOU BEEN ALL QUIET?
HERE I AM TALKING TO YOU.
UM, YEAH. YOU SOUND LIKE SHIT BY THE WAY.
YOU COMIN' DOWN WITH SOMETHING?
MY VOICE IS SOUNDING DOWN?
SOMETHING LIKE THAT.
A-HEM
HWRRAKK
GEH!
AND BETTER NOW?
YEAH, I GUESS.
A FROG HAD BEEN IN MY NECK.
IT IS NOW LEFT.
SQUURRK
--THIS IS SHERIFF CHESTNUT. ANYBODY THERE?
HI, ELVIS.
HEY, ROY, WHERE ARE YOU GUYS NOW?
OUT BY THE LAKE.
HEY, THAT'S PERFECT...

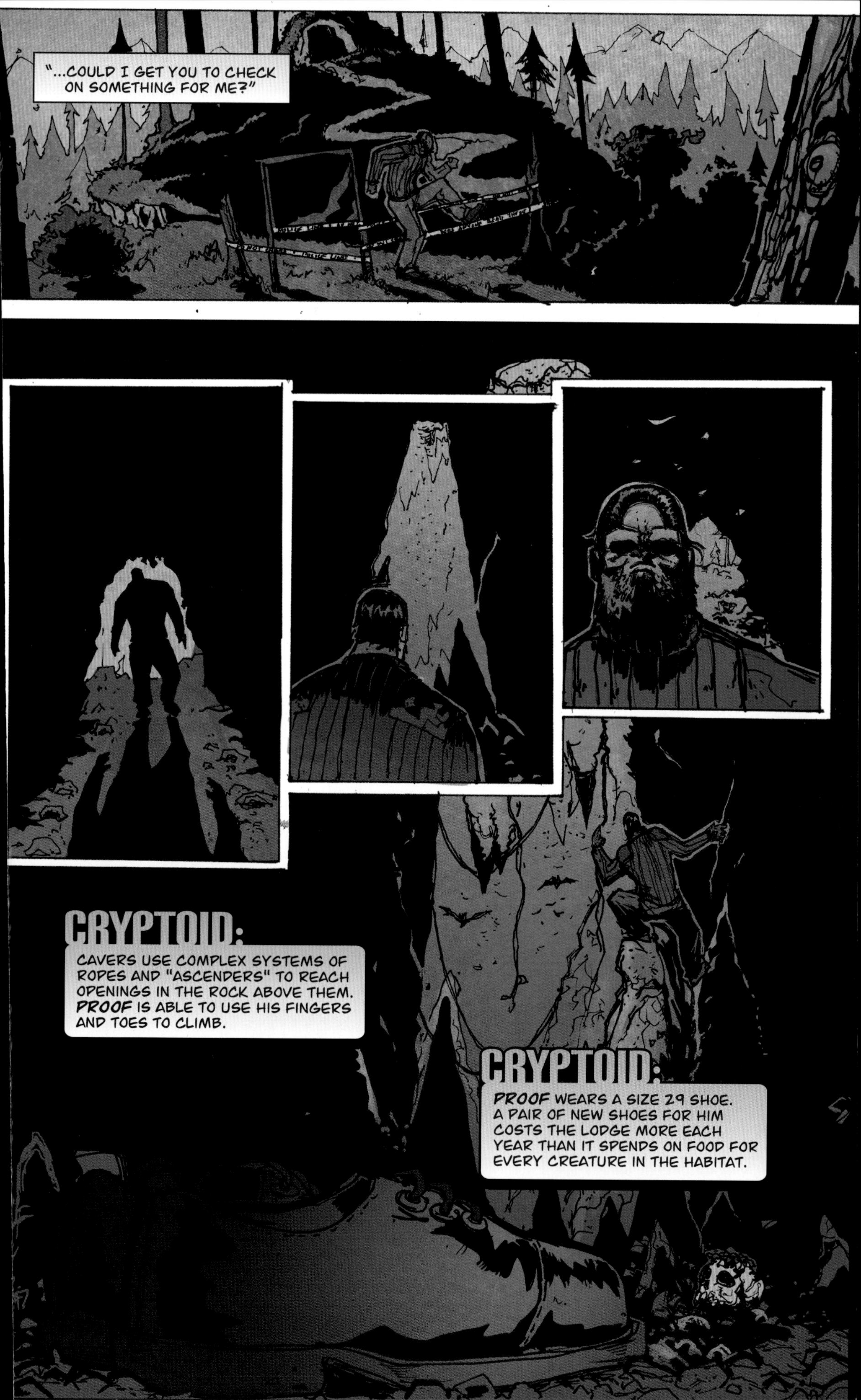
"...COULD I GET YOU TO CHECK ON SOMETHING FOR ME?"
CRYPTOID:
CAVERS USE COMPLEX SYSTEMS OF ROPES AND "ASCENDERS" TO REACH OPENINGS IN THE ROCK ABOVE THEM. PROOF IS ABLE TO USE HIS FINGERS AND TOES TO CLIMB.
CRYPTOID:
PROOF WEARS A SIZE 29 SHOE. A PAIR OF NEW SHOES FOR HIM COSTS THE LODGE MORE EACH YEAR THAN IT SPENDS ON FOOD FOR EVERY CREATURE IN THE HABITAT.

SKRRTCHSKRITCH

KRAK

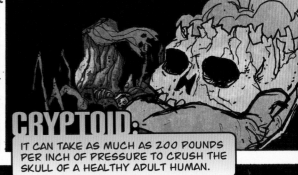

CRYPTOID:
IT CAN TAKE AS MUCH AS 200 POUNDS PER INCH OF PRESSURE TO CRUSH THE SKULL OF A HEALTHY ADULT HUMAN.

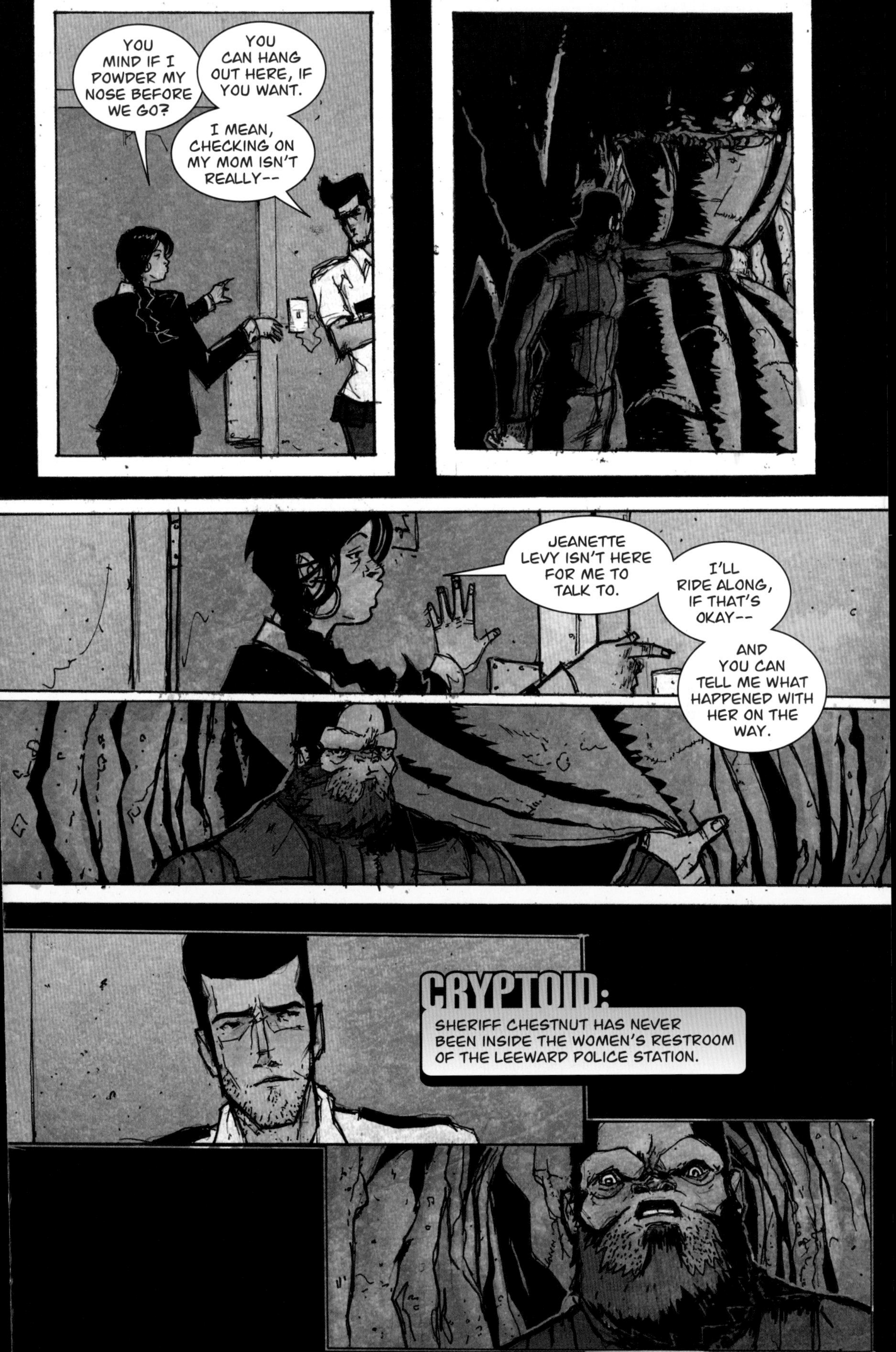
YOU MIND IF I POWDER MY NOSE BEFORE WE GO?
YOU CAN HANG OUT HERE, IF YOU WANT.
I MEAN, CHECKING ON MY MOM ISN'T REALLY--
JEANETTE LEVY ISN'T HERE FOR ME TO TALK TO.
I'LL RIDE ALONG, IF THAT'S OKAY--
AND YOU CAN TELL ME WHAT HAPPENED WITH HER ON THE WAY.
CRYPTOID:
SHERIFF CHESTNUT HAS NEVER BEEN INSIDE THE WOMEN'S RESTROOM OF THE LEEWARD POLICE STATION.

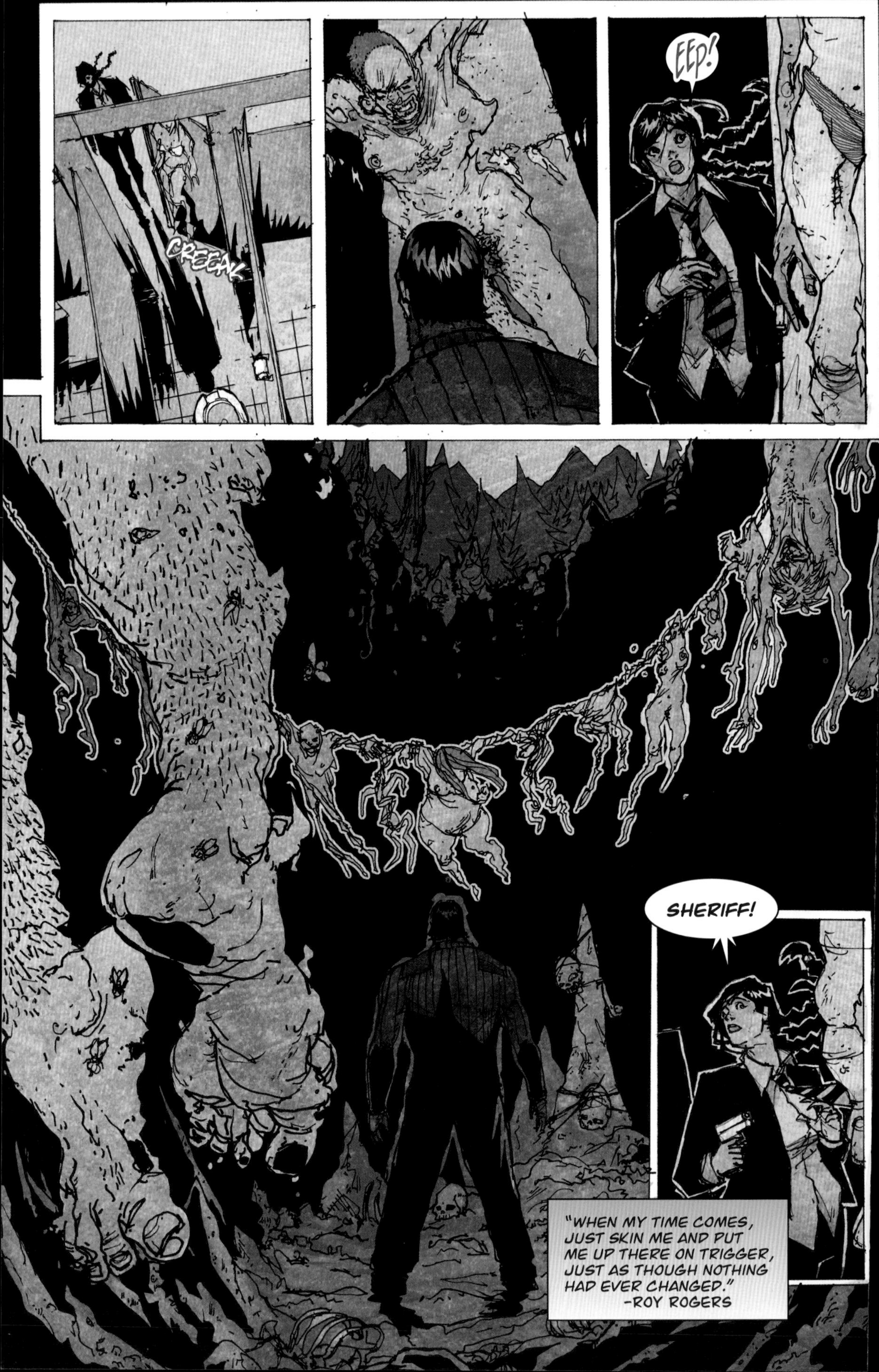
CREEAK
EEP!
SHERIFF!
"WHEN MY TIME COMES, JUST SKIN ME AND PUT ME UP THERE ON TRIGGER, JUST AS THOUGH NOTHING HAD EVER CHANGED."
-ROY ROGERS

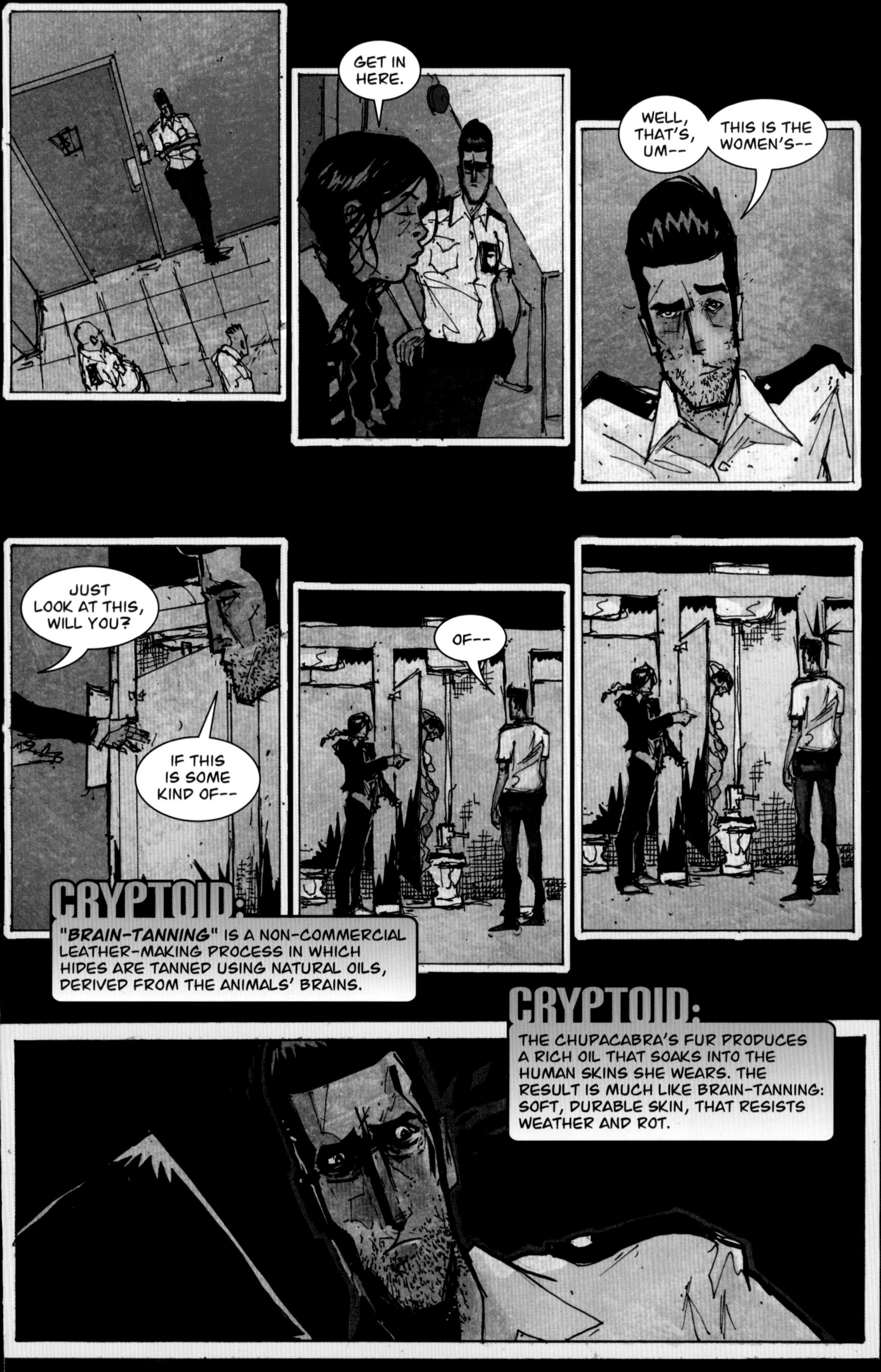
GET IN HERE.
WELL, THAT'S, UM--
THIS IS THE WOMEN'S--
JUST LOOK AT THIS, WILL YOU?
IF THIS IS SOME KIND OF--
OF--
CRYPTOID:
"BRAIN-TANNING" IS A NON-COMMERCIAL LEATHER-MAKING PROCESS IN WHICH HIDES ARE TANNED USING NATURAL OILS, DERIVED FROM THE ANIMALS' BRAINS.
CRYPTOID:
THE CHUPACABRA'S FUR PRODUCES A RICH OIL THAT SOAKS INTO THE HUMAN SKINS SHE WEARS. THE RESULT IS MUCH LIKE BRAIN-TANNING: SOFT, DURABLE SKIN, THAT RESISTS WEATHER AND ROT.

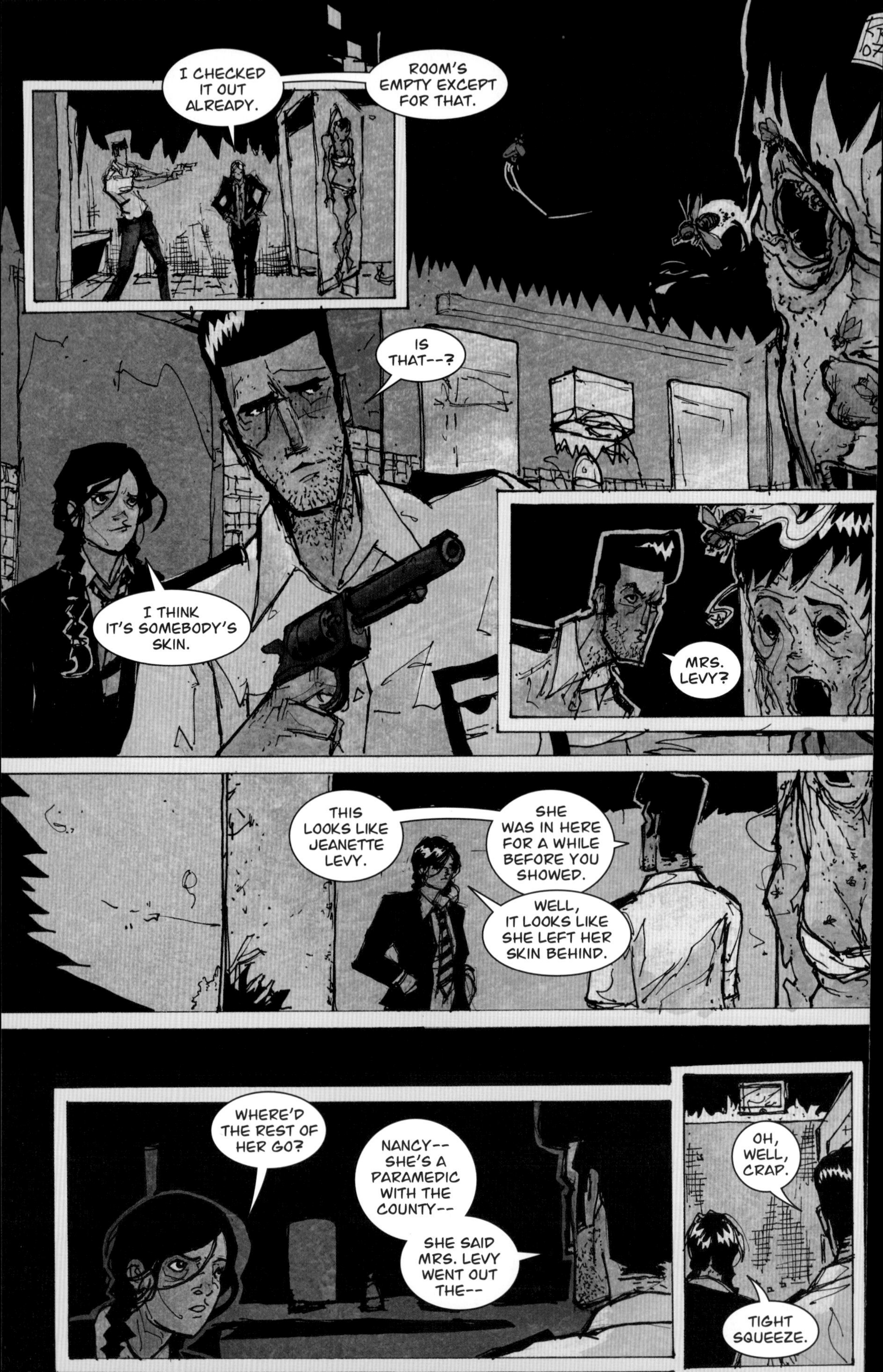
I CHECKED IT OUT ALREADY.
ROOM'S EMPTY EXCEPT FOR THAT.
IS THAT--?
I THINK IT'S SOMEBODY'S SKIN.
MRS. LEVY?
THIS LOOKS LIKE JEANETTE LEVY.
SHE WAS IN HERE FOR A WHILE BEFORE YOU SHOWED.
WELL, IT LOOKS LIKE SHE LEFT HER SKIN BEHIND.
WHERE'D THE REST OF HER GO?
NANCY-- SHE'S A PARAMEDIC WITH THE COUNTY--
SHE SAID MRS. LEVY WENT OUT THE--
OH, WELL, CRAP.
TIGHT SQUEEZE.

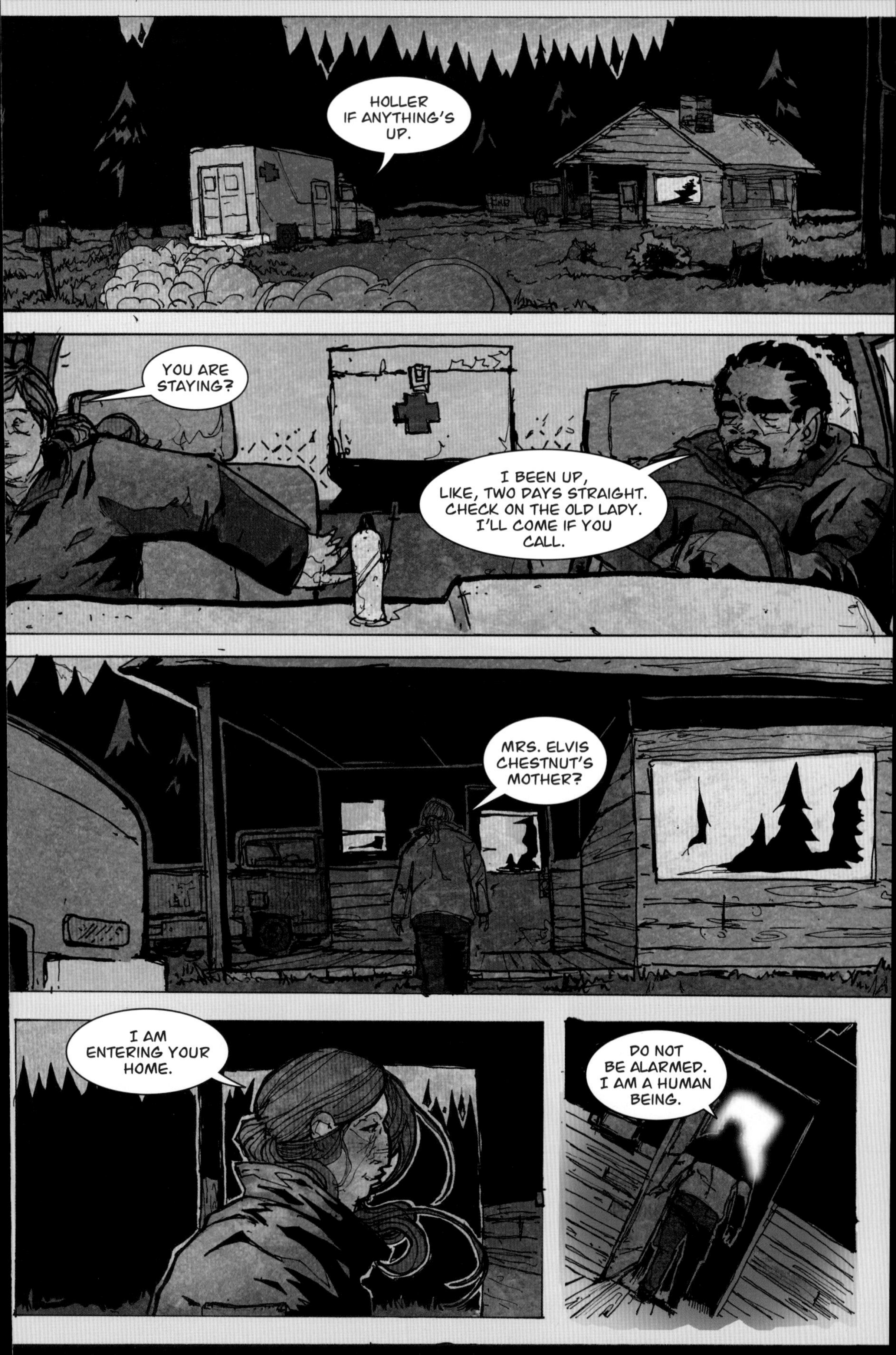
HOLLER IF ANYTHING'S UP.
YOU ARE STAYING?
I BEEN UP, LIKE, TWO DAYS STRAIGHT. CHECK ON THE OLD LADY. I'LL COME IF YOU CALL.
MRS. ELVIS CHESTNUT'S MOTHER?
I AM ENTERING YOUR HOME.
DO NOT BE ALARMED. I AM A HUMAN BEING.

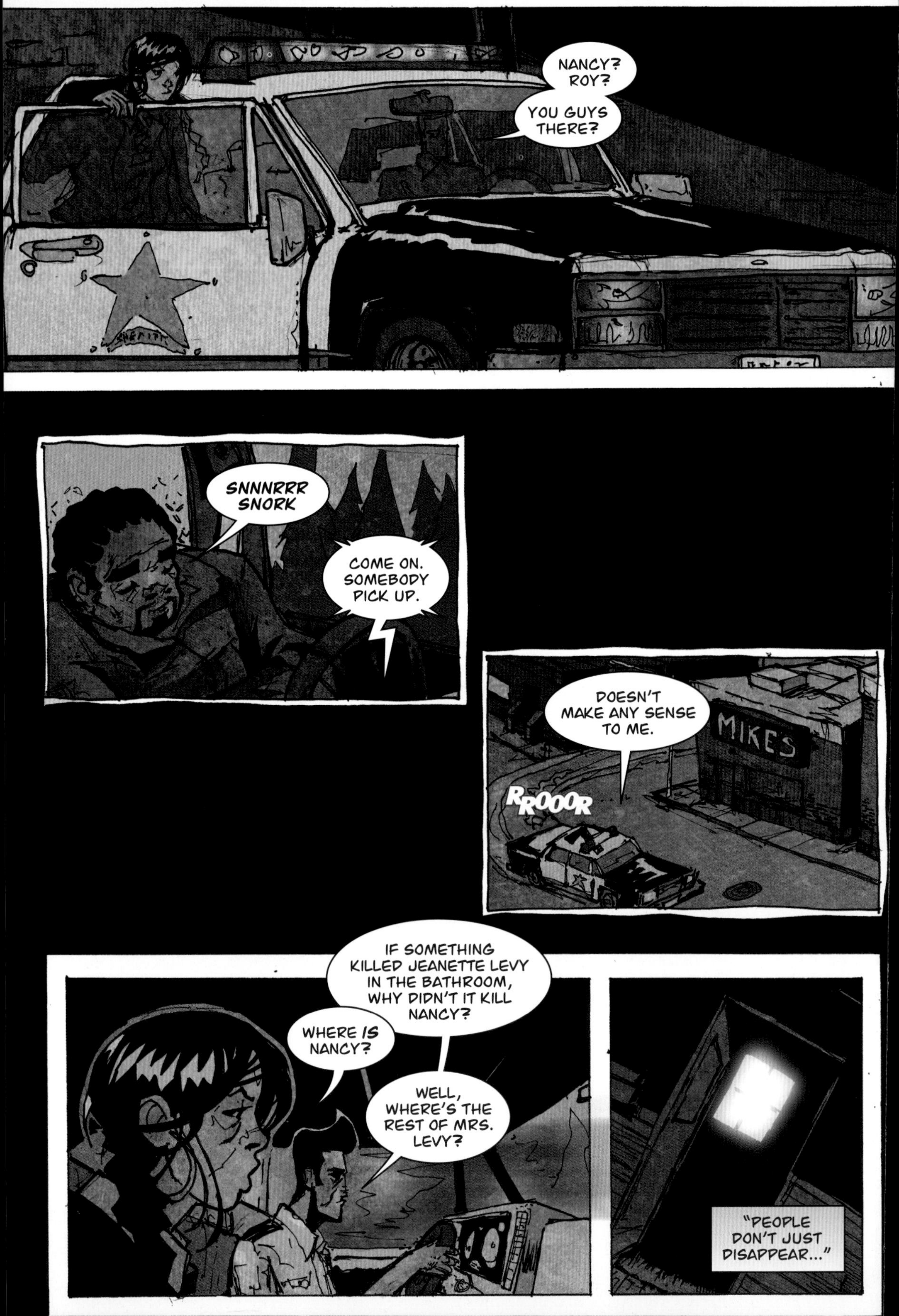
NANCY? ROY?
YOU GUYS THERE?
SNNNRRR SNORK
COME ON. SOMEBODY PICK UP.
DOESN'T MAKE ANY SENSE TO ME.
MIKES
RROOOR
IF SOMETHING KILLED JEANETTE LEVY IN THE BATHROOM, WHY DIDN'T IT KILL NANCY?
WHERE *IS* NANCY?
WELL, WHERE'S THE REST OF MRS. LEVY?
"PEOPLE DON'T JUST DISAPPEAR..."

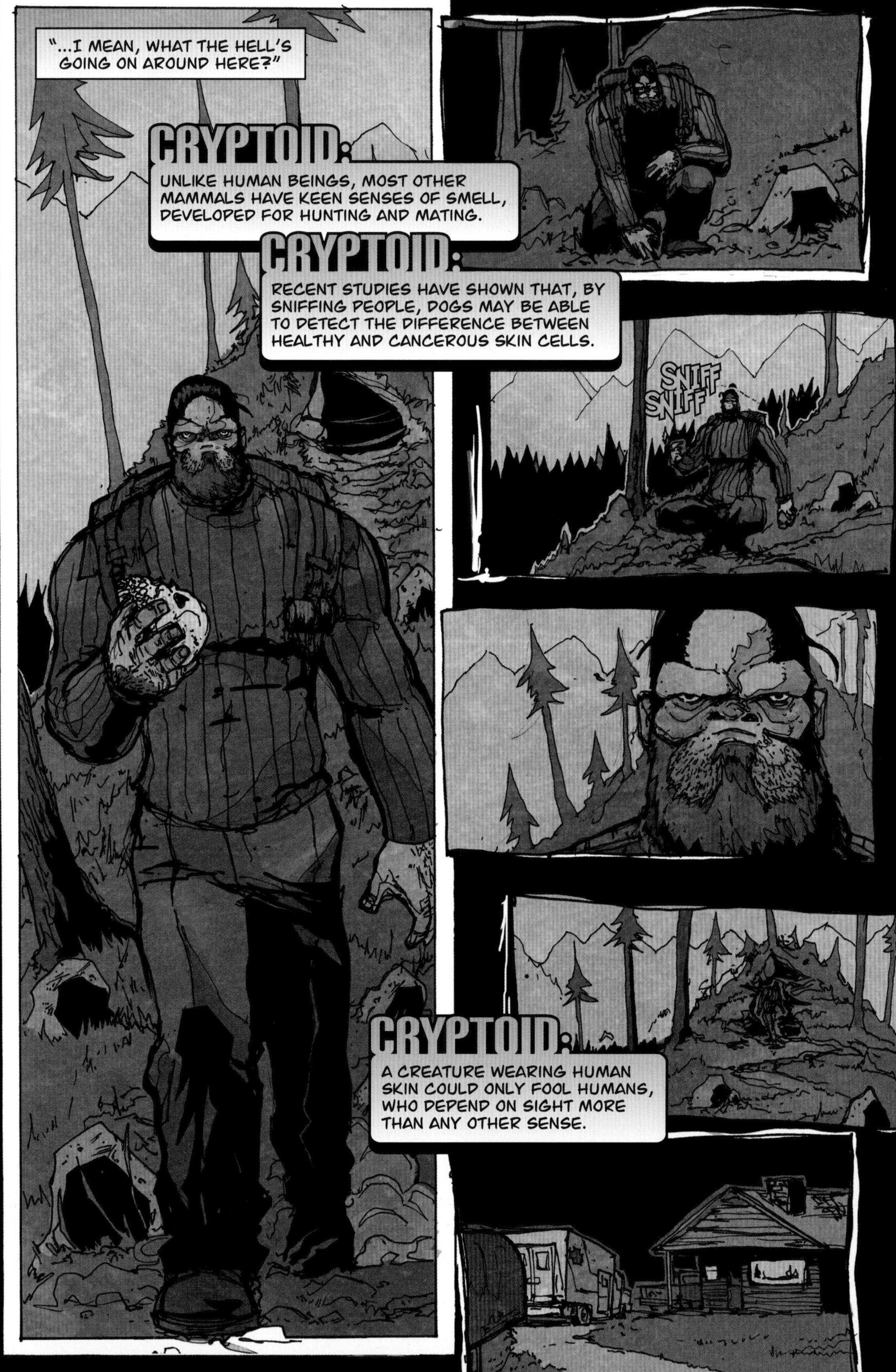

"...I MEAN, WHAT THE HELL'S GOING ON AROUND HERE?"
CRYPTOID:
UNLIKE HUMAN BEINGS, MOST OTHER MAMMALS HAVE KEEN SENSES OF SMELL, DEVELOPED FOR HUNTING AND MATING.
CRYPTOID:
RECENT STUDIES HAVE SHOWN THAT, BY SNIFFING PEOPLE, DOGS MAY BE ABLE TO DETECT THE DIFFERENCE BETWEEN HEALTHY AND CANCEROUS SKIN CELLS.
SNIFF SNIFF
CRYPTOID:
A CREATURE WEARING HUMAN SKIN COULD ONLY FOOL HUMANS, WHO DEPEND ON SIGHT MORE THAN ANY OTHER SENSE.

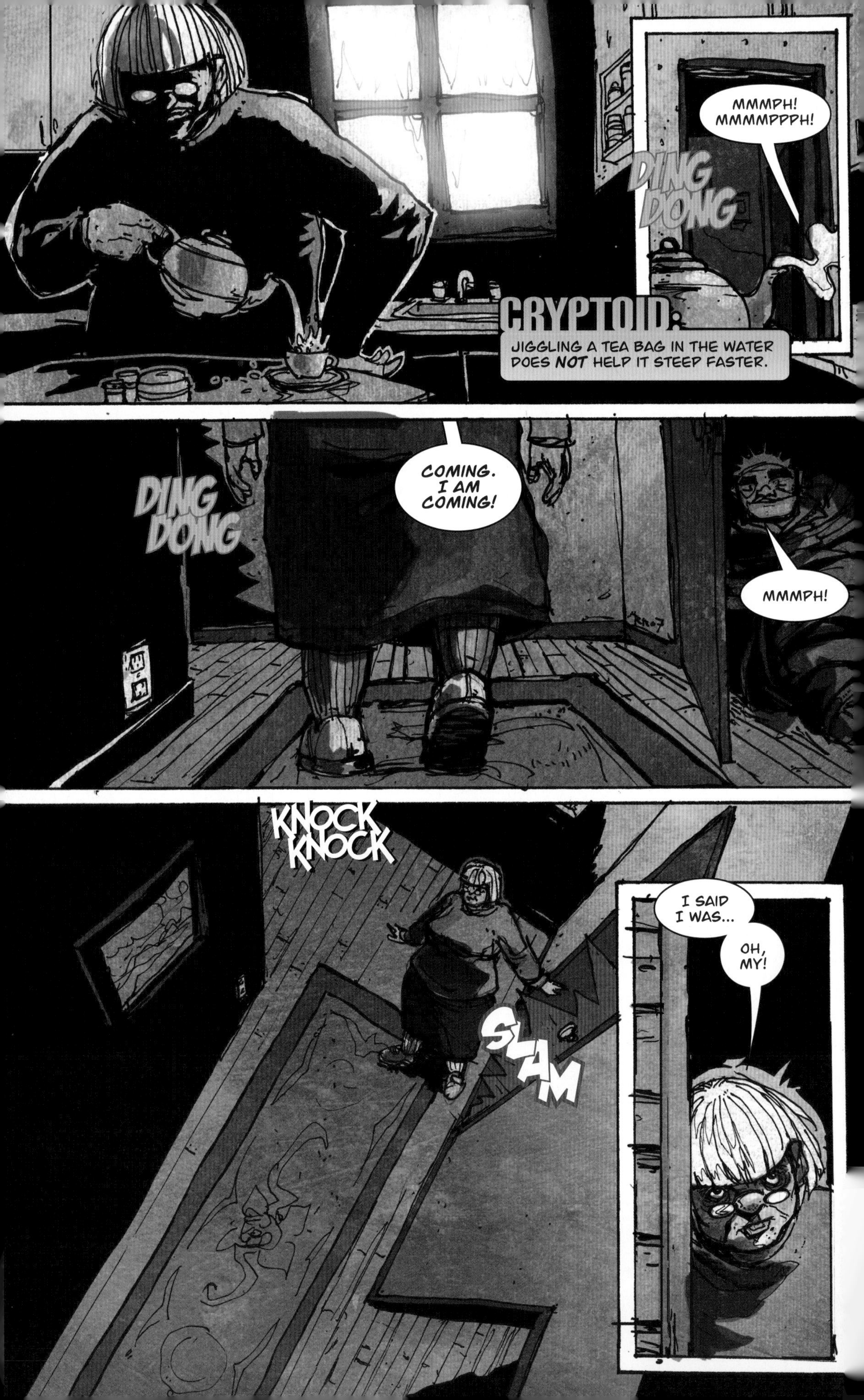
DING DONG
MMMPH! MMMMPPPH!
CRYPTOID:
JIGGLING A TEA BAG IN THE WATER DOES NOT HELP IT STEEP FASTER.
DING DONG
COMING. I AM COMING!
MMMPH!
KNOCK KNOCK
SLAM
I SAID I WAS...
OH, MY!

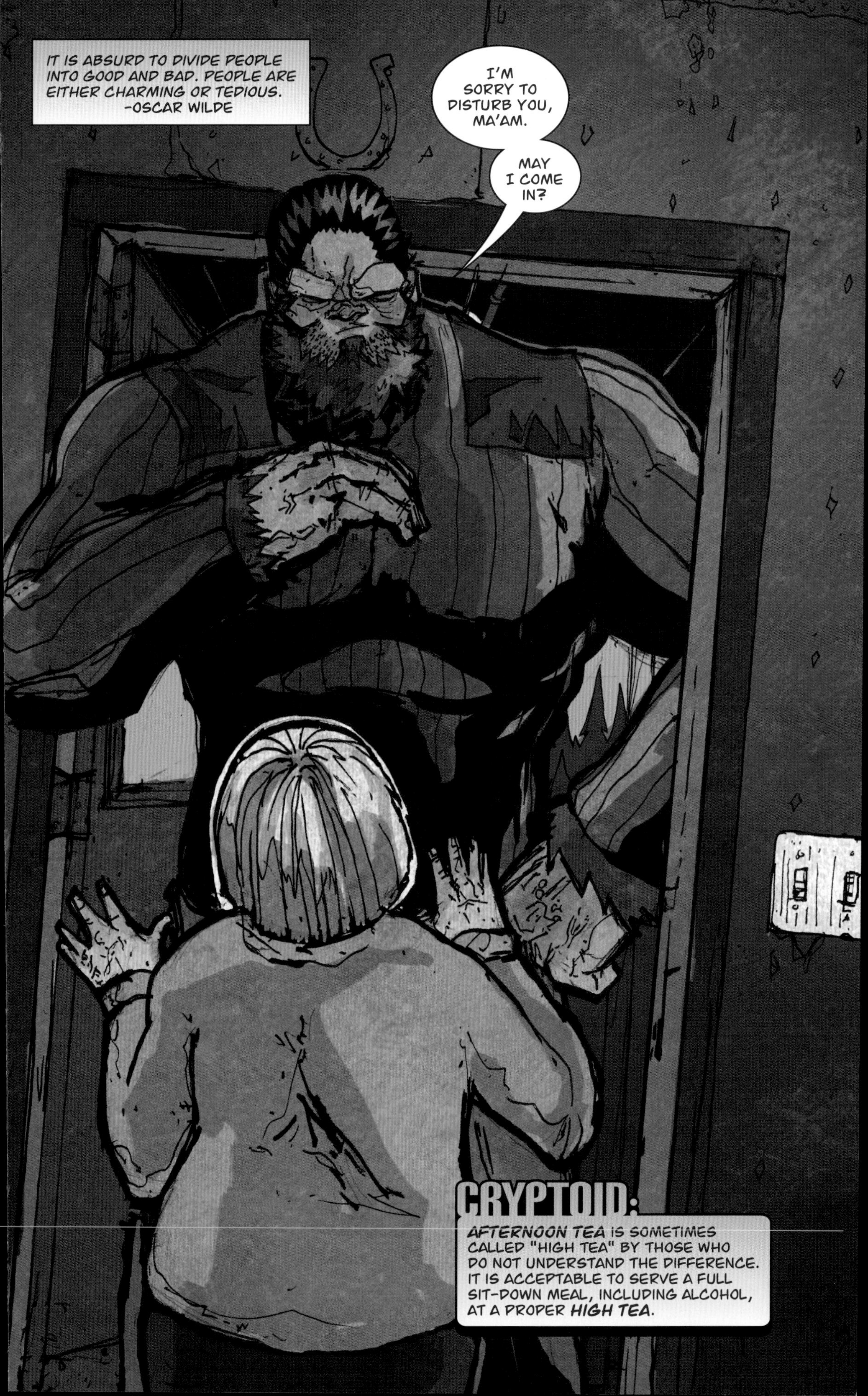

IT IS ABSURD TO DIVIDE PEOPLE INTO GOOD AND BAD. PEOPLE ARE EITHER CHARMING OR TEDIOUS. -OSCAR WILDE
I'M SORRY TO DISTURB YOU, MA'AM.
MAY I COME IN?
CRYPTOID:
AFTERNOON TEA IS SOMETIMES CALLED "HIGH TEA" BY THOSE WHO DO NOT UNDERSTAND THE DIFFERENCE. IT IS ACCEPTABLE TO SERVE A FULL SIT-DOWN MEAL, INCLUDING ALCOHOL, AT A PROPER HIGH TEA.

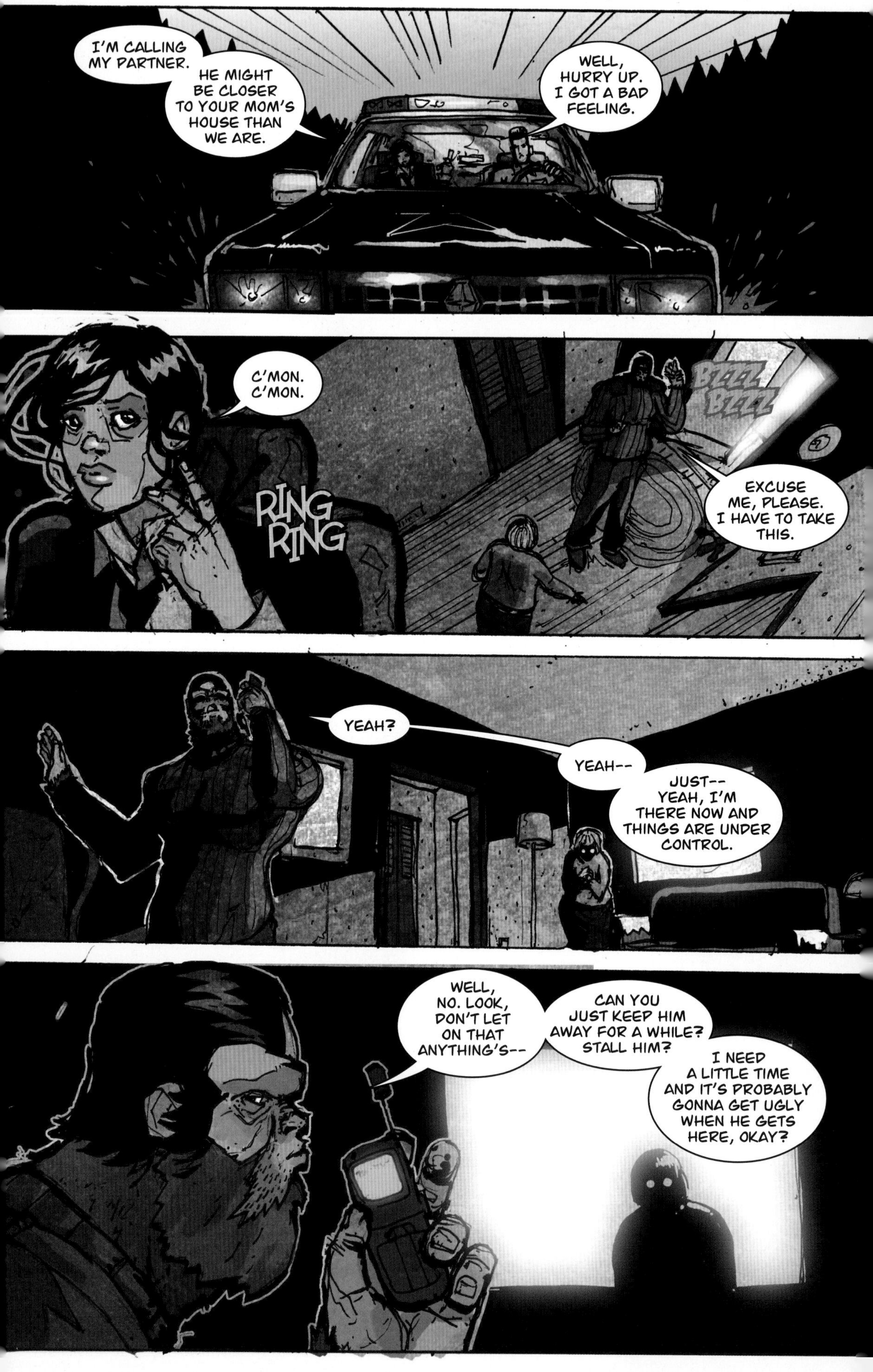
I'M CALLING MY PARTNER.
HE MIGHT BE CLOSER TO YOUR MOM'S HOUSE THAN WE ARE.
WELL, HURRY UP. I GOT A BAD FEELING.
C'MON. C'MON.
RING RING
BZZZ BZZZ
EXCUSE ME, PLEASE. I HAVE TO TAKE THIS.
YEAH?
YEAH--
JUST-- YEAH, I'M THERE NOW AND THINGS ARE UNDER CONTROL.
WELL, NO. LOOK, DON'T LET ON THAT ANYTHING'S--
CAN YOU JUST KEEP HIM AWAY FOR A WHILE? STALL HIM?
I NEED A LITTLE TIME AND IT'S PROBABLY GONNA GET UGLY WHEN HE GETS HERE, OKAY?

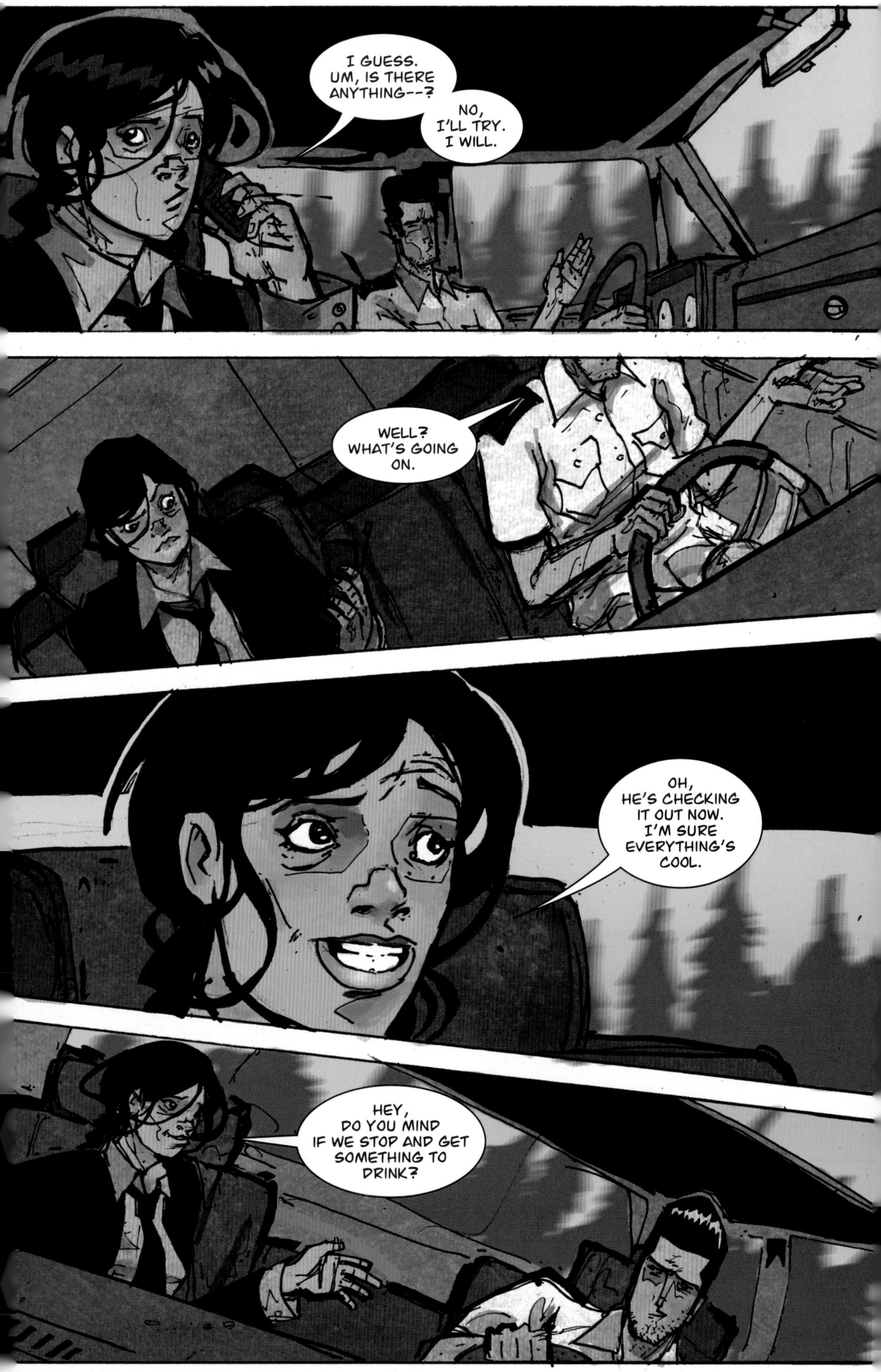
I GUESS. UM, IS THERE ANYTHING--?
NO, I'LL TRY. I WILL.
WELL? WHAT'S GOING ON.
OH, HE'S CHECKING IT OUT NOW. I'M SURE EVERYTHING'S COOL.
HEY, DO YOU MIND IF WE STOP AND GET SOMETHING TO DRINK?

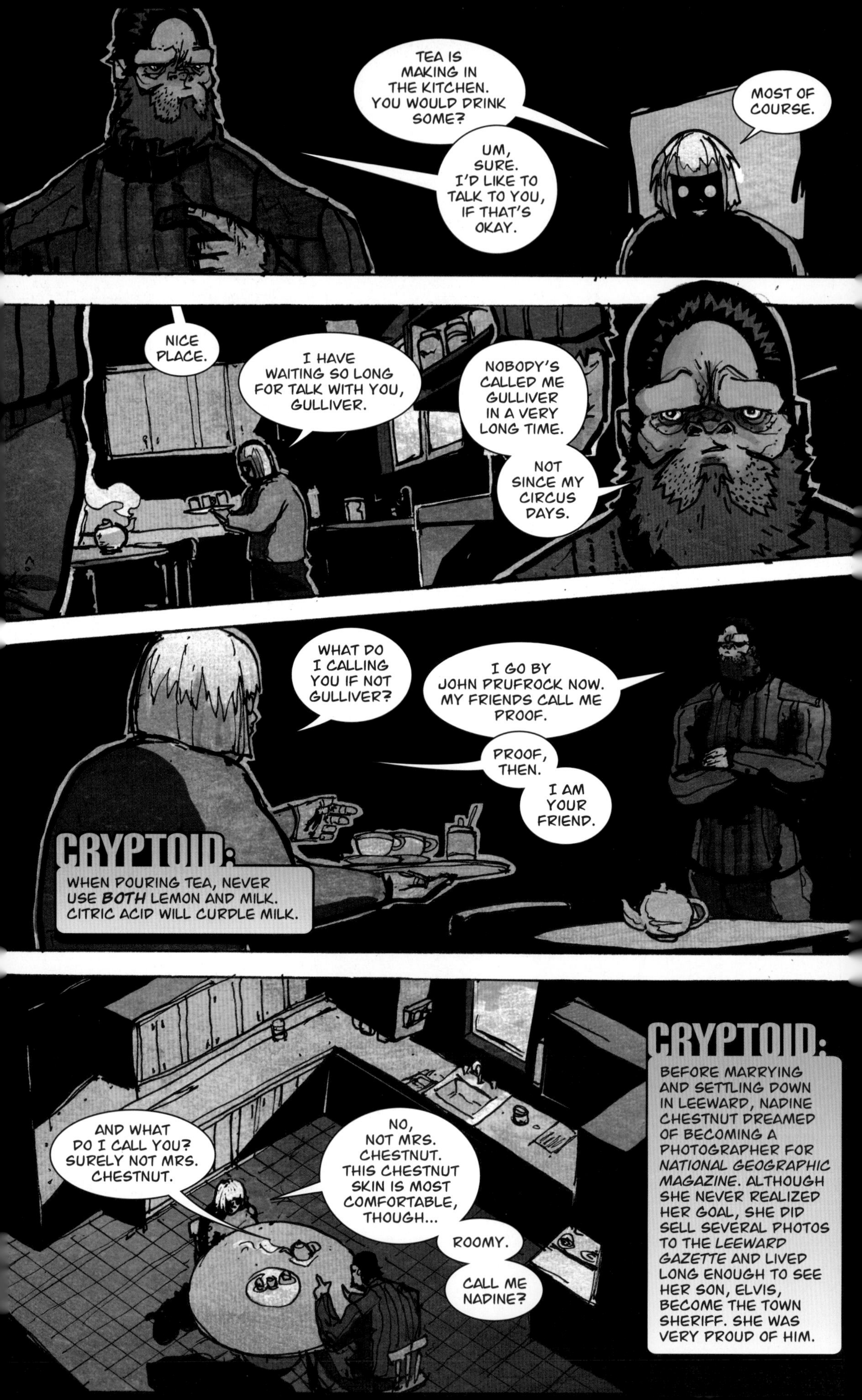

TEA IS MAKING IN THE KITCHEN. YOU WOULD DRINK SOME?
UM, SURE. I'D LIKE TO TALK TO YOU, IF THAT'S OKAY.
MOST OF COURSE.
NICE PLACE.
I HAVE WAITING SO LONG FOR TALK WITH YOU, GULLIVER.
NOBODY'S CALLED ME GULLIVER IN A VERY LONG TIME.
NOT SINCE MY CIRCUS DAYS.
WHAT DO I CALLING YOU IF NOT GULLIVER?
I GO BY JOHN PRUFROCK NOW. MY FRIENDS CALL ME PROOF.
PROOF, THEN.
I AM YOUR FRIEND.
CRYPTOID:
WHEN POURING TEA, NEVER USE *BOTH* LEMON AND MILK. CITRIC ACID WILL CURDLE MILK.
AND WHAT DO I CALL YOU? SURELY NOT MRS. CHESTNUT.
NO, NOT MRS. CHESTNUT. THIS CHESTNUT SKIN IS MOST COMFORTABLE, THOUGH...
ROOMY.
CALL ME NADINE?
CRYPTOID:
BEFORE MARRYING AND SETTLING DOWN IN LEEWARD, NADINE CHESTNUT DREAMED OF BECOMING A PHOTOGRAPHER FOR *NATIONAL GEOGRAPHIC MAGAZINE*. ALTHOUGH SHE NEVER REALIZED HER GOAL, SHE DID SELL SEVERAL PHOTOS TO THE *LEEWARD GAZETTE* AND LIVED LONG ENOUGH TO SEE HER SON, ELVIS, BECOME THE TOWN SHERIFF. SHE WAS VERY PROUD OF HIM.

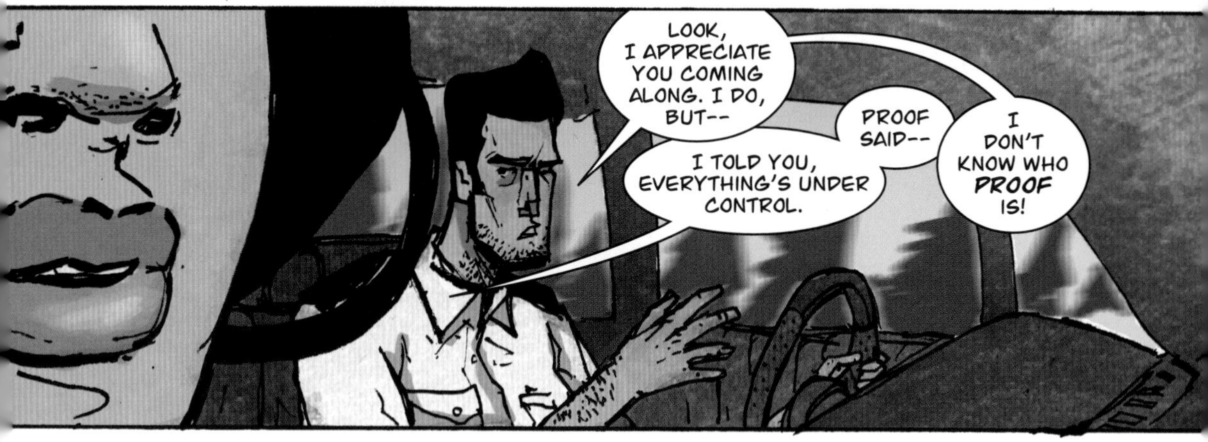
LOOK, I APPRECIATE YOU COMING ALONG. I DO, BUT--
I TOLD YOU, EVERYTHING'S UNDER CONTROL.
PROOF SAID--
I DON'T KNOW WHO **PROOF** IS!

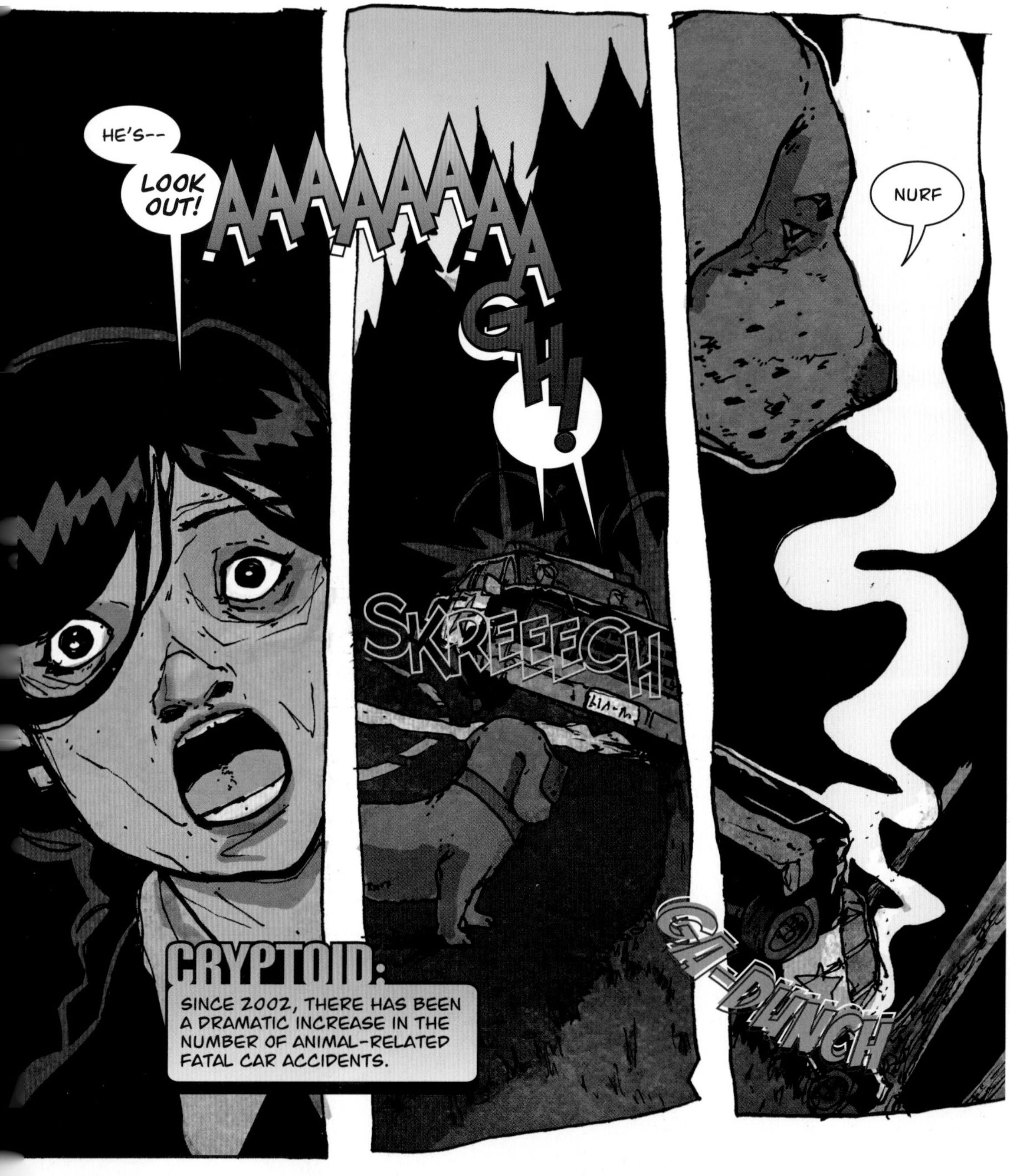
HE'S--
LOOK OUT!
AAAAAAAAAGH!
SKREEECH
NURF
CA-DUNCH
CRYPTOID:
SINCE 2002, THERE HAS BEEN A DRAMATIC INCREASE IN THE NUMBER OF ANIMAL-RELATED FATAL CAR ACCIDENTS.

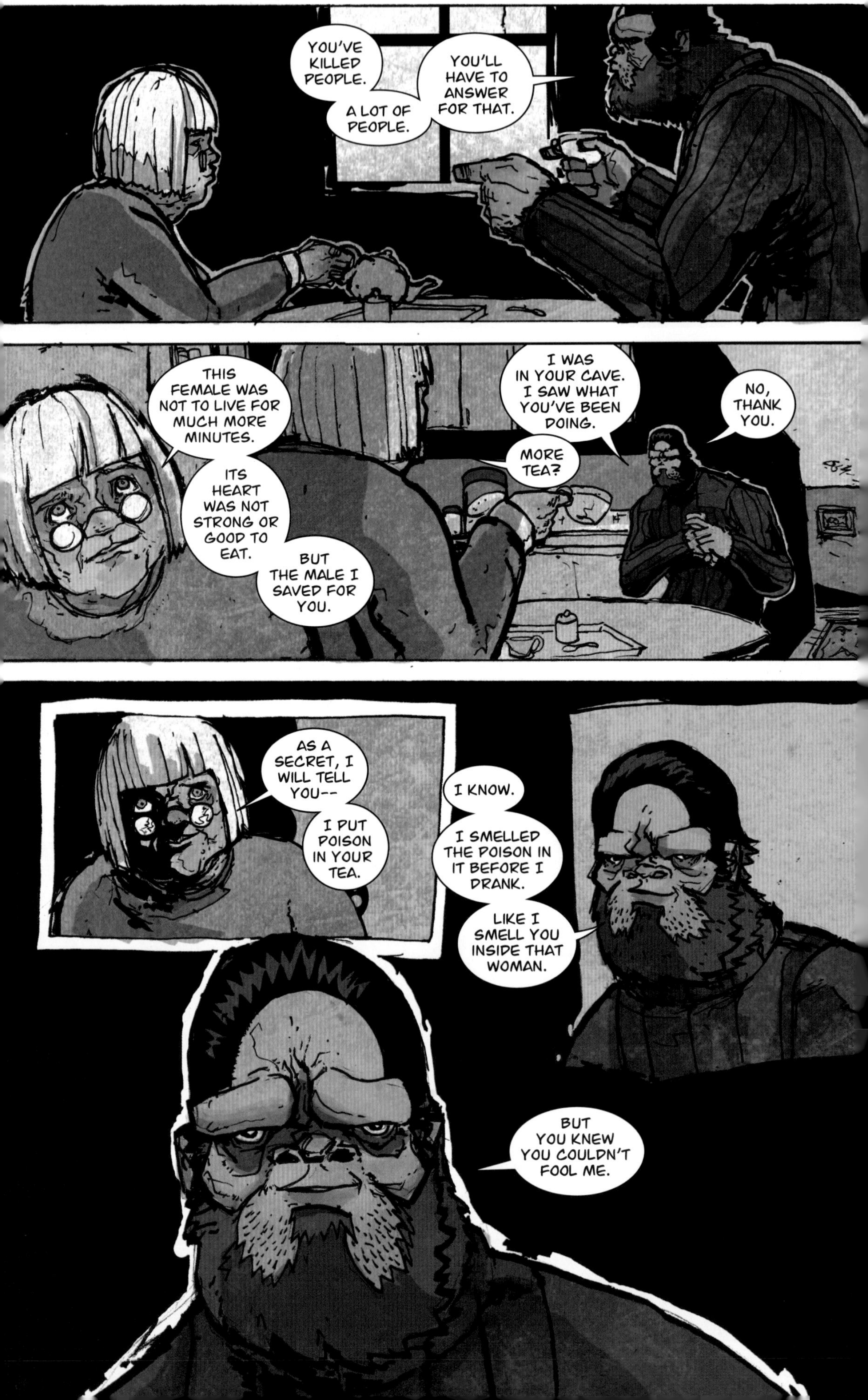

YOU'VE KILLED PEOPLE.
A LOT OF PEOPLE.
YOU'LL HAVE TO ANSWER FOR THAT.
THIS FEMALE WAS NOT TO LIVE FOR MUCH MORE MINUTES.
ITS HEART WAS NOT STRONG OR GOOD TO EAT.
BUT THE MALE I SAVED FOR YOU.
I WAS IN YOUR CAVE. I SAW WHAT YOU'VE BEEN DOING.
MORE TEA?
NO, THANK YOU.
AS A SECRET, I WILL TELL YOU--
I PUT POISON IN YOUR TEA.
I KNOW.
I SMELLED THE POISON IN IT BEFORE I DRANK.
LIKE I SMELL YOU INSIDE THAT WOMAN.
BUT YOU KNEW YOU COULDN'T FOOL ME.

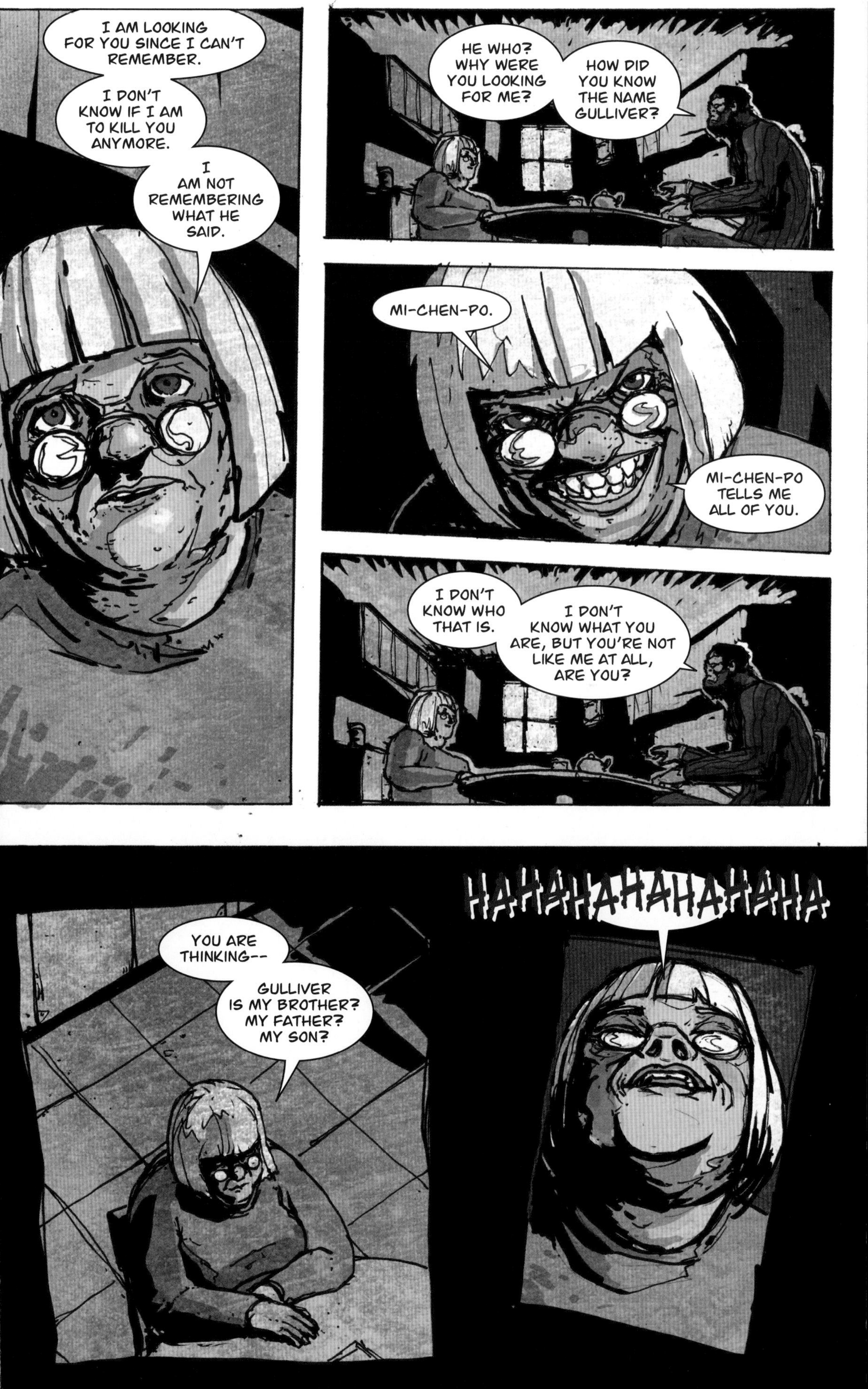
I AM LOOKING FOR YOU SINCE I CAN'T REMEMBER.
I DON'T KNOW IF I AM TO KILL YOU ANYMORE.
I AM NOT REMEMBERING WHAT HE SAID.
HE WHO? WHY WERE YOU LOOKING FOR ME?
HOW DID YOU KNOW THE NAME GULLIVER?
MI-CHEN-PO.
MI-CHEN-PO TELLS ME ALL OF YOU.
I DON'T KNOW WHO THAT IS.
I DON'T KNOW WHAT YOU ARE, BUT YOU'RE NOT LIKE ME AT ALL, ARE YOU?
YOU ARE THINKING--
GULLIVER IS MY BROTHER? MY FATHER? MY SON?
HAHAHAHAHAHAHAHA

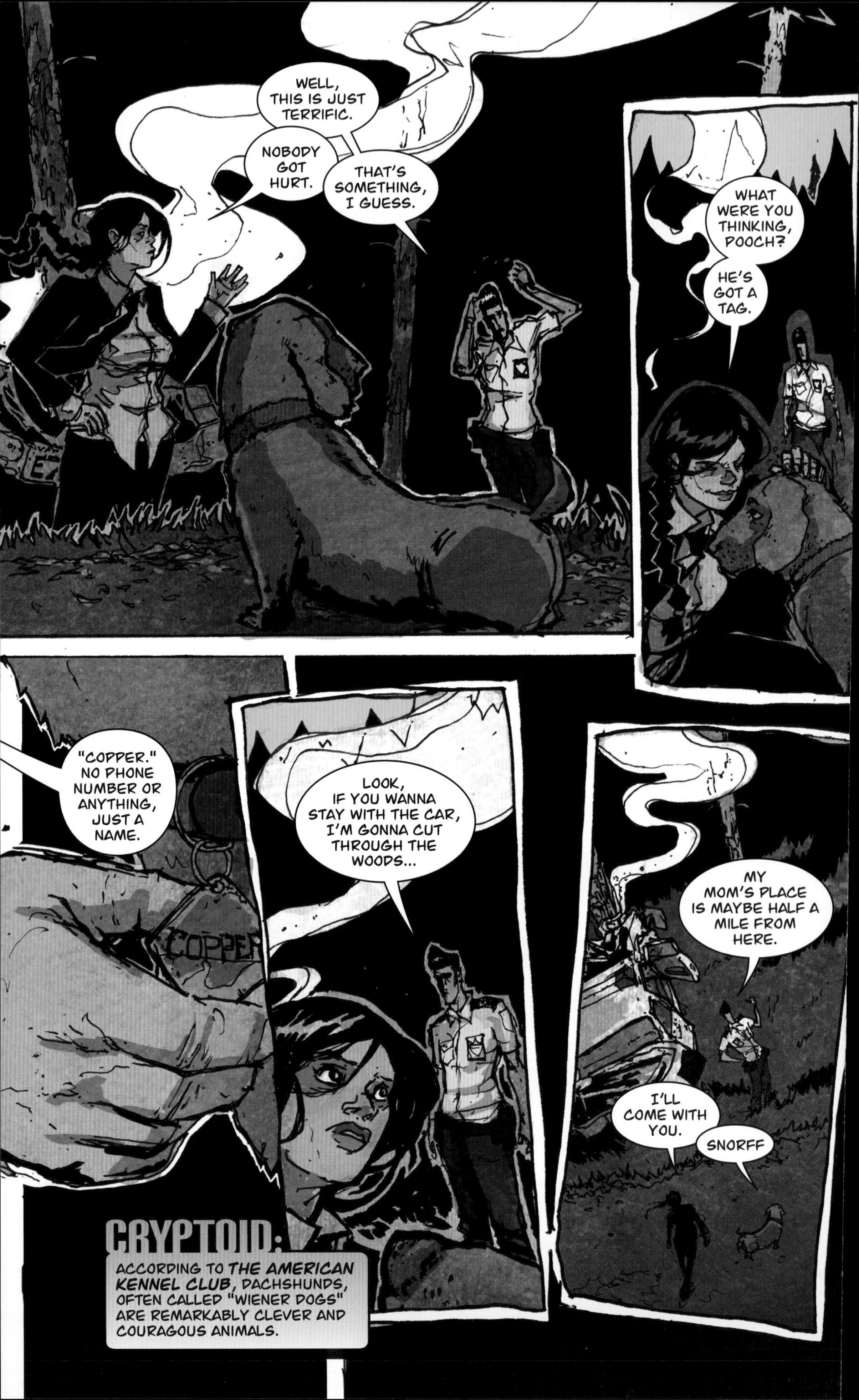

WELL, THIS IS JUST TERRIFIC.
NOBODY GOT HURT.
THAT'S SOMETHING, I GUESS.
WHAT WERE YOU THINKING, POOCH?
HE'S GOT A TAG.
"COPPER." NO PHONE NUMBER OR ANYTHING, JUST A NAME.
COPPER
LOOK, IF YOU WANNA STAY WITH THE CAR, I'M GONNA CUT THROUGH THE WOODS...
MY MOM'S PLACE IS MAYBE HALF A MILE FROM HERE.
I'LL COME WITH YOU.
SNORFF
CRYPTOID:
ACCORDING TO THE AMERICAN KENNEL CLUB, DACHSHUNDS, OFTEN CALLED "WIENER DOGS" ARE REMARKABLY CLEVER AND COURAGOUS ANIMALS.

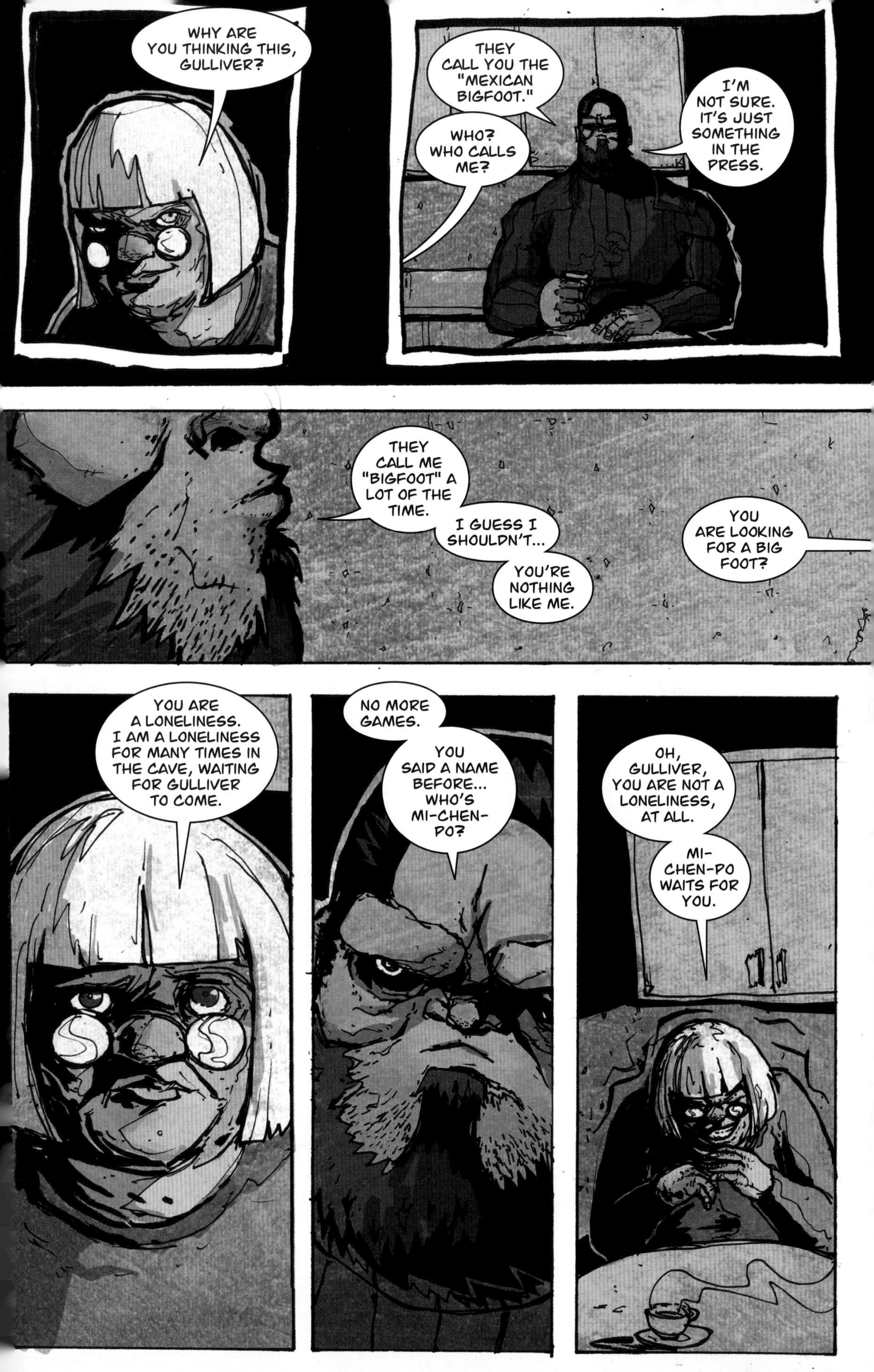
WHY ARE YOU THINKING THIS, GULLIVER?
THEY CALL YOU THE "MEXICAN BIGFOOT."
WHO? WHO CALLS ME?
I'M NOT SURE. IT'S JUST SOMETHING IN THE PRESS.
THEY CALL ME "BIGFOOT" A LOT OF THE TIME.
I GUESS I SHOULDN'T...
YOU'RE NOTHING LIKE ME.
YOU ARE LOOKING FOR A BIG FOOT?
YOU ARE A LONELINESS. I AM A LONELINESS FOR MANY TIMES IN THE CAVE, WAITING FOR GULLIVER TO COME.
NO MORE GAMES.
YOU SAID A NAME BEFORE... WHO'S MI-CHEN-PO?
OH, GULLIVER, YOU ARE NOT A LONELINESS, AT ALL.
MI-CHEN-PO WAITS FOR YOU.

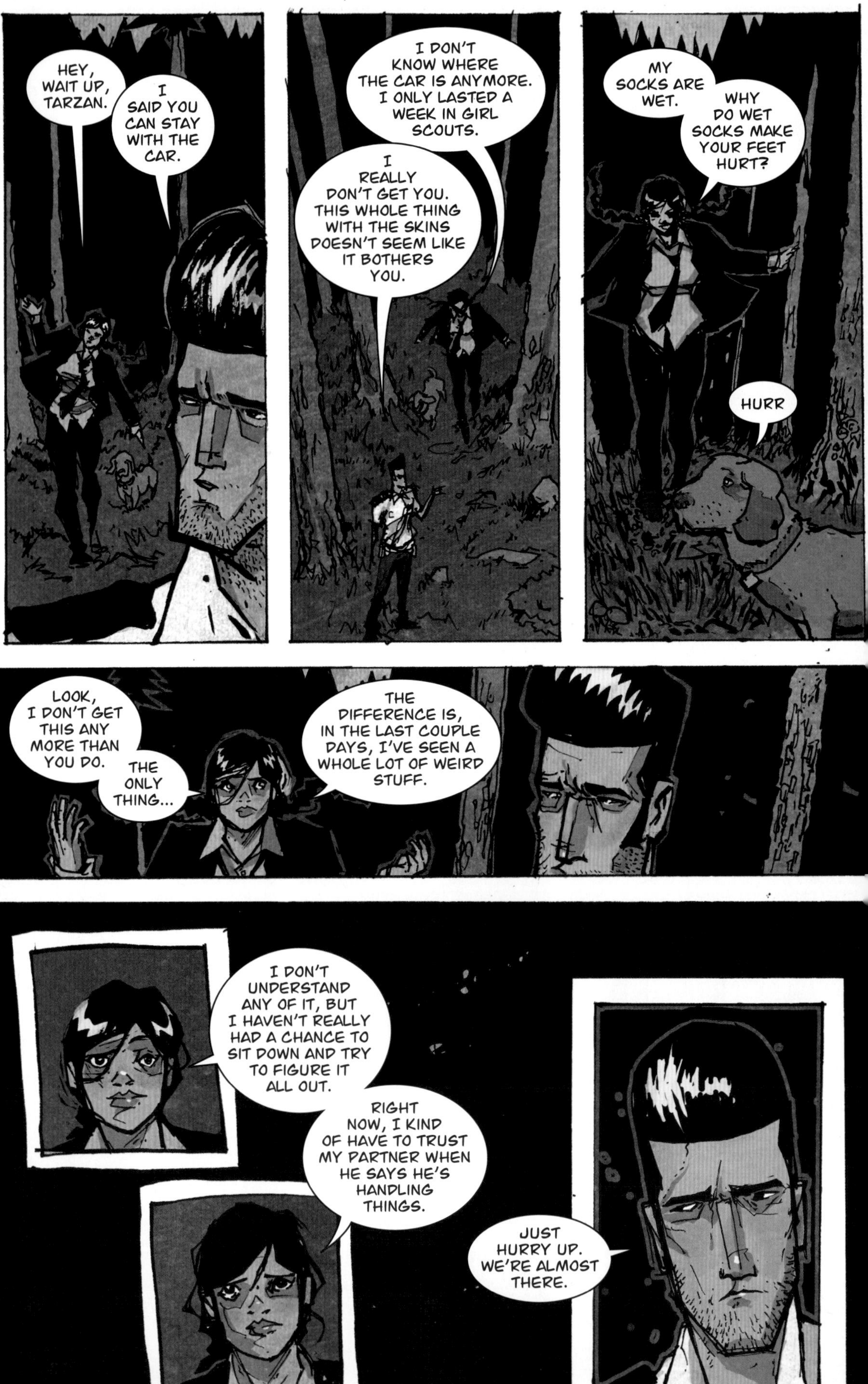
HEY, WAIT UP, TARZAN.
I SAID YOU CAN STAY WITH THE CAR.
I DON'T KNOW WHERE THE CAR IS ANYMORE. I ONLY LASTED A WEEK IN GIRL SCOUTS.
I REALLY DON'T GET YOU. THIS WHOLE THING WITH THE SKINS DOESN'T SEEM LIKE IT BOTHERS YOU.
MY SOCKS ARE WET.
WHY DO WET SOCKS MAKE YOUR FEET HURT?
HURR
LOOK, I DON'T GET THIS ANY MORE THAN YOU DO.
THE ONLY THING...
THE DIFFERENCE IS, IN THE LAST COUPLE DAYS, I'VE SEEN A WHOLE LOT OF WEIRD STUFF.
I DON'T UNDERSTAND ANY OF IT, BUT I HAVEN'T REALLY HAD A CHANCE TO SIT DOWN AND TRY TO FIGURE IT ALL OUT.
RIGHT NOW, I KIND OF HAVE TO TRUST MY PARTNER WHEN HE SAYS HE'S HANDLING THINGS.
JUST HURRY UP. WE'RE ALMOST THERE.

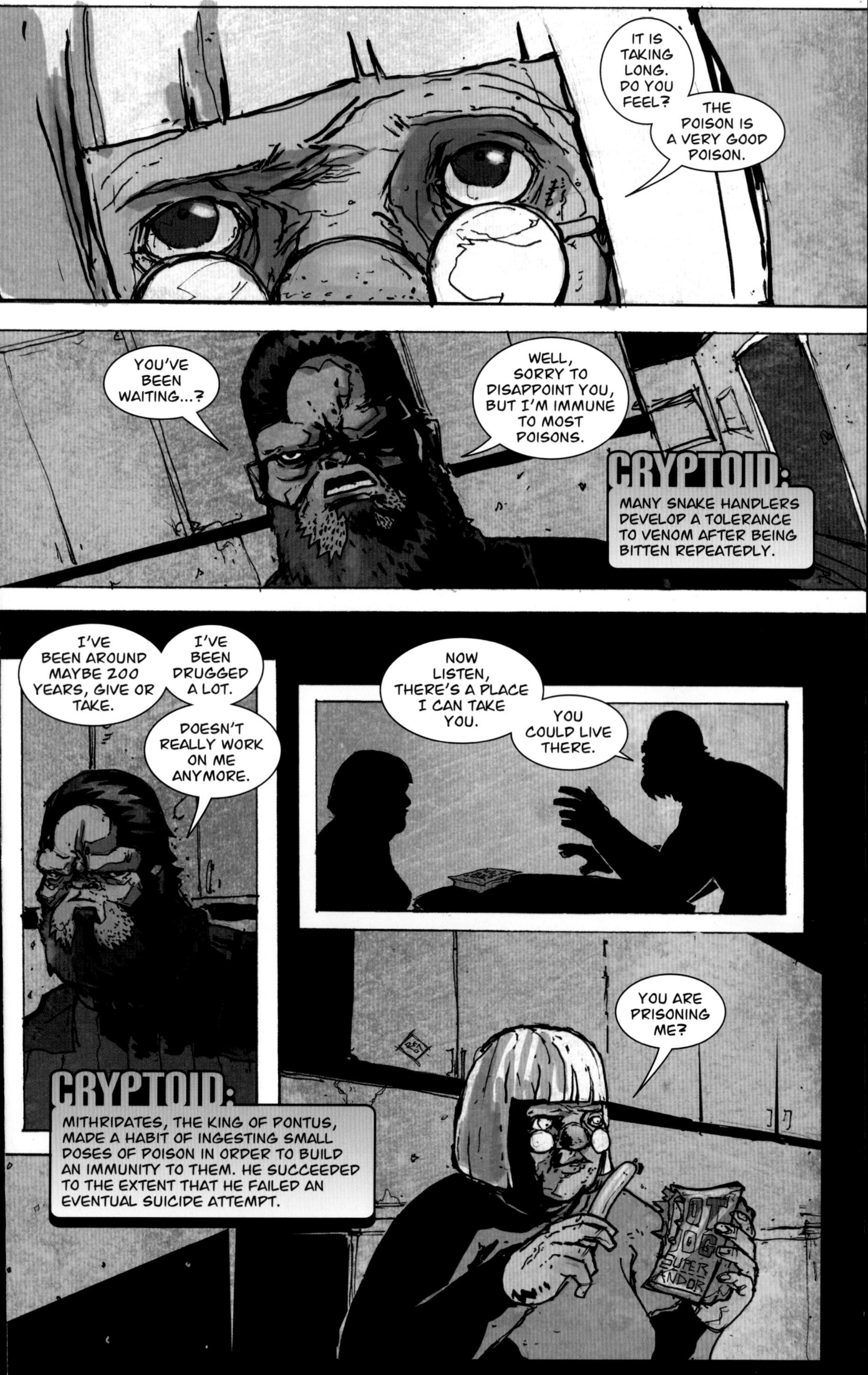

IT IS TAKING LONG. DO YOU FEEL?
THE POISON IS A VERY GOOD POISON.
YOU'VE BEEN WAITING...?
WELL, SORRY TO DISAPPOINT YOU, BUT I'M IMMUNE TO MOST POISONS.
CRYPTOID:
MANY SNAKE HANDLERS DEVELOP A TOLERANCE TO VENOM AFTER BEING BITTEN REPEATEDLY.
I'VE BEEN AROUND MAYBE 200 YEARS, GIVE OR TAKE.
I'VE BEEN DRUGGED A LOT.
DOESN'T REALLY WORK ON ME ANYMORE.
NOW LISTEN, THERE'S A PLACE I CAN TAKE YOU.
YOU COULD LIVE THERE.
YOU ARE PRISONING ME?
CRYPTOID:
MITHRIDATES, THE KING OF PONTUS, MADE A HABIT OF INGESTING SMALL DOSES OF POISON IN ORDER TO BUILD AN IMMUNITY TO THEM. HE SUCCEEDED TO THE EXTENT THAT HE FAILED AN EVENTUAL SUICIDE ATTEMPT.

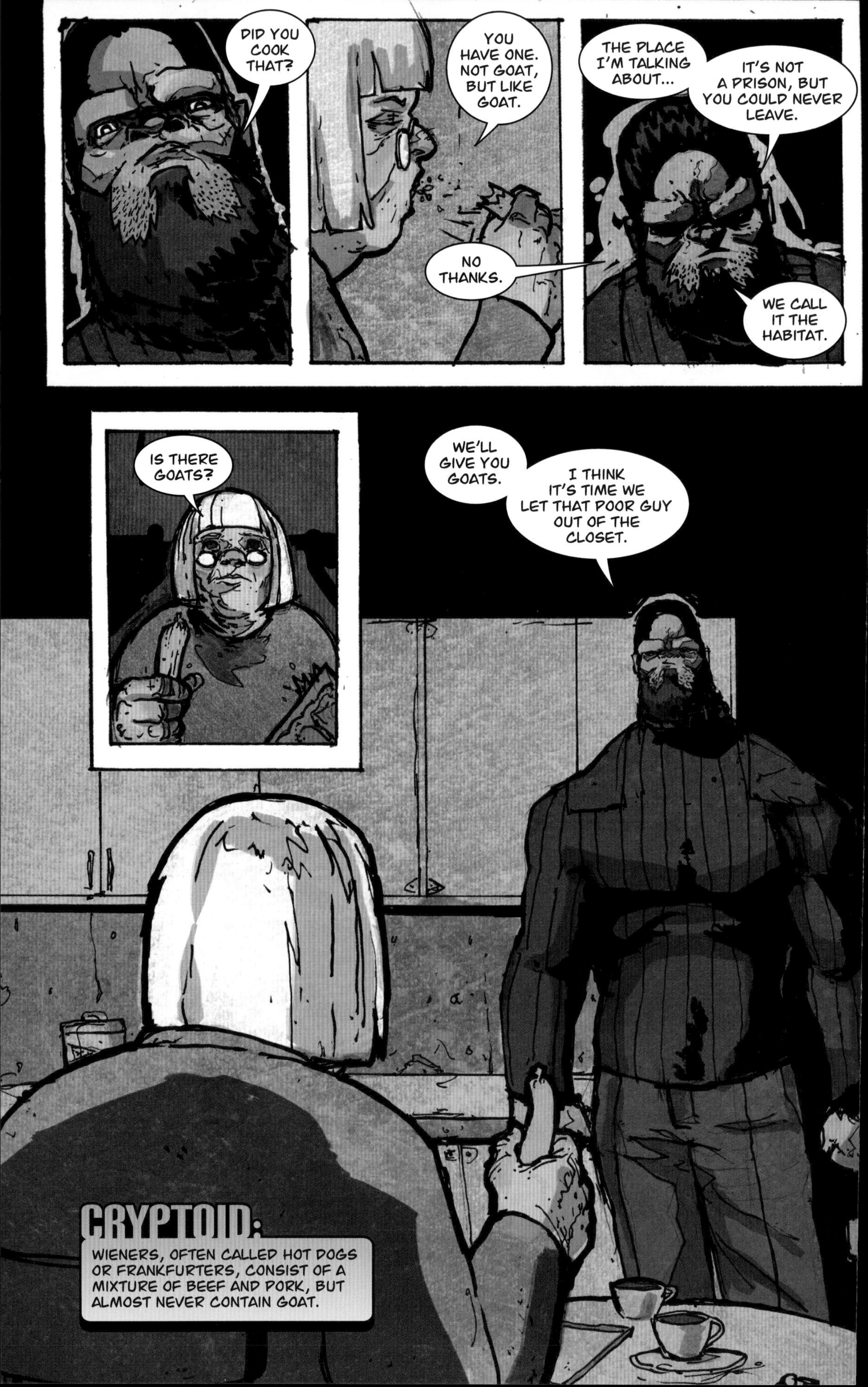
DID YOU COOK THAT?
YOU HAVE ONE. NOT GOAT, BUT LIKE GOAT.
NO THANKS.
THE PLACE I'M TALKING ABOUT...
IT'S NOT A PRISON, BUT YOU COULD NEVER LEAVE.
WE CALL IT THE HABITAT.
IS THERE GOATS?
WE'LL GIVE YOU GOATS.
I THINK IT'S TIME WE LET THAT POOR GUY OUT OF THE CLOSET.
CRYPTOID:
WIENERS, OFTEN CALLED HOT DOGS OR FRANKFURTERS, CONSIST OF A MIXTURE OF BEEF AND PORK, BUT ALMOST NEVER CONTAIN GOAT.

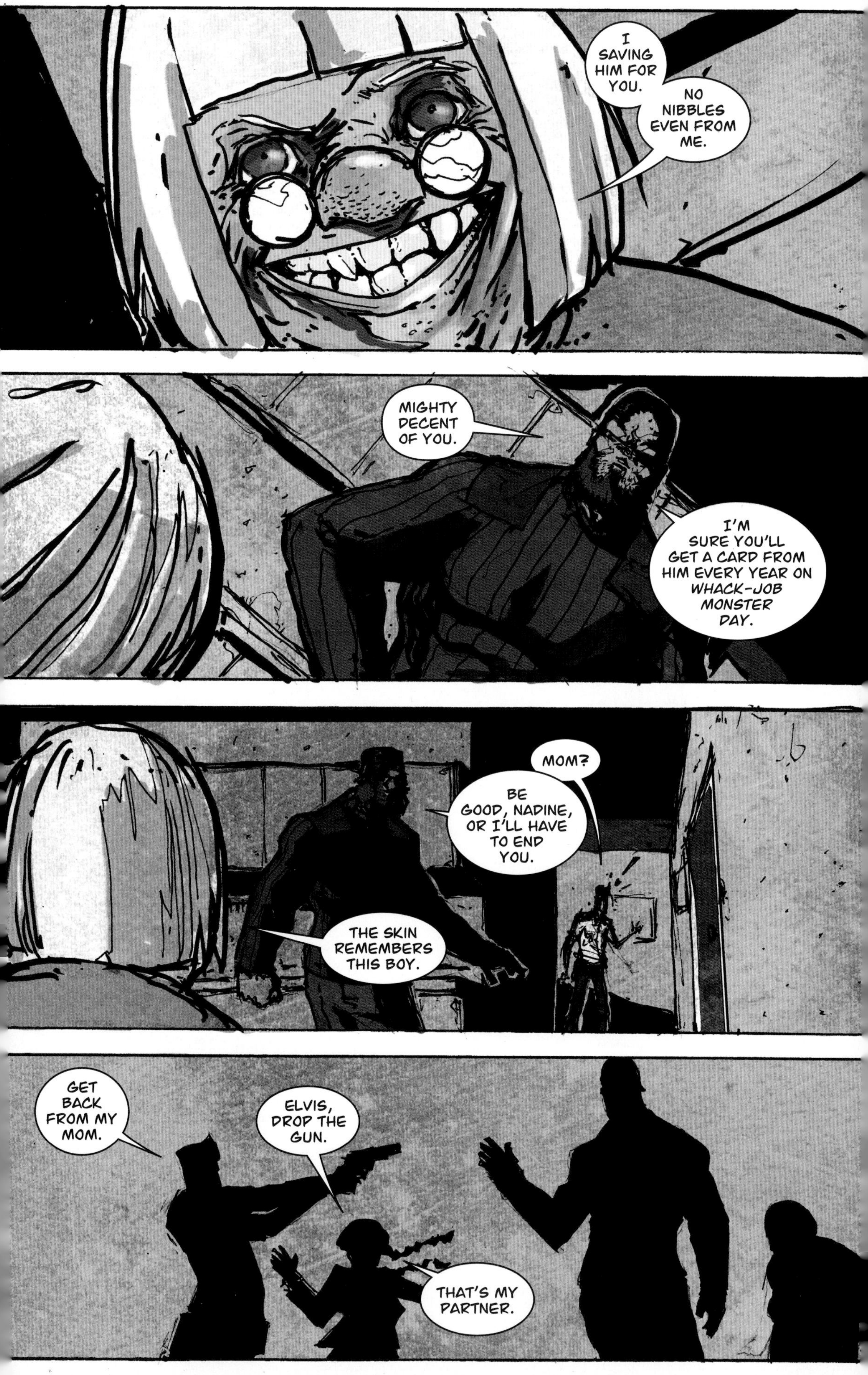
I SAVING HIM FOR YOU.
NO NIBBLES EVEN FROM ME.
MIGHTY DECENT OF YOU.
I'M SURE YOU'LL GET A CARD FROM HIM EVERY YEAR ON WHACK-JOB MONSTER DAY.
MOM?
BE GOOD, NADINE, OR I'LL HAVE TO END YOU.
THE SKIN REMEMBERS THIS BOY.
GET BACK FROM MY MOM.
ELVIS, DROP THE GUN.
THAT'S MY PARTNER.

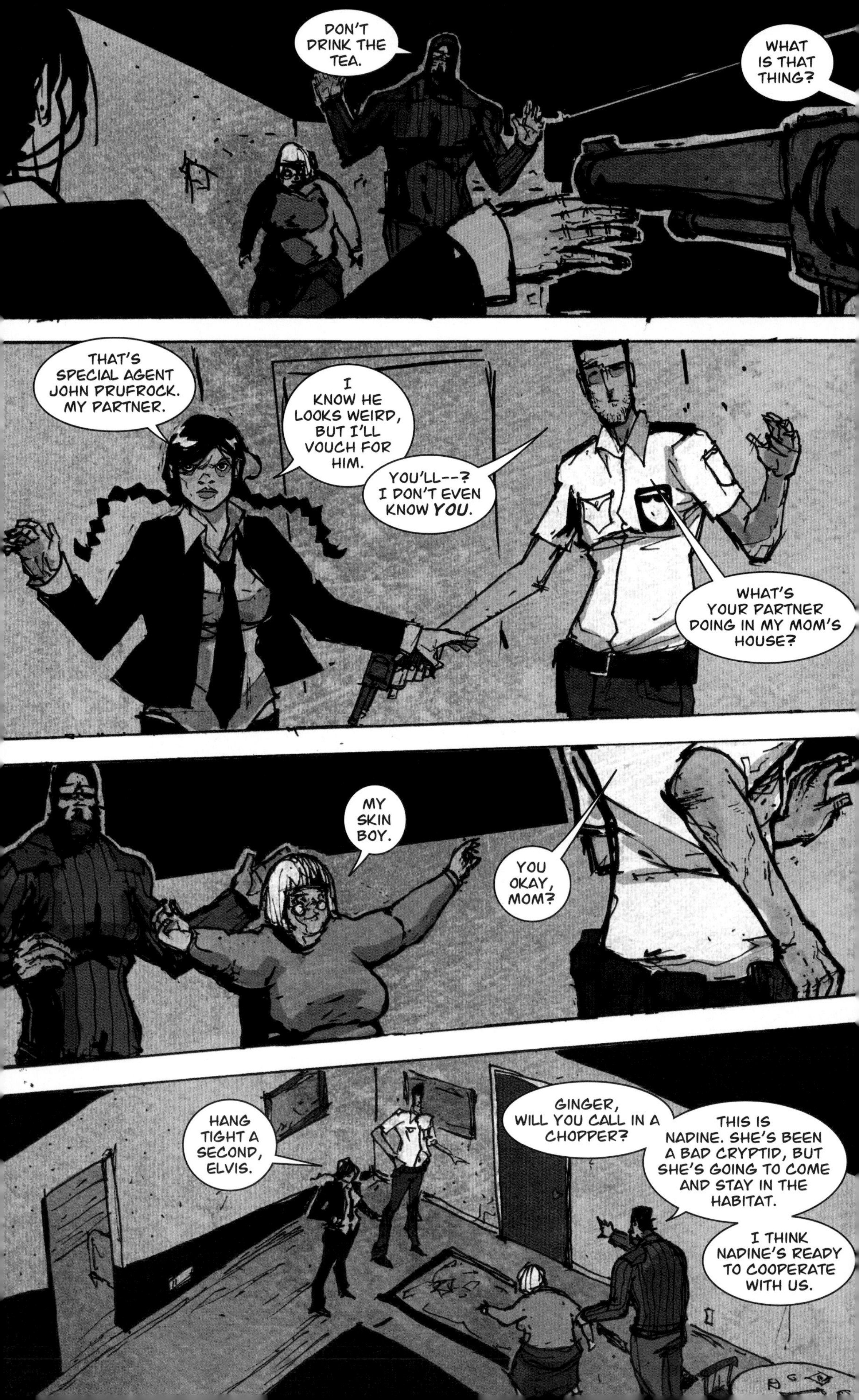

DON'T DRINK THE TEA.
WHAT IS THAT THING?
THAT'S SPECIAL AGENT JOHN PRUFROCK. MY PARTNER.
I KNOW HE LOOKS WEIRD, BUT I'LL VOUCH FOR HIM.
YOU'LL--? I DON'T EVEN KNOW YOU.
WHAT'S YOUR PARTNER DOING IN MY MOM'S HOUSE?
MY SKIN BOY.
YOU OKAY, MOM?
HANG TIGHT A SECOND, ELVIS.
GINGER, WILL YOU CALL IN A CHOPPER?
THIS IS NADINE. SHE'S BEEN A BAD CRYPTID, BUT SHE'S GOING TO COME AND STAY IN THE HABITAT.
I THINK NADINE'S READY TO COOPERATE WITH US.

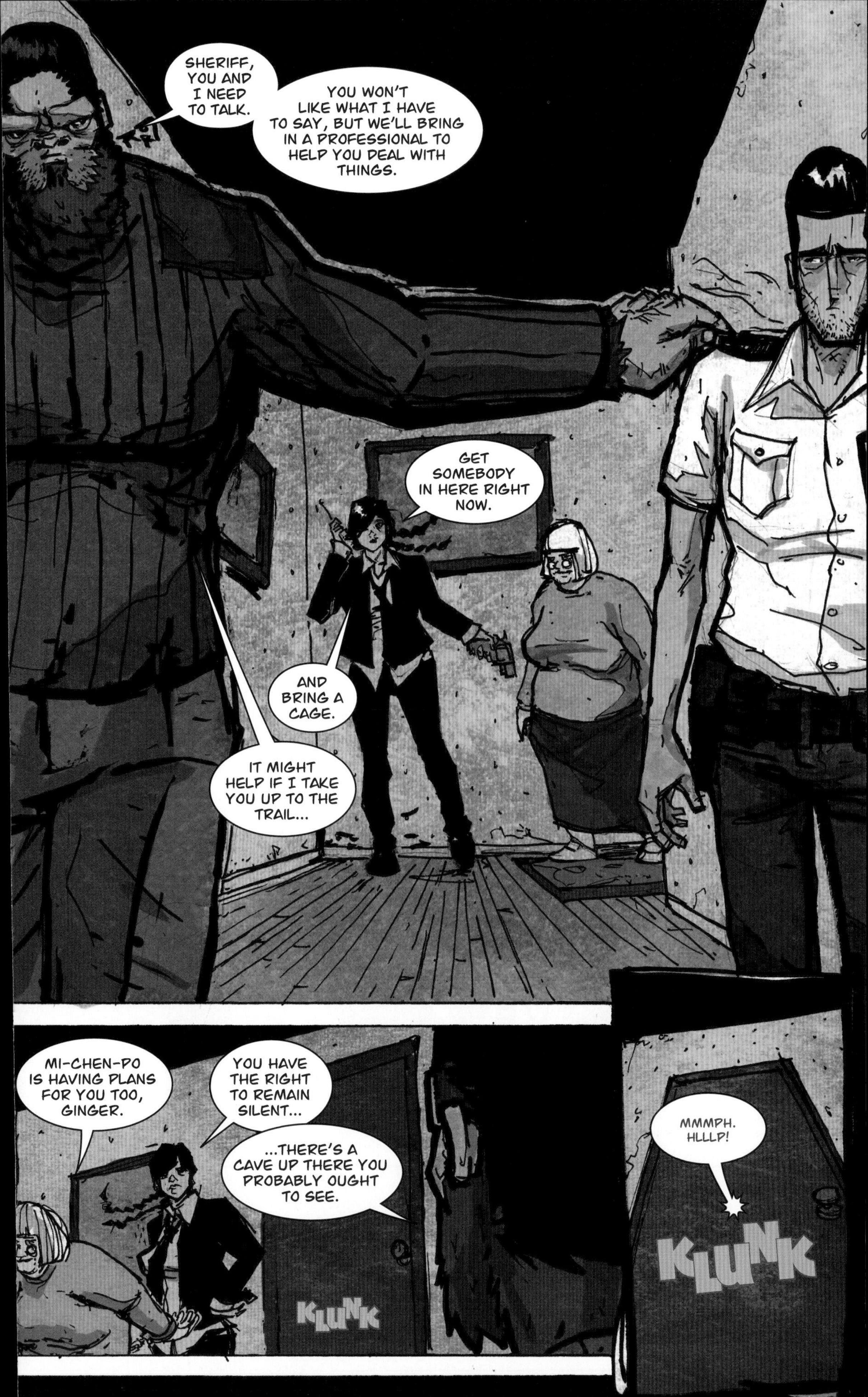
SHERIFF, YOU AND I NEED TO TALK.
YOU WON'T LIKE WHAT I HAVE TO SAY, BUT WE'LL BRING IN A PROFESSIONAL TO HELP YOU DEAL WITH THINGS.
GET SOMEBODY IN HERE RIGHT NOW.
AND BRING A CAGE.
IT MIGHT HELP IF I TAKE YOU UP TO THE TRAIL...
MI-CHEN-PO IS HAVING PLANS FOR YOU TOO, GINGER.
YOU HAVE THE RIGHT TO REMAIN SILENT...
...THERE'S A CAVE UP THERE YOU PROBABLY OUGHT TO SEE.
KLUNK
MMMPH. HLLLP!
KLUNK

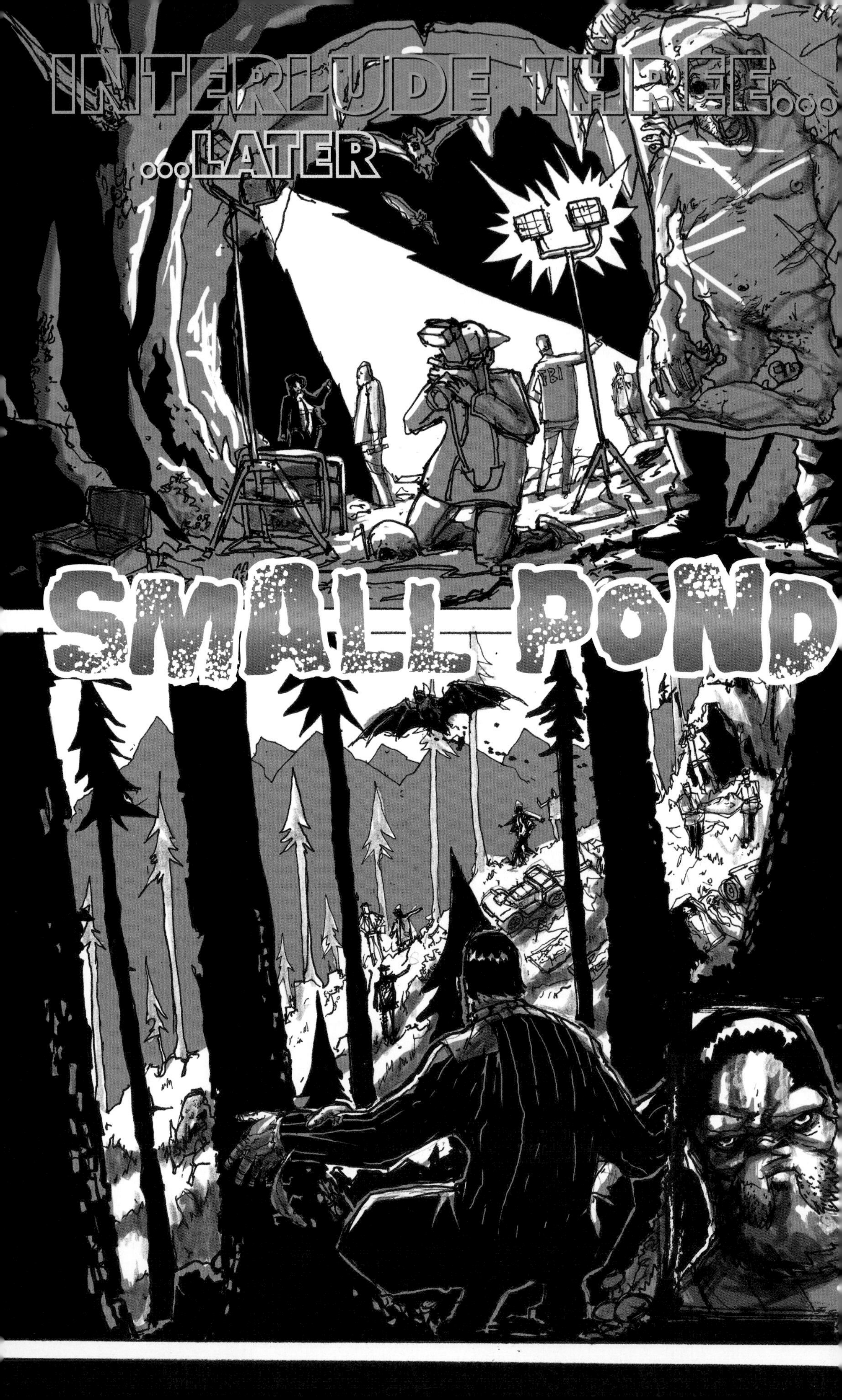
INTERLUDE THREE...
...LATER
FBI
SMALL POND

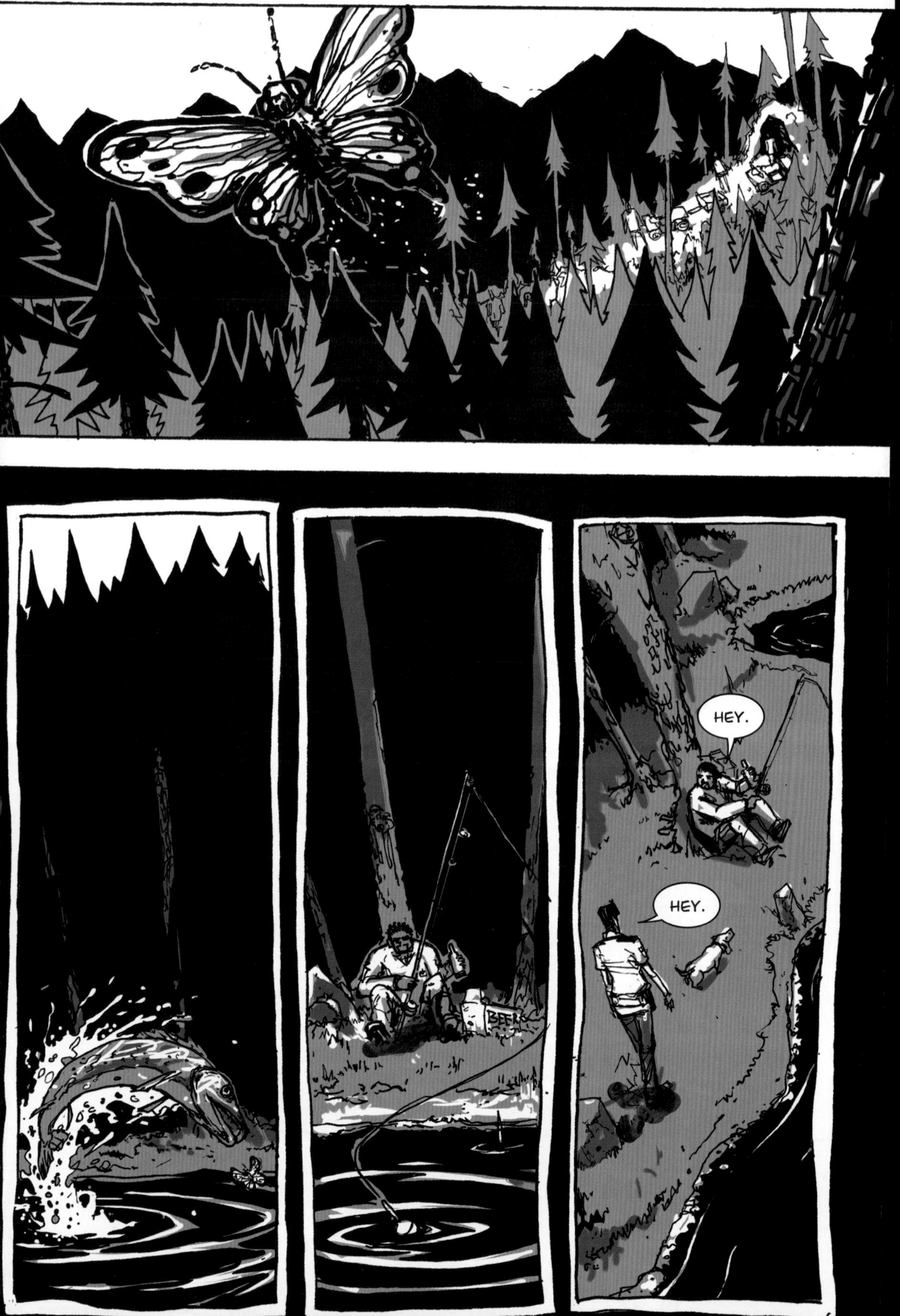
BEER
HEY.
HEY.

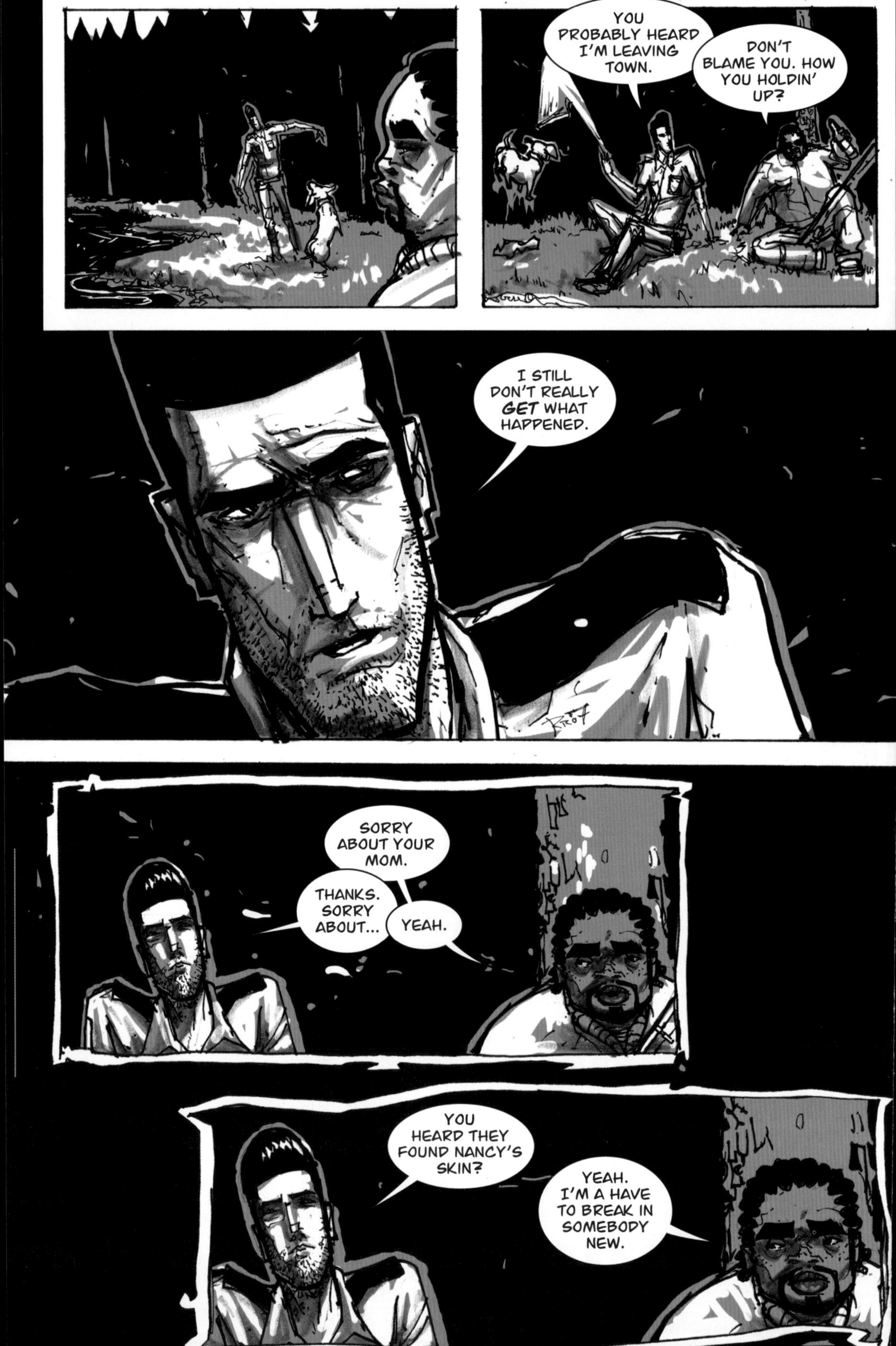
YOU PROBABLY HEARD I'M LEAVING TOWN.
DON'T BLAME YOU. HOW YOU HOLDIN' UP?
I STILL DON'T REALLY GET WHAT HAPPENED.
SORRY ABOUT YOUR MOM.
THANKS. SORRY ABOUT...
YEAH.
YOU HEARD THEY FOUND NANCY'S SKIN?
YEAH. I'M A HAVE TO BREAK IN SOMEBODY NEW.

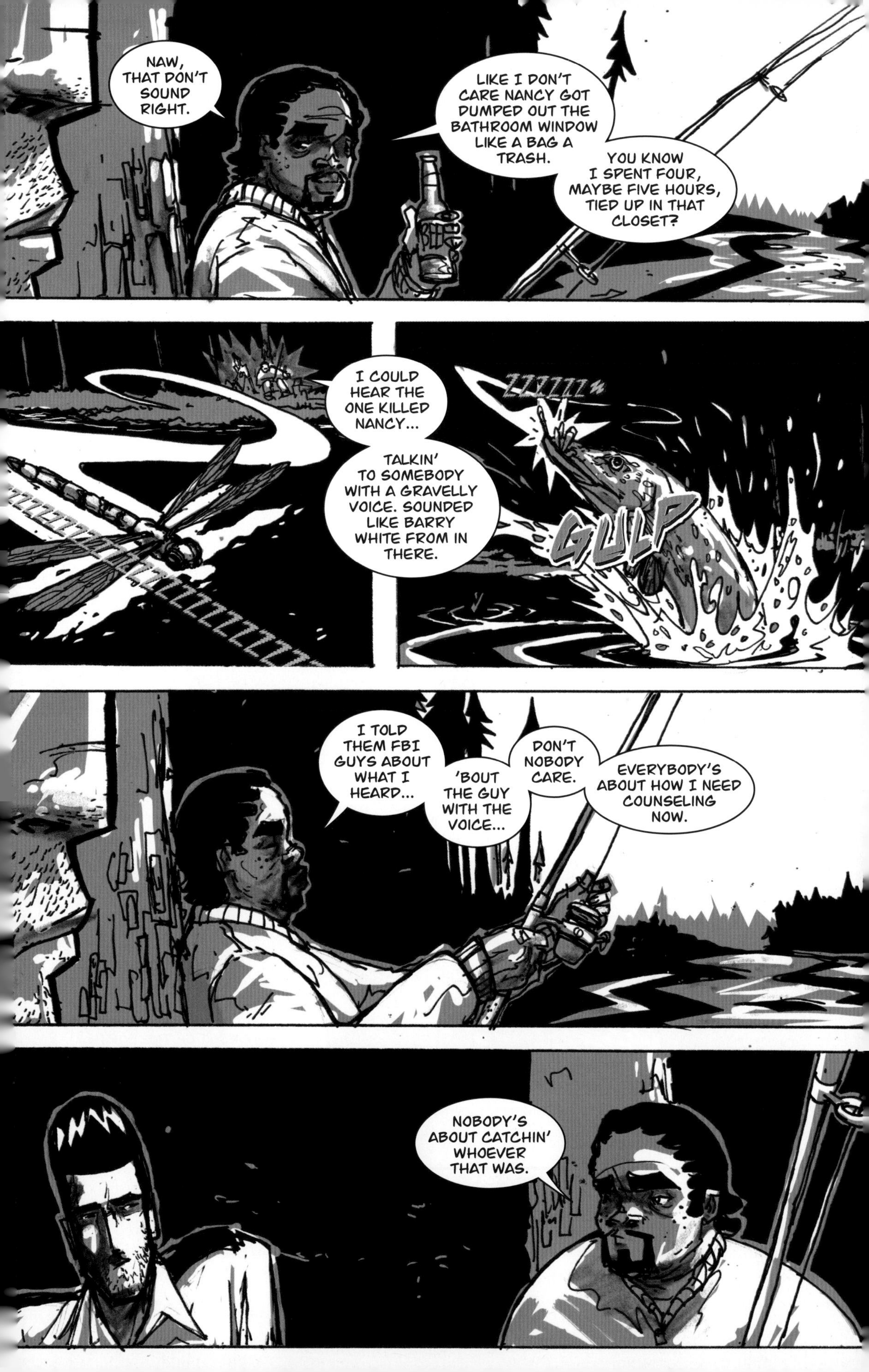
NAW, THAT DON'T SOUND RIGHT.
LIKE I DON'T CARE NANCY GOT DUMPED OUT THE BATHROOM WINDOW LIKE A BAG A TRASH.
YOU KNOW I SPENT FOUR, MAYBE FIVE HOURS, TIED UP IN THAT CLOSET?
I COULD HEAR THE ONE KILLED NANCY...
TALKIN' TO SOMEBODY WITH A GRAVELLY VOICE. SOUNDED LIKE BARRY WHITE FROM IN THERE.
ZZZZZZZ
GULP
I TOLD THEM FBI GUYS ABOUT WHAT I HEARD...
'BOUT THE GUY WITH THE VOICE...
DON'T NOBODY CARE.
EVERYBODY'S ABOUT HOW I NEED COUNSELING NOW.
NOBODY'S ABOUT CATCHIN' WHOEVER THAT WAS.

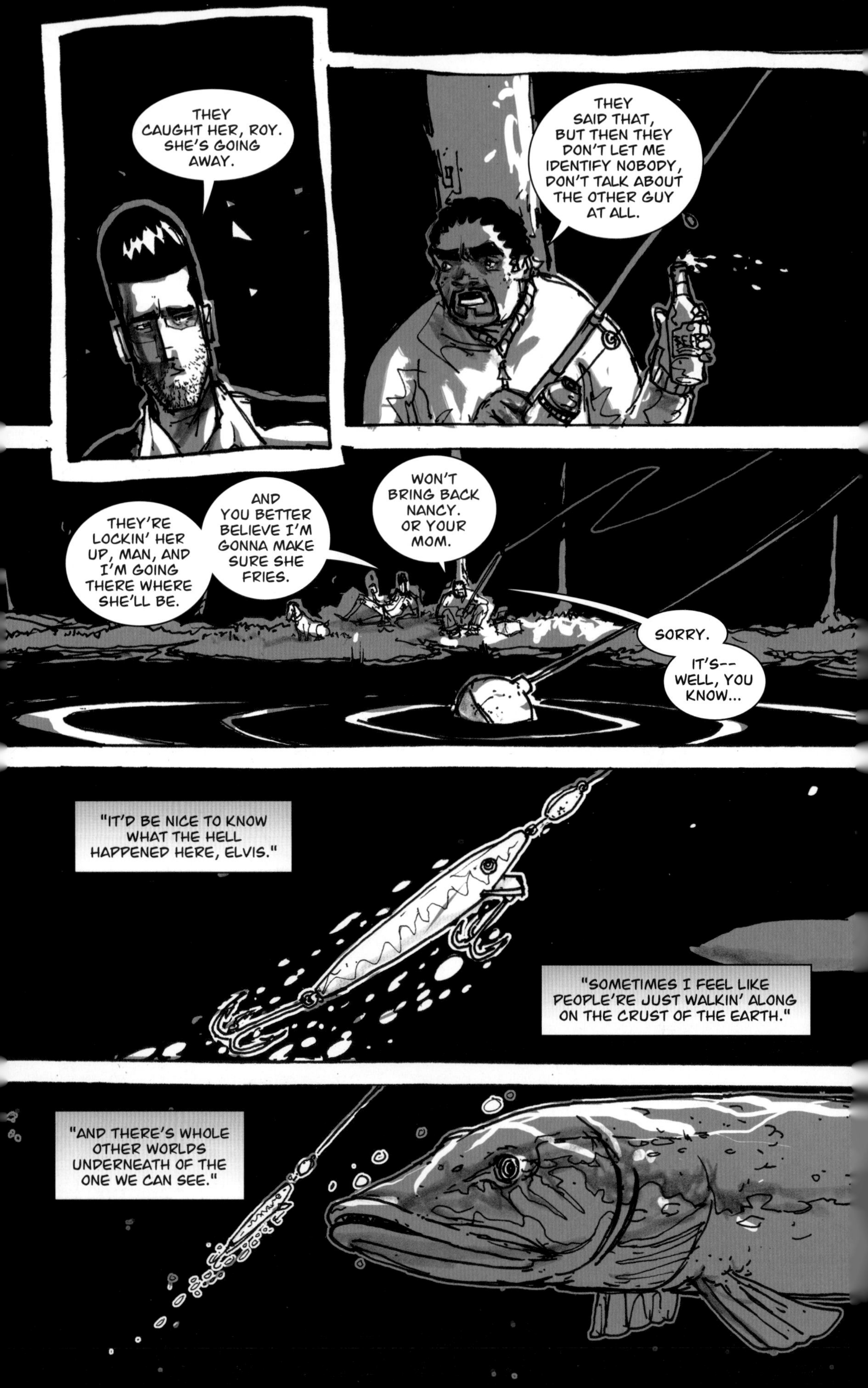
THEY CAUGHT HER, ROY. SHE'S GOING AWAY.
THEY SAID THAT, BUT THEN THEY DON'T LET ME IDENTIFY NOBODY, DON'T TALK ABOUT THE OTHER GUY AT ALL.
THEY'RE LOCKIN' HER UP, MAN, AND I'M GOING THERE WHERE SHE'LL BE.
AND YOU BETTER BELIEVE I'M GONNA MAKE SURE SHE FRIES.
WON'T BRING BACK NANCY. OR YOUR MOM.
SORRY.
IT'S-- WELL, YOU KNOW...
"IT'D BE NICE TO KNOW WHAT THE HELL HAPPENED HERE, ELVIS."
"SOMETIMES I FEEL LIKE PEOPLE'RE JUST WALKIN' ALONG ON THE CRUST OF THE EARTH."
"AND THERE'S WHOLE OTHER WORLDS UNDERNEATH OF THE ONE WE CAN SEE."

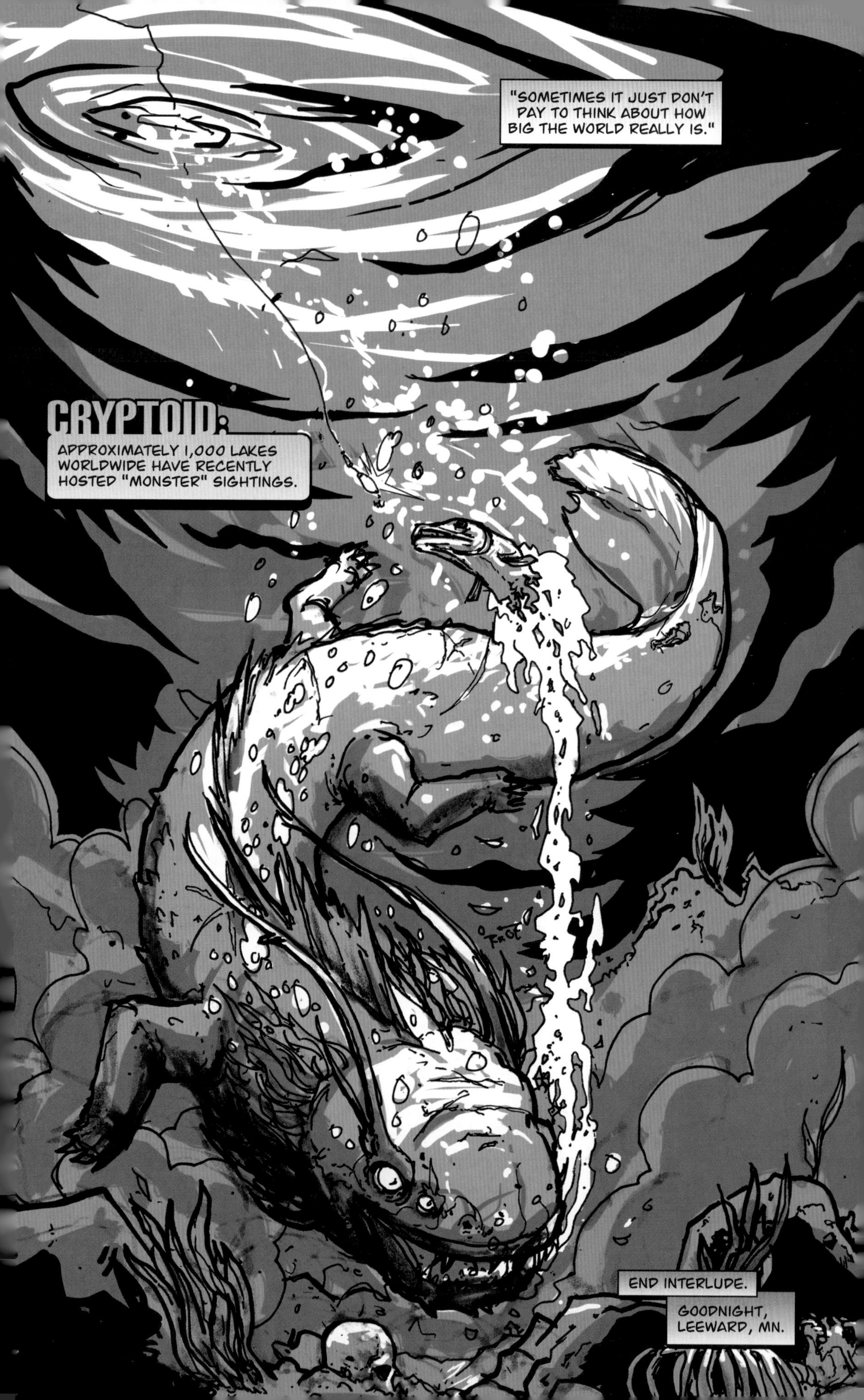
"SOMETIMES IT JUST DON'T PAY TO THINK ABOUT HOW BIG THE WORLD REALLY IS."
CRYPTOID:
APPROXIMATELY 1,000 LAKES WORLDWIDE HAVE RECENTLY HOSTED "MONSTER" SIGHTINGS.
END INTERLUDE.
GOODNIGHT, LEEWARD, MN.

THE LODGE

KNOCK KNOCK

MONDAY

PROOF? ARE YOU HOME?

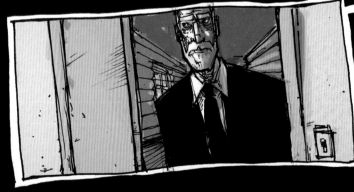

HEY, THERE, GIRL. WHERE'S OUR BIG BOY?

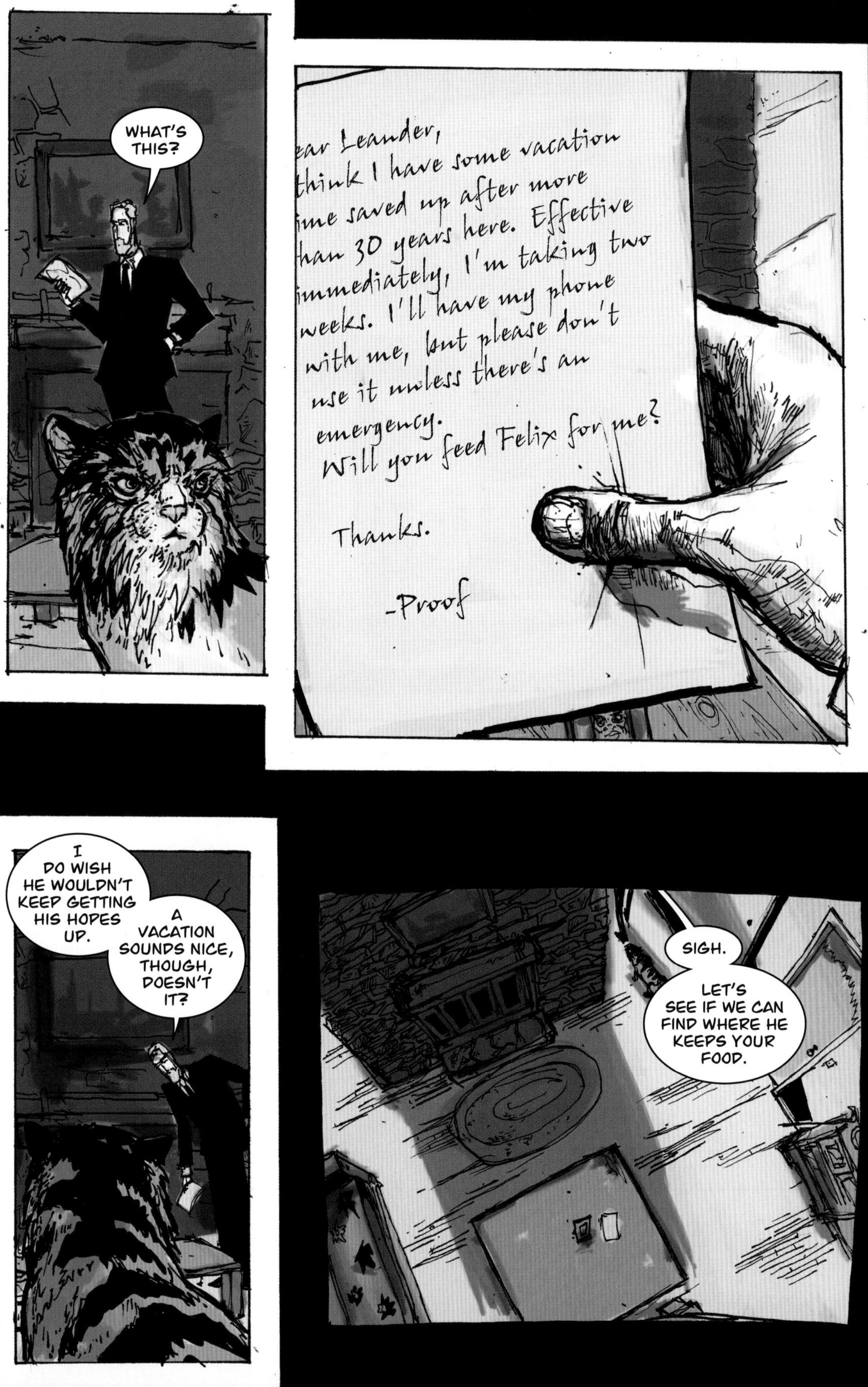
WHAT'S THIS?
ear Leander,
think I have some vacation
ime saved up after more
han 30 years here. Effective
immediately, I'm taking two
weeks. I'll have my phone
with me, but please don't
use it unless there's an
emergency.
Will you feed Felix for me?
Thanks.
-Proof
I DO WISH HE WOULDN'T KEEP GETTING HIS HOPES UP.
A VACATION SOUNDS NICE, THOUGH, DOESN'T IT?
SIGH.
LET'S SEE IF WE CAN FIND WHERE HE KEEPS YOUR FOOD.

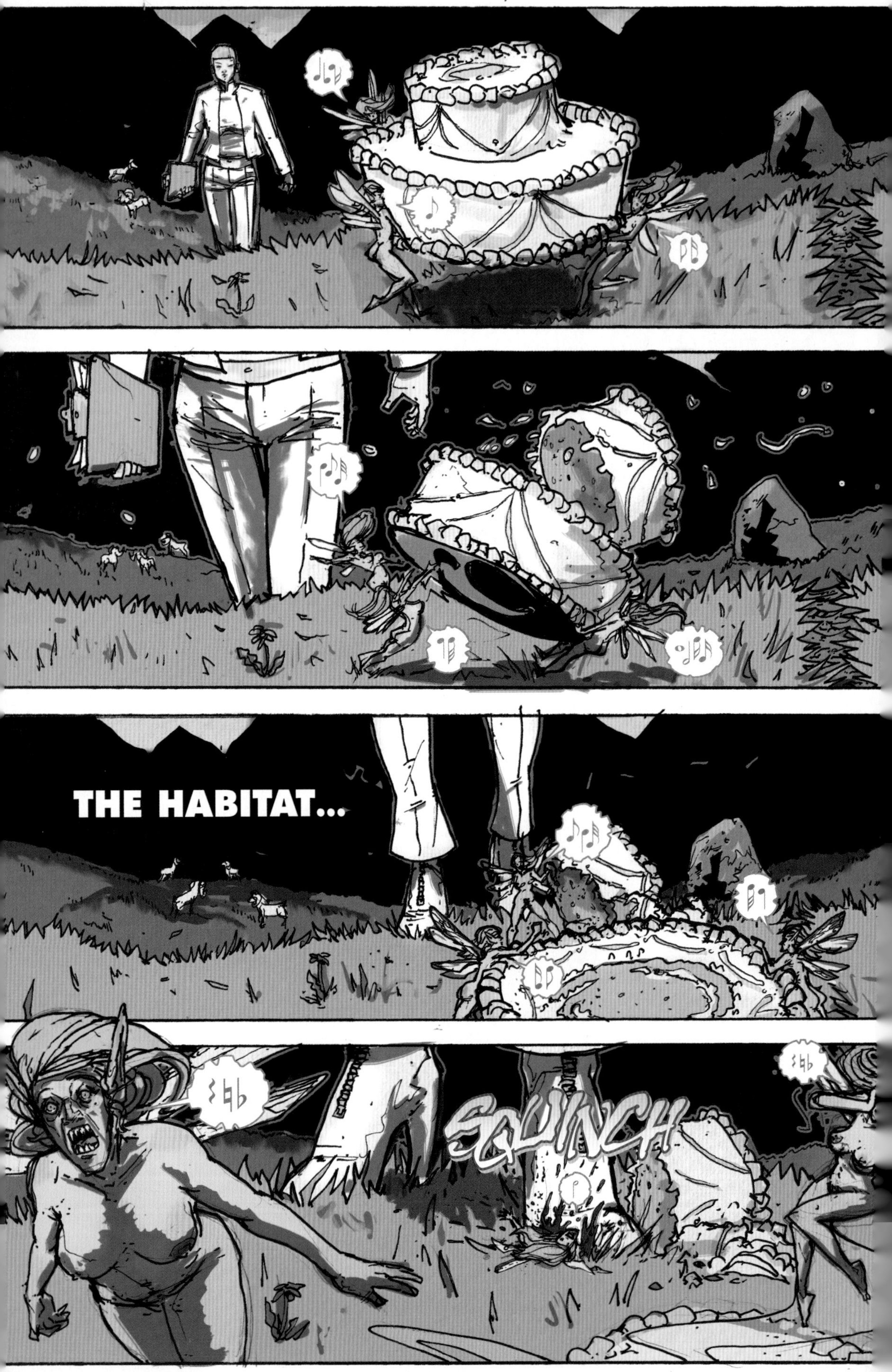
THE HABITAT...
SQUINCH

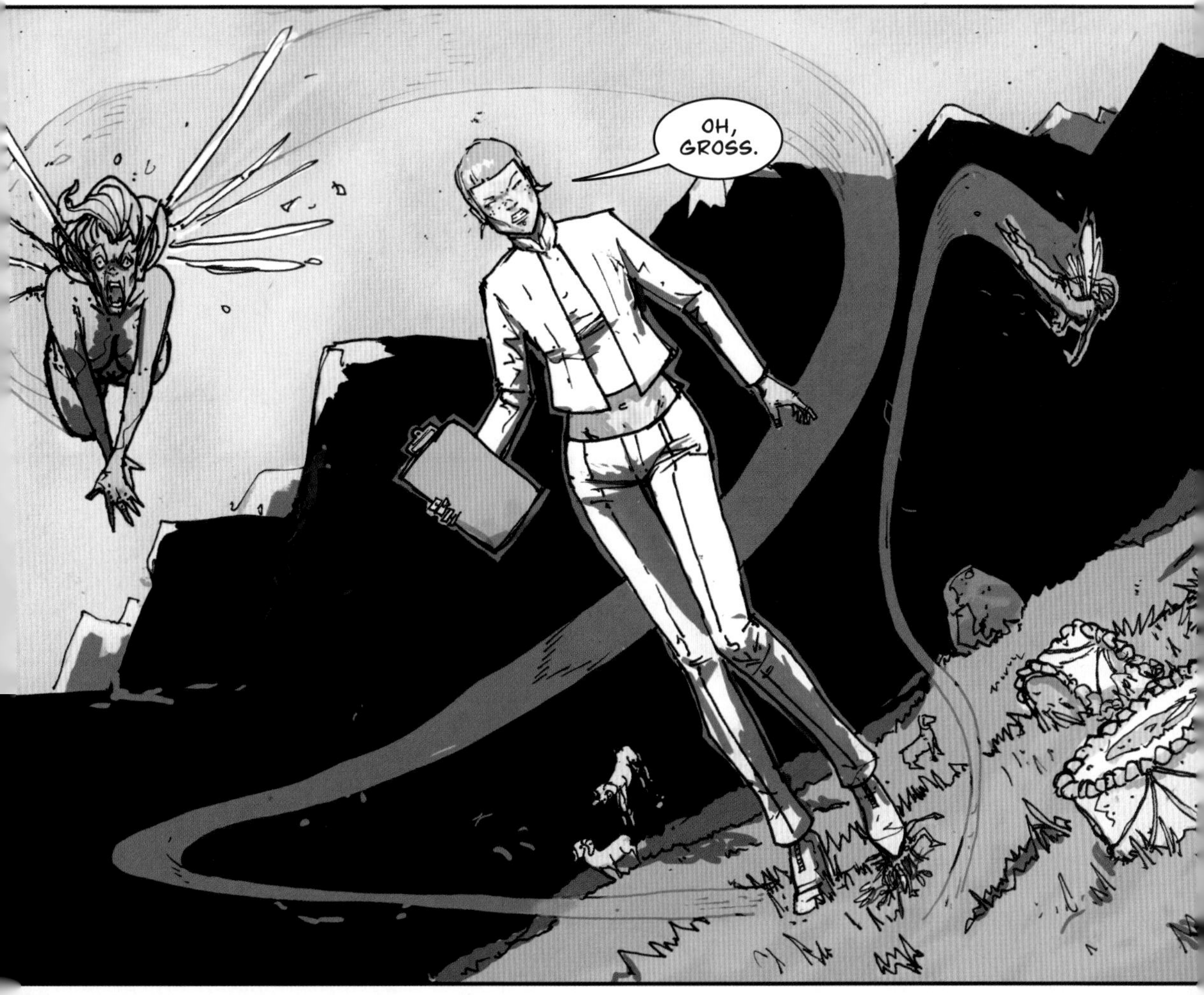
OH, GROSS.

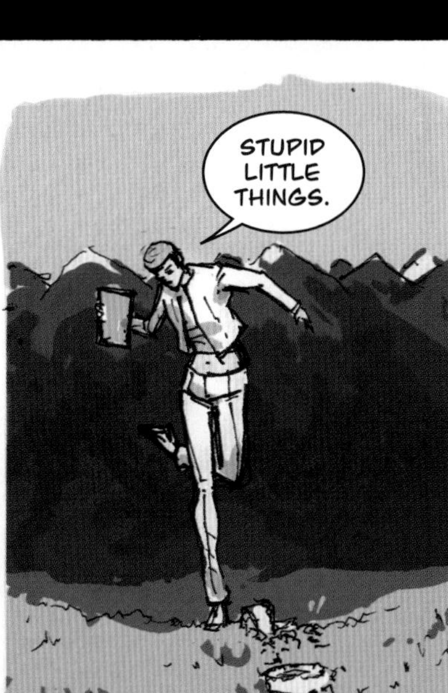
STUPID LITTLE THINGS.

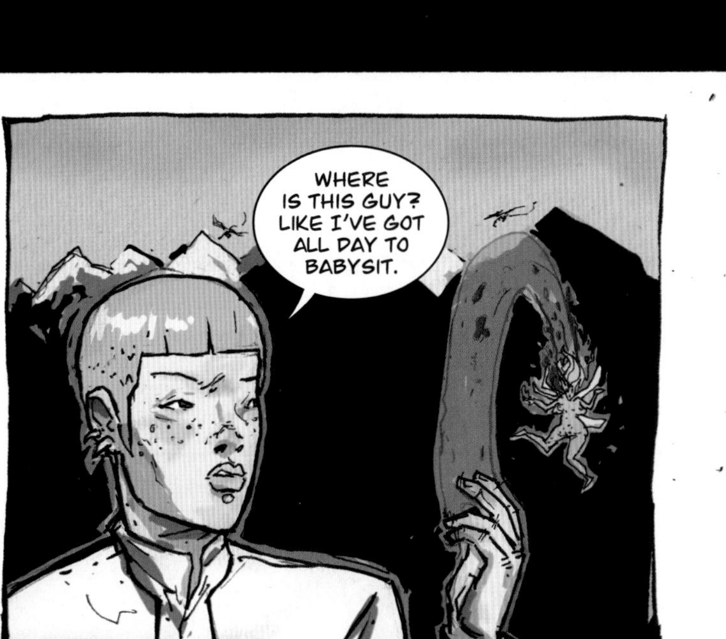
WHERE IS THIS GUY? LIKE I'VE GOT ALL DAY TO BABYSIT.

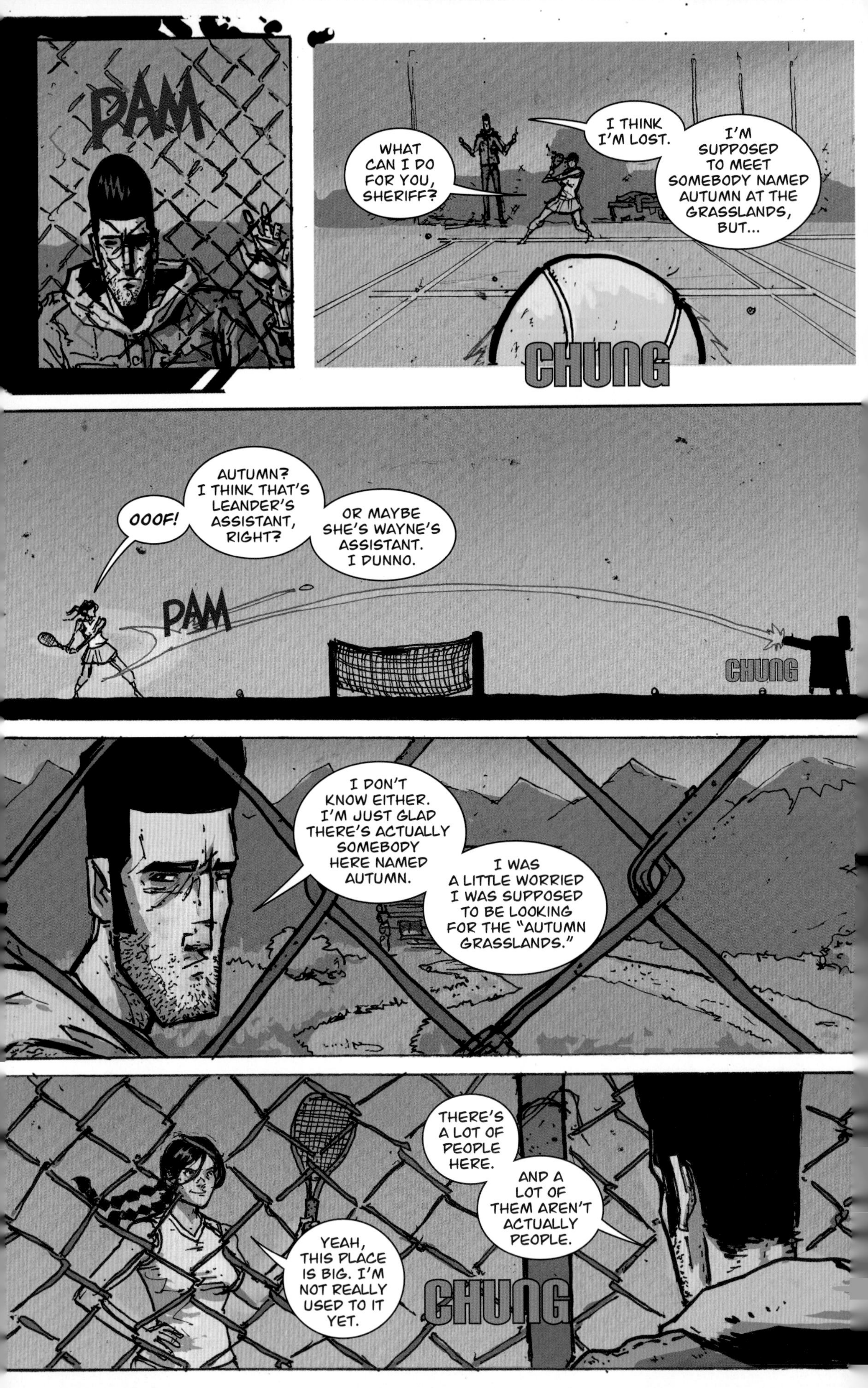
PAM
WHAT CAN I DO FOR YOU, SHERIFF?
I THINK I'M LOST.
I'M SUPPOSED TO MEET SOMEBODY NAMED AUTUMN AT THE GRASSLANDS, BUT...
CHUNG
OOOF!
AUTUMN? I THINK THAT'S LEANDER'S ASSISTANT, RIGHT?
OR MAYBE SHE'S WAYNE'S ASSISTANT. I DUNNO.
PAM
CHUNG
I DON'T KNOW EITHER. I'M JUST GLAD THERE'S ACTUALLY SOMEBODY HERE NAMED AUTUMN.
I WAS A LITTLE WORRIED I WAS SUPPOSED TO BE LOOKING FOR THE "AUTUMN GRASSLANDS."
THERE'S A LOT OF PEOPLE HERE.
AND A LOT OF THEM AREN'T ACTUALLY PEOPLE.
YEAH, THIS PLACE IS BIG. I'M NOT REALLY USED TO IT YET.
CHUNG

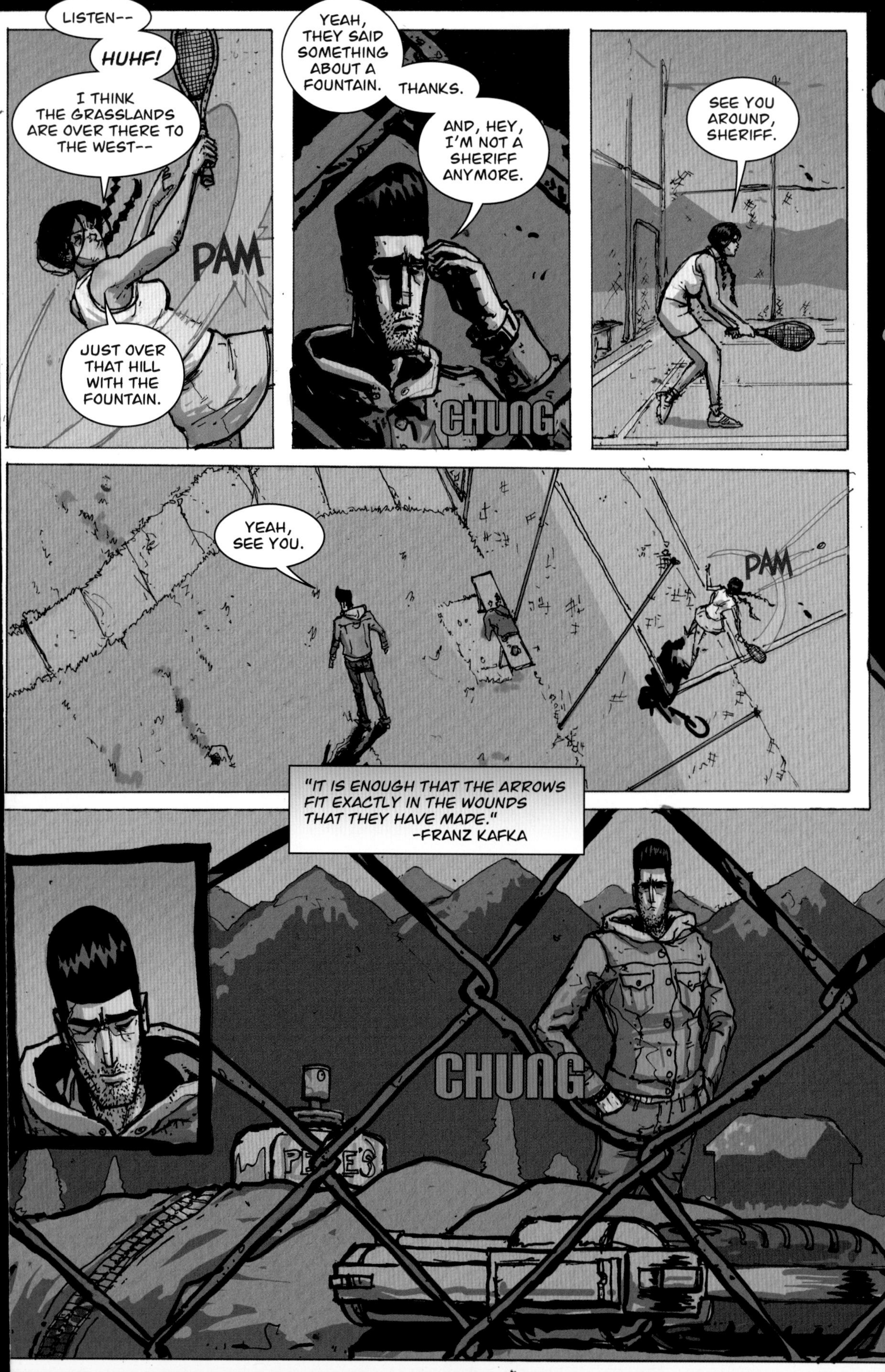

LISTEN--
HUHF!
I THINK THE GRASSLANDS ARE OVER THERE TO THE WEST--
PAM
JUST OVER THAT HILL WITH THE FOUNTAIN.
YEAH, THEY SAID SOMETHING ABOUT A FOUNTAIN.
THANKS.
AND, HEY, I'M NOT A SHERIFF ANYMORE.
CHUNG
SEE YOU AROUND, SHERIFF.
YEAH, SEE YOU.
PAM
"IT IS ENOUGH THAT THE ARROWS FIT EXACTLY IN THE WOUNDS THAT THEY HAVE MADE."
-FRANZ KAFKA
CHUNG
PETE'S

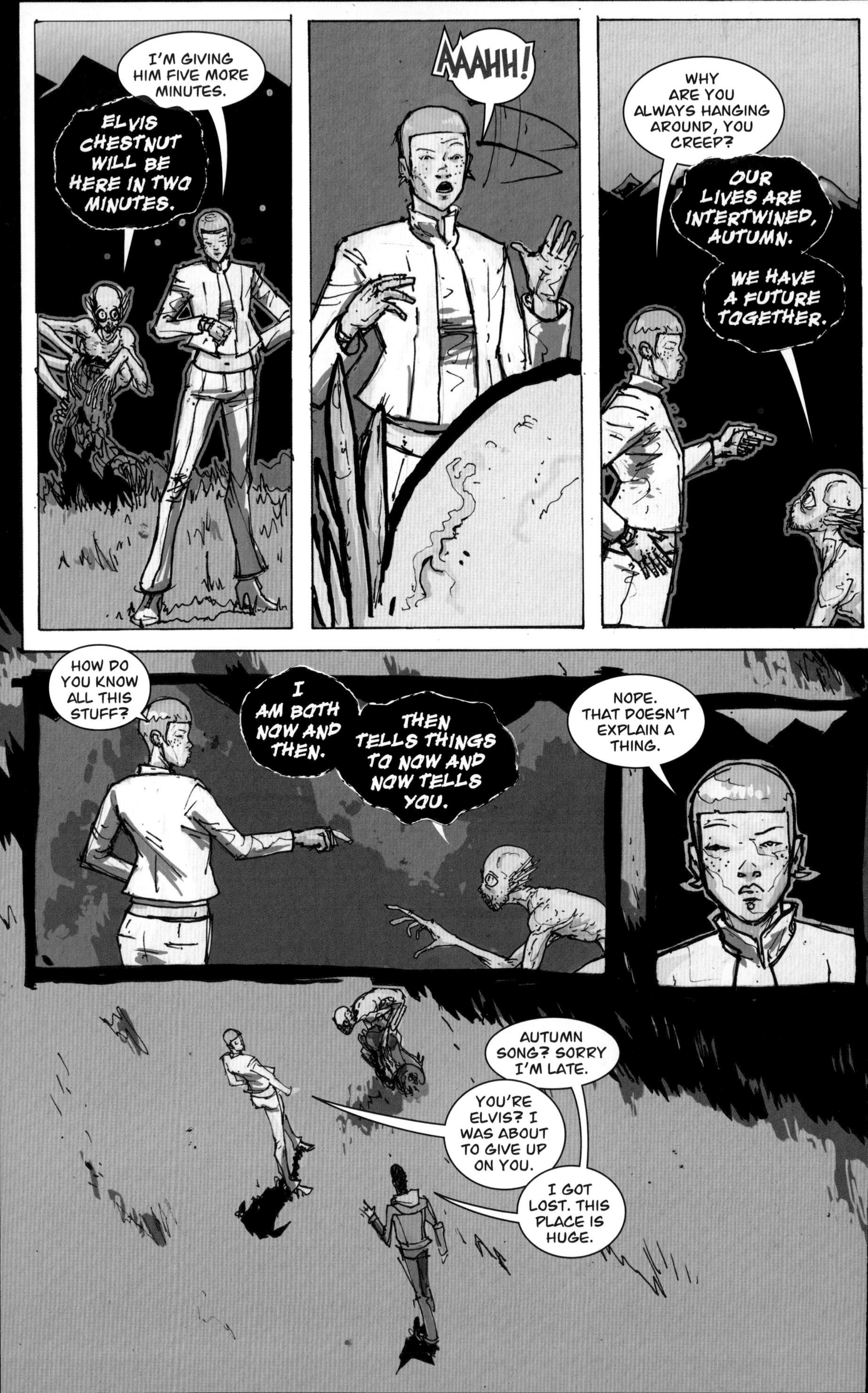

I'M GIVING HIM FIVE MORE MINUTES.
ELVIS CHESTNUT WILL BE HERE IN TWO MINUTES.
AAAHH!
WHY ARE YOU ALWAYS HANGING AROUND, YOU CREEP?
OUR LIVES ARE INTERTWINED, AUTUMN.
WE HAVE A FUTURE TOGETHER.
HOW DO YOU KNOW ALL THIS STUFF?
I AM BOTH NOW AND THEN.
THEN TELLS THINGS TO NOW AND NOW TELLS YOU.
NOPE. THAT DOESN'T EXPLAIN A THING.
AUTUMN SONG? SORRY I'M LATE.
YOU'RE ELVIS? I WAS ABOUT TO GIVE UP ON YOU.
I GOT LOST. THIS PLACE IS HUGE.

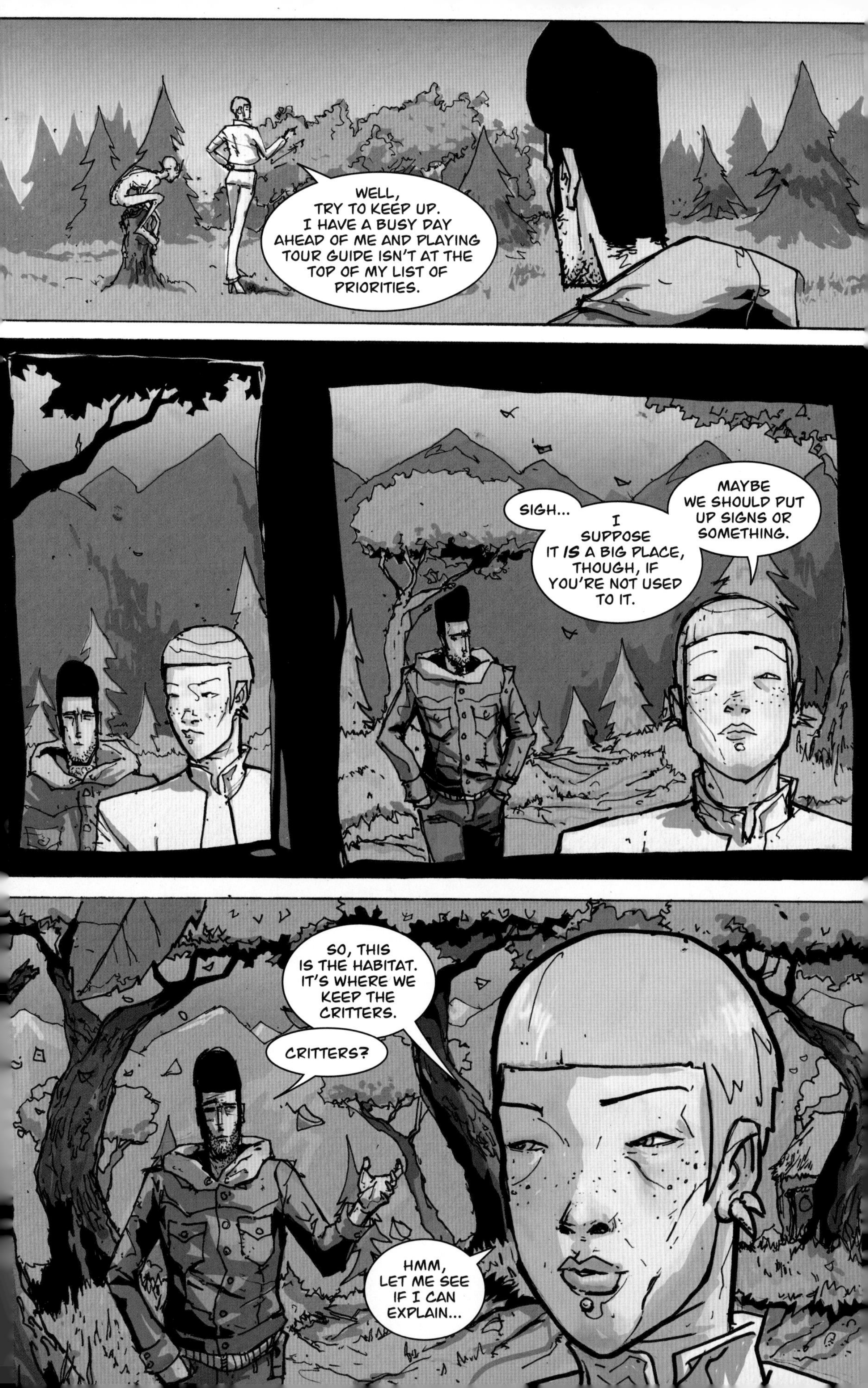
WELL, TRY TO KEEP UP. I HAVE A BUSY DAY AHEAD OF ME AND PLAYING TOUR GUIDE ISN'T AT THE TOP OF MY LIST OF PRIORITIES.
SIGH...
I SUPPOSE IT *IS* A BIG PLACE, THOUGH, IF YOU'RE NOT USED TO IT.
MAYBE WE SHOULD PUT UP SIGNS OR SOMETHING.
SO, THIS IS THE HABITAT. IT'S WHERE WE KEEP THE CRITTERS.
CRITTERS?
HMM, LET ME SEE IF I CAN EXPLAIN...

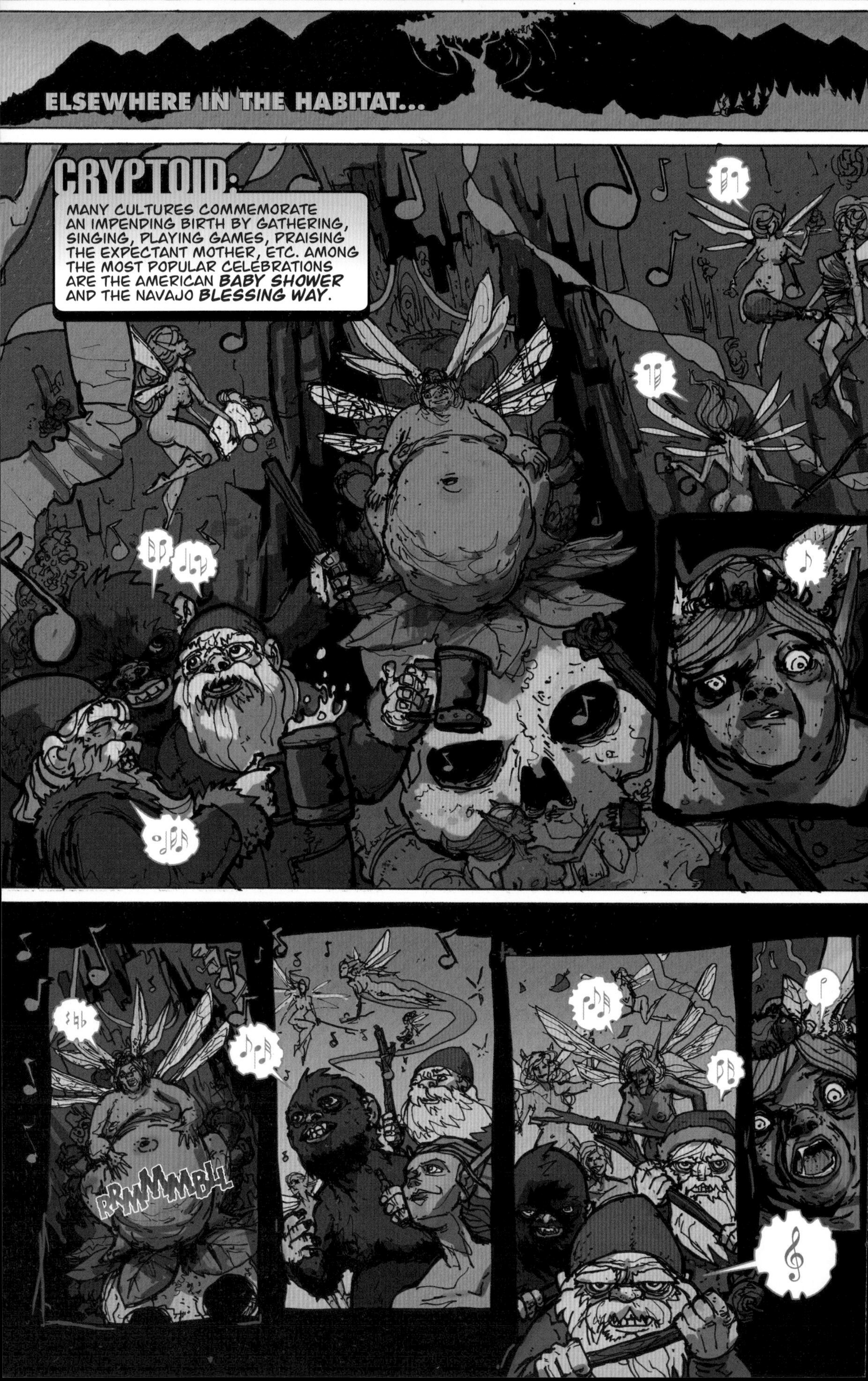
ELSEWHERE IN THE HABITAT...
CRYPTOID:
MANY CULTURES COMMEMORATE AN IMPENDING BIRTH BY GATHERING, SINGING, PLAYING GAMES, PRAISING THE EXPECTANT MOTHER, ETC. AMONG THE MOST POPULAR CELEBRATIONS ARE THE AMERICAN BABY SHOWER AND THE NAVAJO BLESSING WAY.
RRWMMMBLL

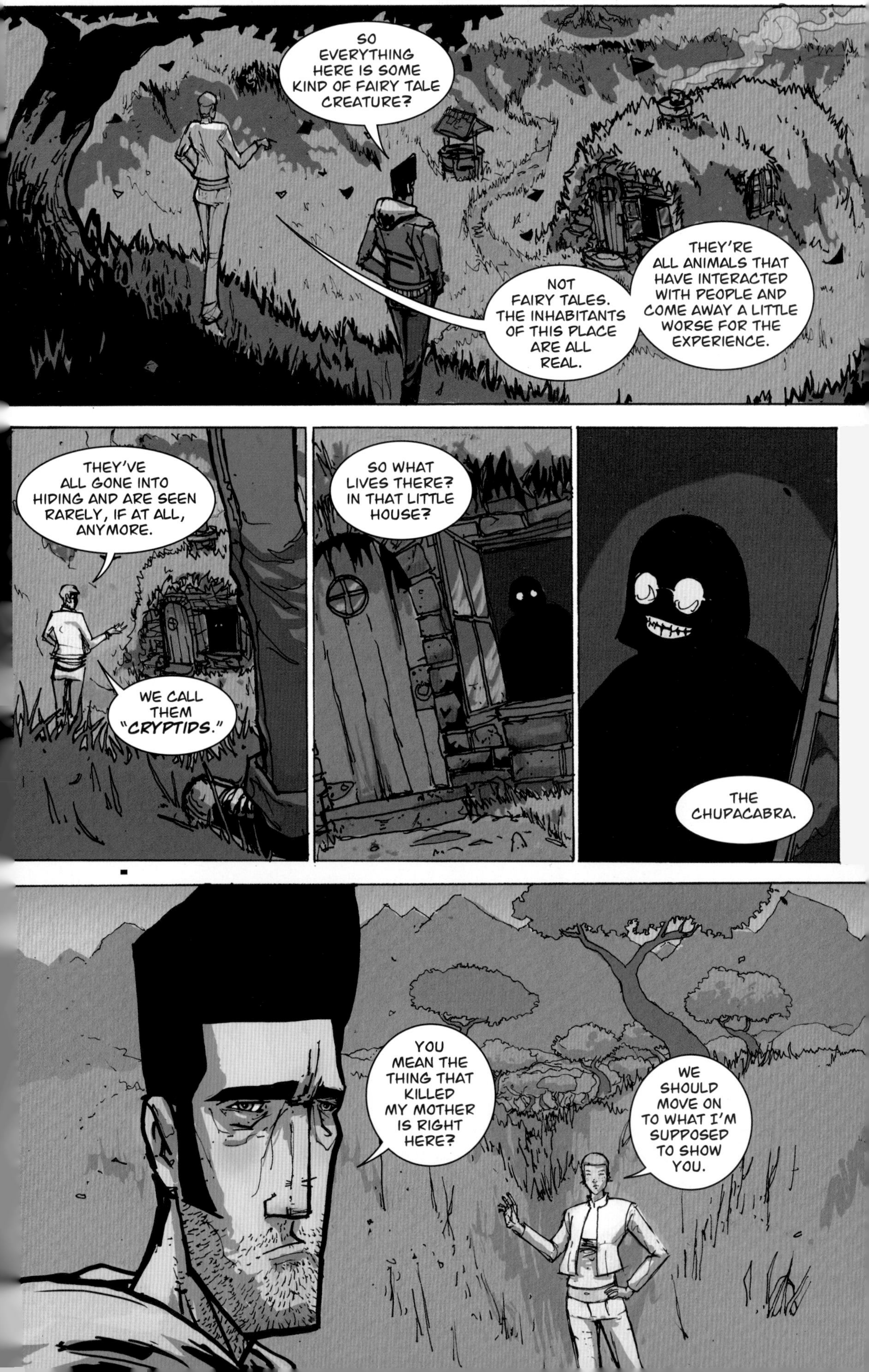
SO EVERYTHING HERE IS SOME KIND OF FAIRY TALE CREATURE?
NOT FAIRY TALES. THE INHABITANTS OF THIS PLACE ARE ALL REAL.
THEY'RE ALL ANIMALS THAT HAVE INTERACTED WITH PEOPLE AND COME AWAY A LITTLE WORSE FOR THE EXPERIENCE.
THEY'VE ALL GONE INTO HIDING AND ARE SEEN RARELY, IF AT ALL, ANYMORE.
WE CALL THEM "CRYPTIDS."
SO WHAT LIVES THERE? IN THAT LITTLE HOUSE?
THE CHUPACABRA.
YOU MEAN THE THING THAT KILLED MY MOTHER IS RIGHT HERE?
WE SHOULD MOVE ON TO WHAT I'M SUPPOSED TO SHOW YOU.

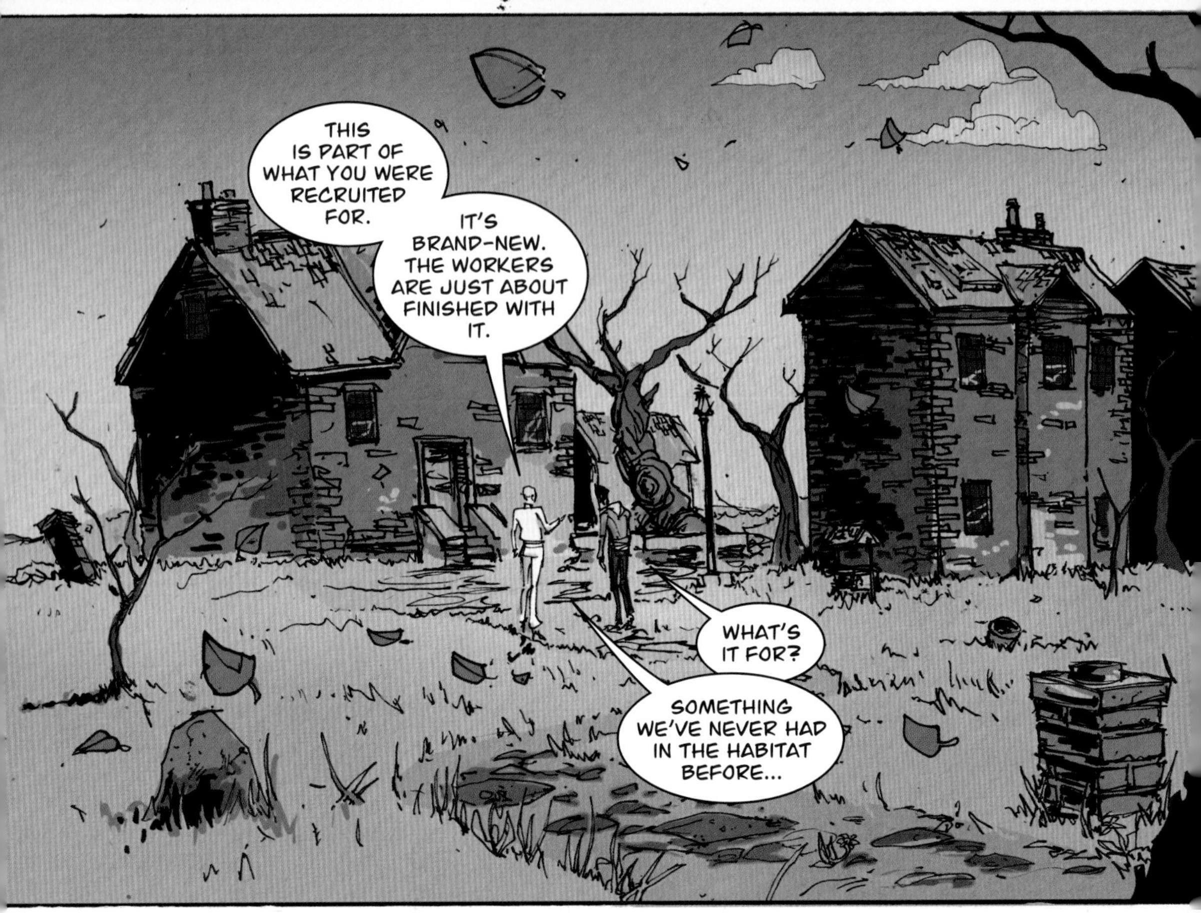
THIS IS PART OF WHAT YOU WERE RECRUITED FOR.
IT'S BRAND-NEW. THE WORKERS ARE JUST ABOUT FINISHED WITH IT.
WHAT'S IT FOR?
SOMETHING WE'VE NEVER HAD IN THE HABITAT BEFORE...

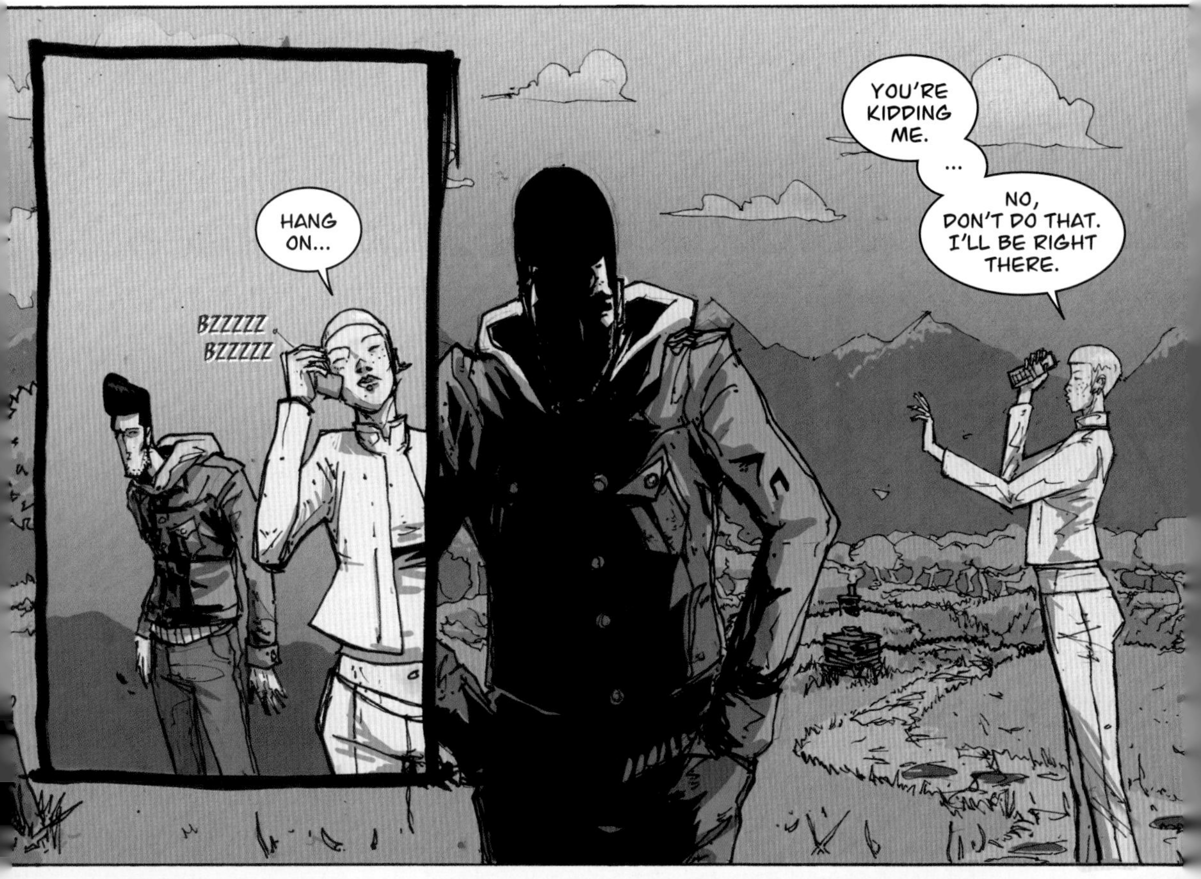
BZZZZZ BZZZZZ
HANG ON...
YOU'RE KIDDING ME.
...
NO, DON'T DO THAT. I'LL BE RIGHT THERE.

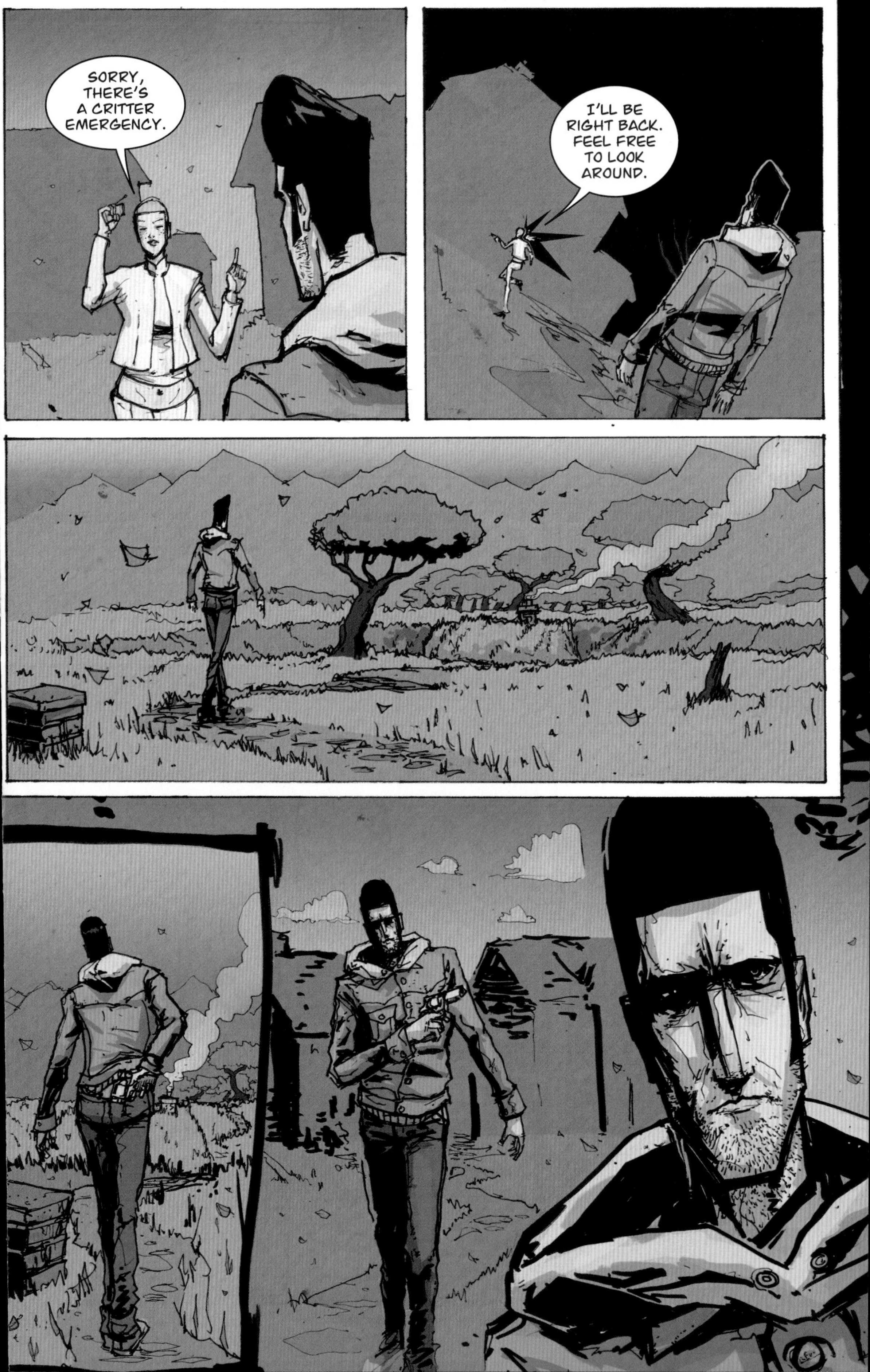
SORRY, THERE'S A CRITTER EMERGENCY.
I'LL BE RIGHT BACK. FEEL FREE TO LOOK AROUND.

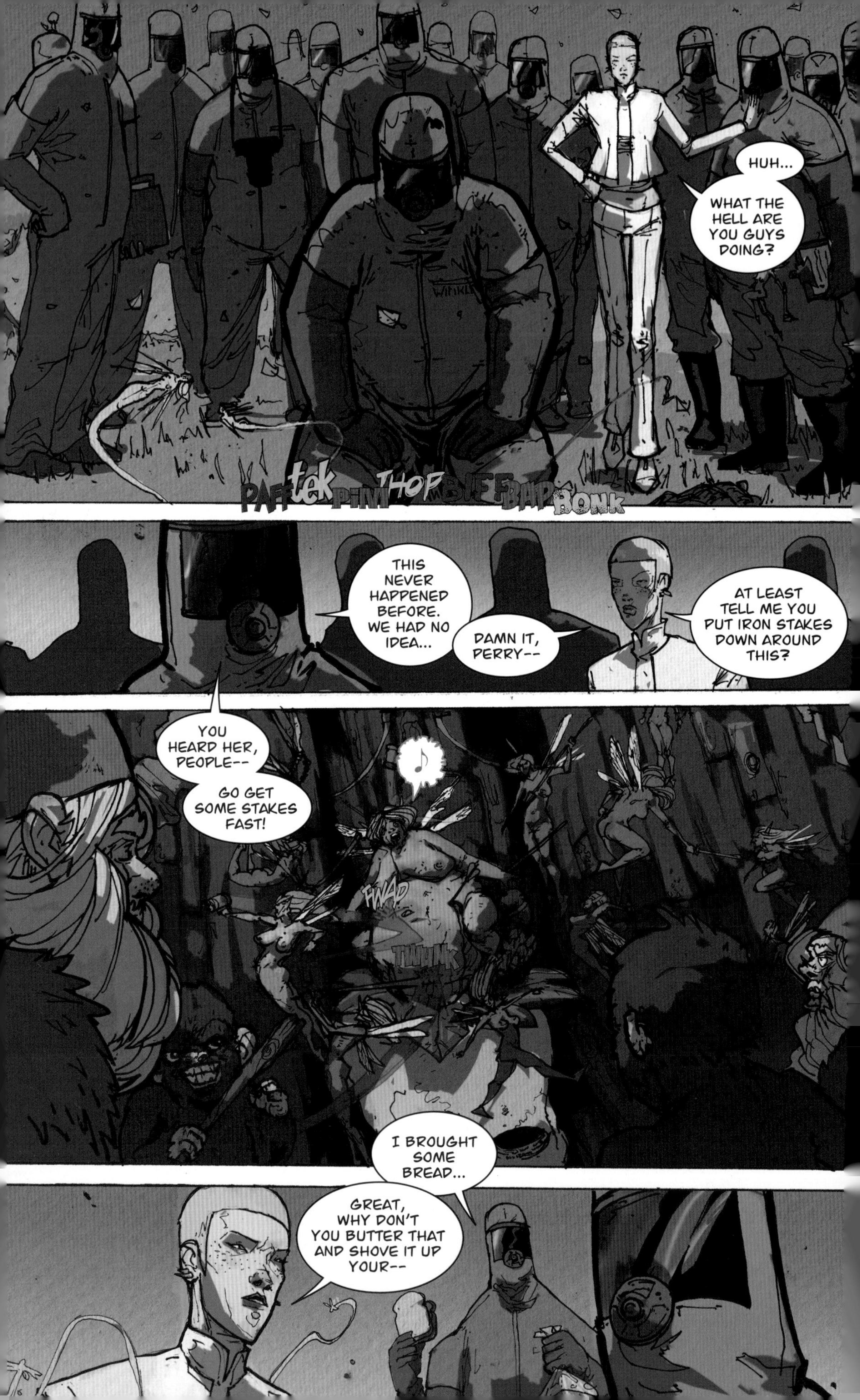
HUH...
WHAT THE HELL ARE YOU GUYS DOING?
PAFF tek PIM THOP BIFF BAP BONK
THIS NEVER HAPPENED BEFORE. WE HAD NO IDEA...
DAMN IT, PERRY--
AT LEAST TELL ME YOU PUT IRON STAKES DOWN AROUND THIS?
YOU HEARD HER, PEOPLE--
GO GET SOME STAKES FAST!
FWAP
TWUNK
I BROUGHT SOME BREAD...
GREAT, WHY DON'T YOU BUTTER THAT AND SHOVE IT UP YOUR--

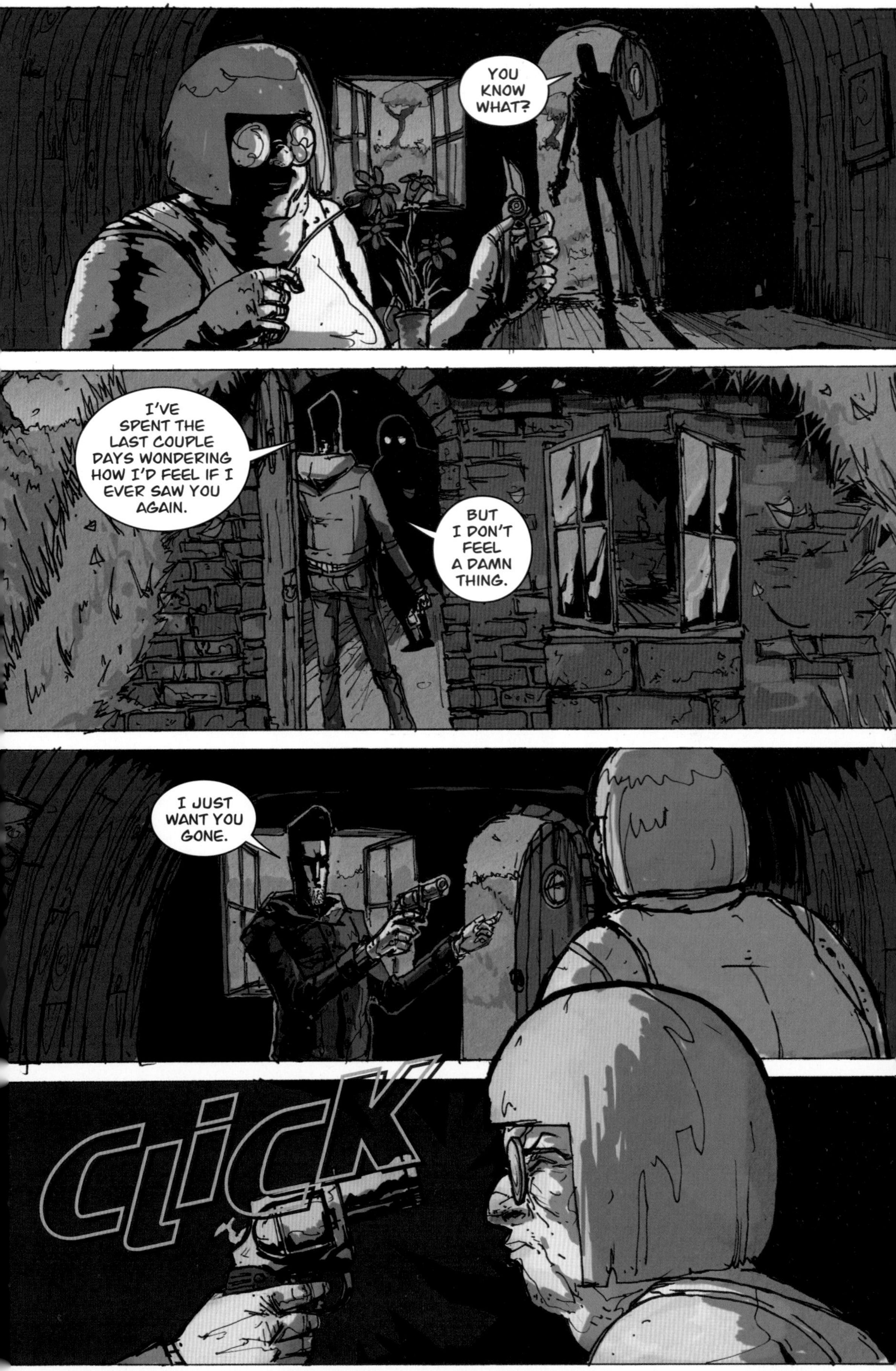
YOU KNOW WHAT?
I'VE SPENT THE LAST COUPLE DAYS WONDERING HOW I'D FEEL IF I EVER SAW YOU AGAIN.
BUT I DON'T FEEL A DAMN THING.
I JUST WANT YOU GONE.
CLICK

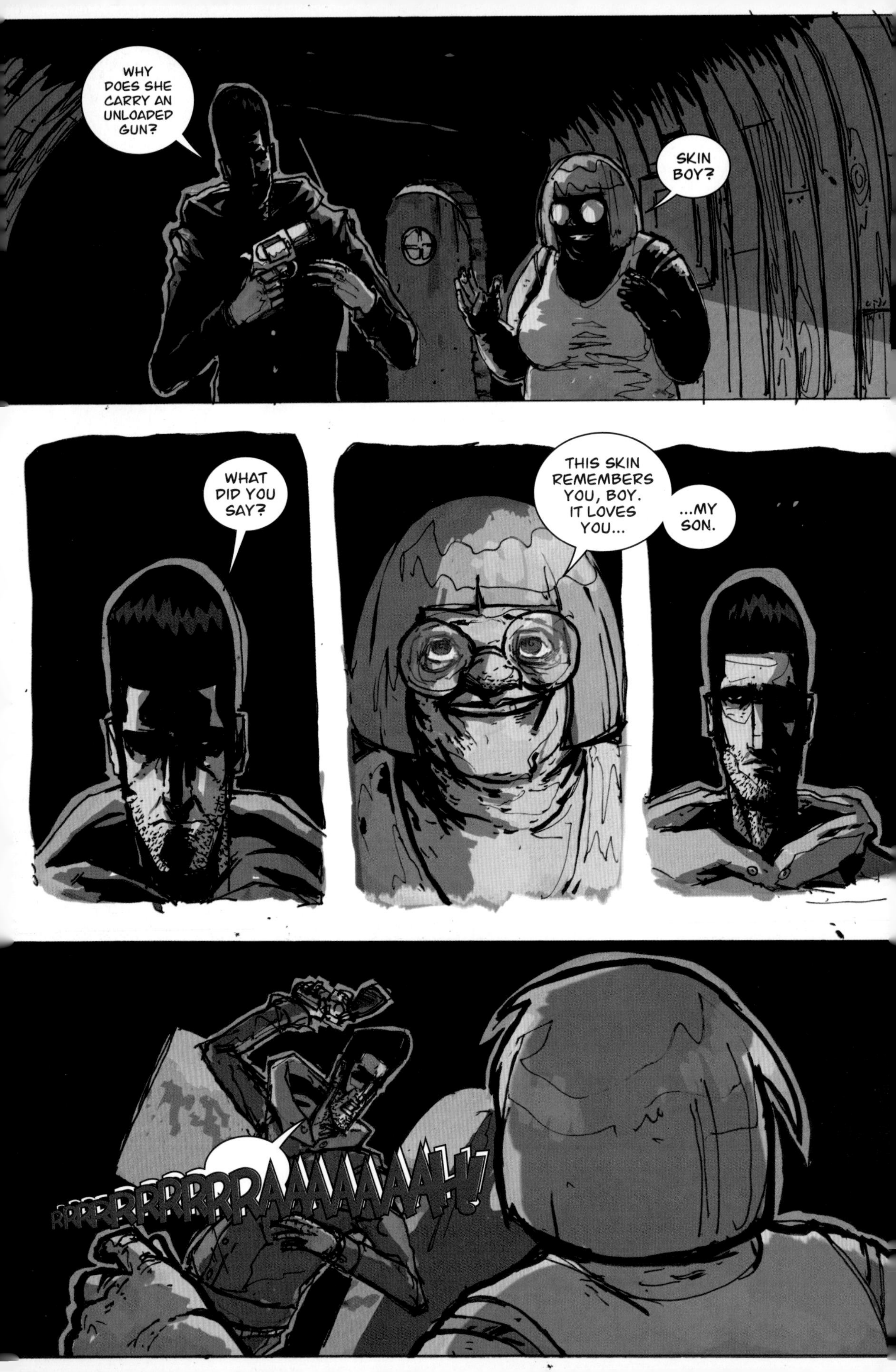
WHY DOES SHE CARRY AN UNLOADED GUN?
SKIN BOY?
WHAT DID YOU SAY?
THIS SKIN REMEMBERS YOU, BOY. IT LOVES YOU...
...MY SON.
RRRRRRRRRRRAAAAAAAAH!

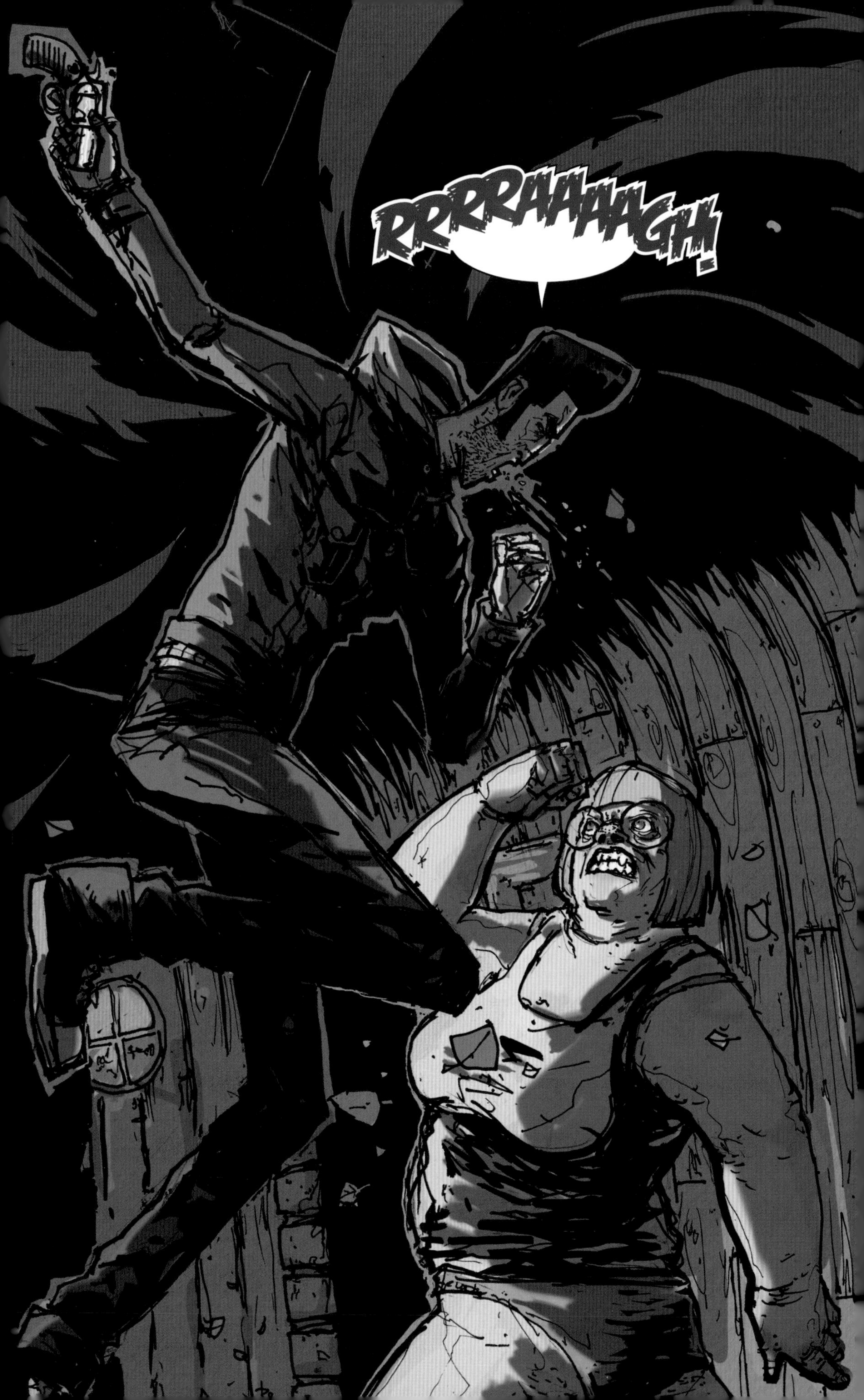
RRRRAAAAAGH!

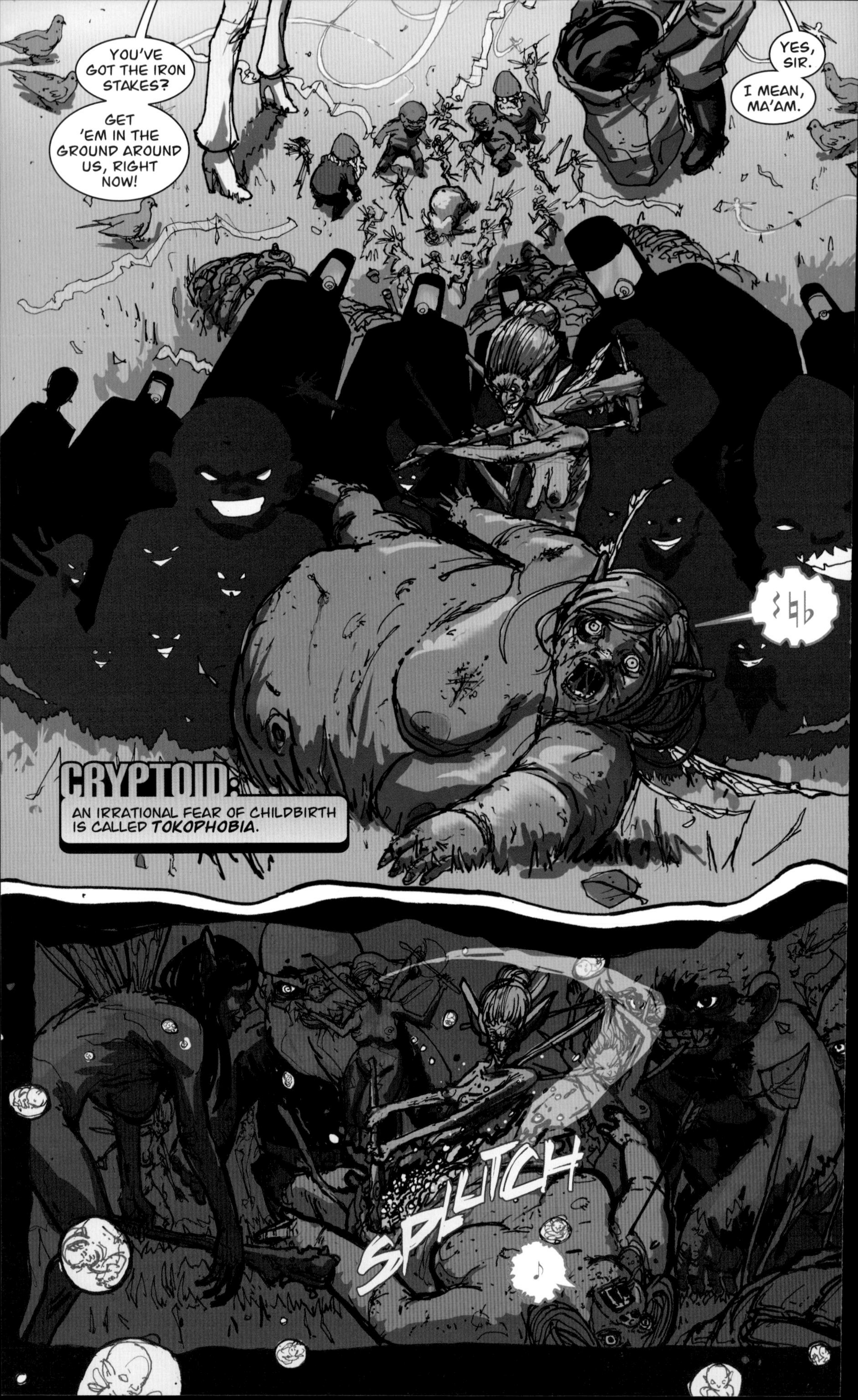
YOU'VE GOT THE IRON STAKES?
GET 'EM IN THE GROUND AROUND US, RIGHT NOW!
YES, SIR.
I MEAN, MA'AM.
CRYPTOID:
AN IRRATIONAL FEAR OF CHILDBIRTH IS CALLED TOKOPHOBIA.
SPLUTCH

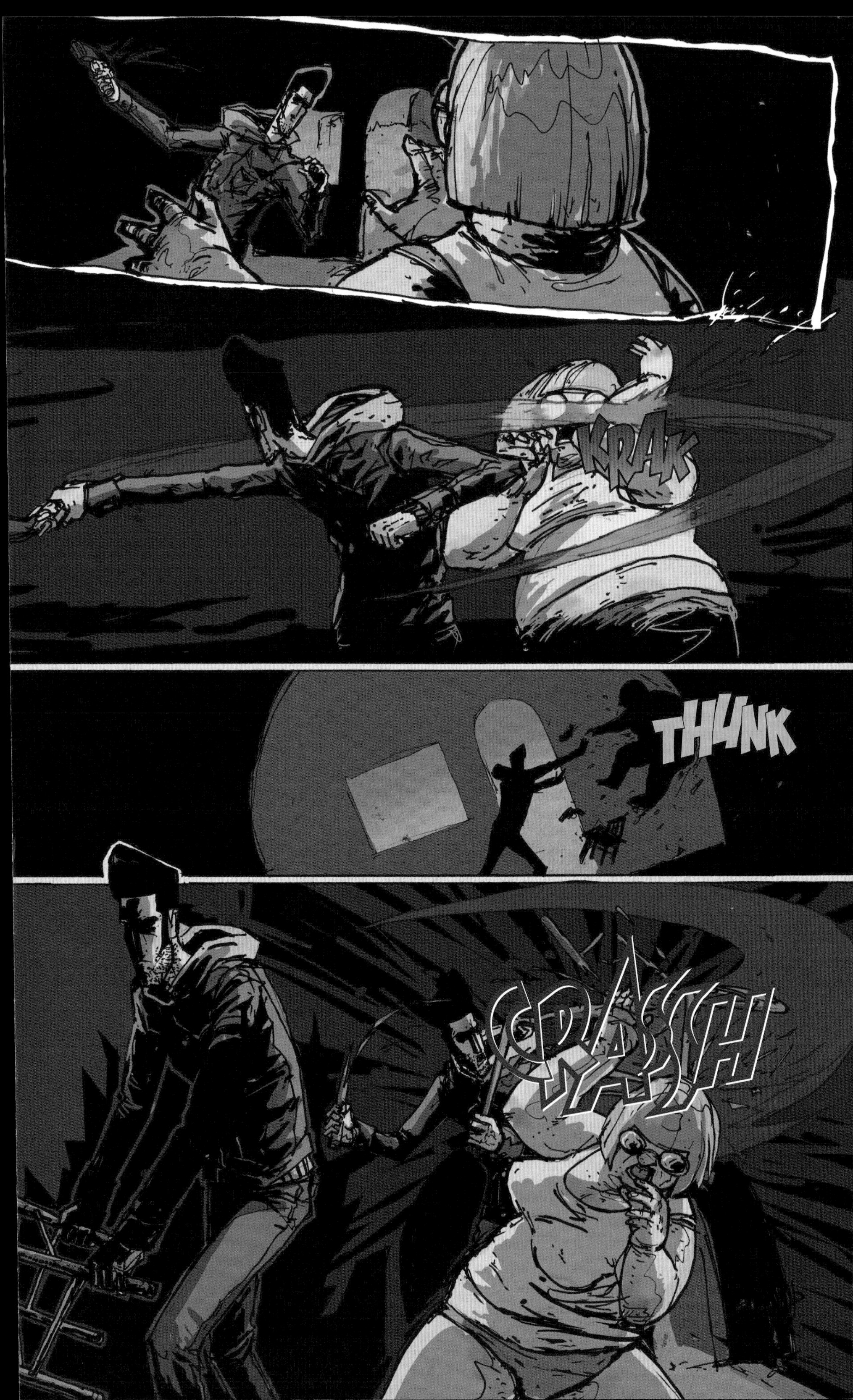
KRAK
THUNK
CRASH

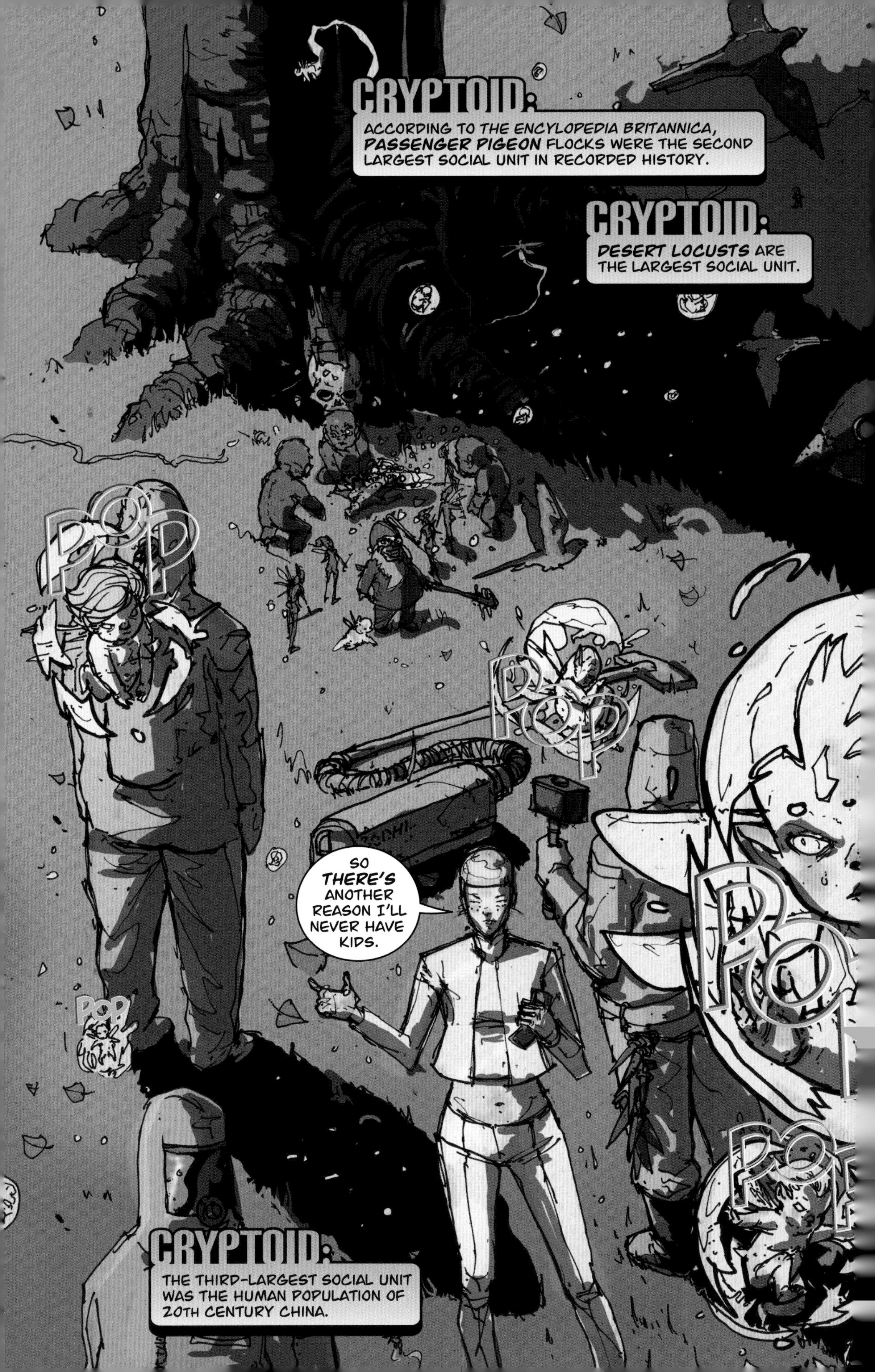
CRYPTOID:
ACCORDING TO THE ENCYLOPEDIA BRITANNICA, PASSENGER PIGEON FLOCKS WERE THE SECOND LARGEST SOCIAL UNIT IN RECORDED HISTORY.
CRYPTOID:
DESERT LOCUSTS ARE THE LARGEST SOCIAL UNIT.
POP
POP
SO THERE'S ANOTHER REASON I'LL NEVER HAVE KIDS.
POP
POP
POP
CRYPTOID:
THE THIRD-LARGEST SOCIAL UNIT WAS THE HUMAN POPULATION OF 20TH CENTURY CHINA.

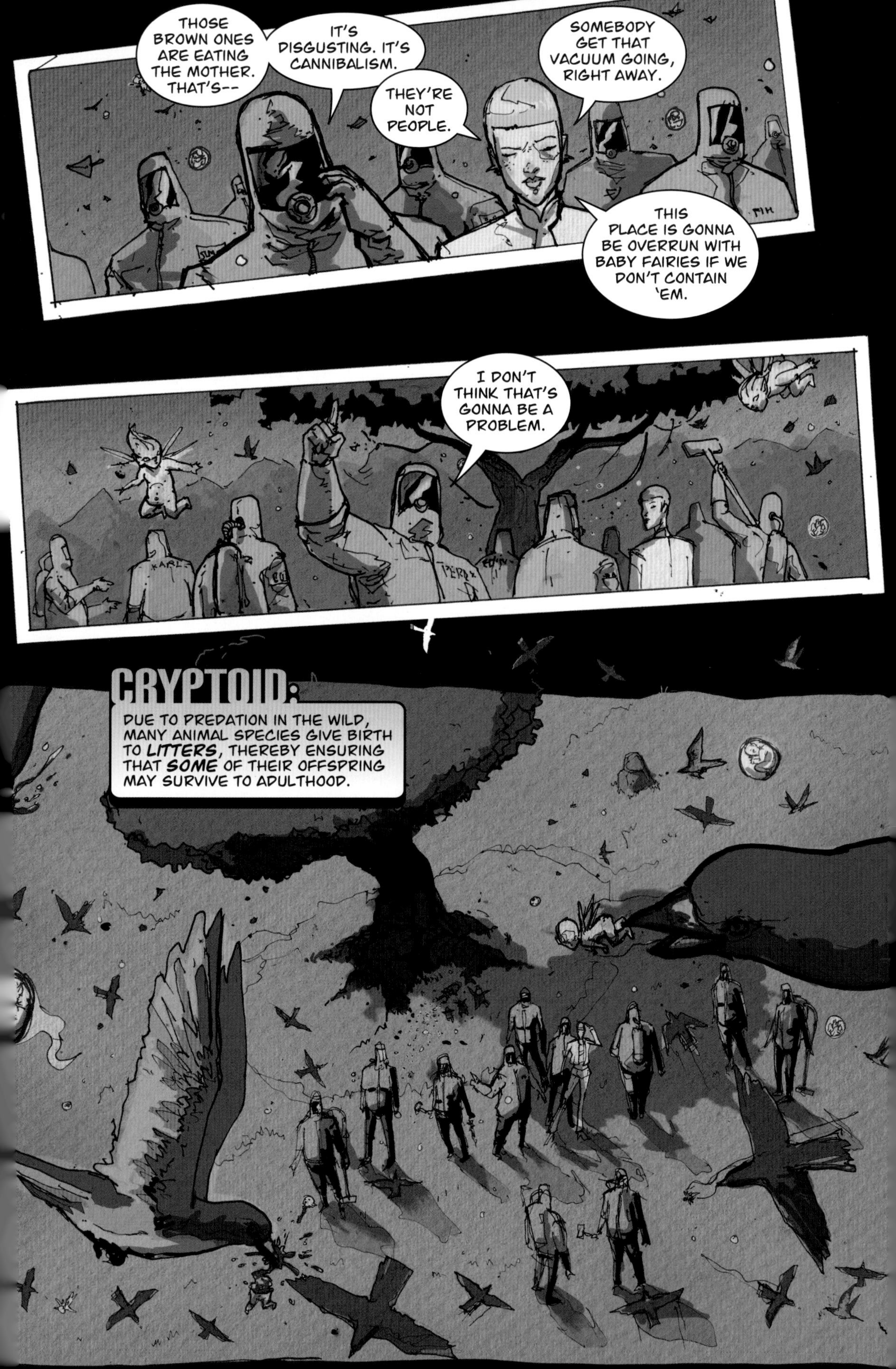
THOSE BROWN ONES ARE EATING THE MOTHER. THAT'S--
IT'S DISGUSTING. IT'S CANNIBALISM.
THEY'RE NOT PEOPLE.
SOMEBODY GET THAT VACUUM GOING, RIGHT AWAY.
THIS PLACE IS GONNA BE OVERRUN WITH BABY FAIRIES IF WE DON'T CONTAIN 'EM.
I DON'T THINK THAT'S GONNA BE A PROBLEM.
CRYPTOID:
DUE TO PREDATION IN THE WILD, MANY ANIMAL SPECIES GIVE BIRTH TO LITTERS, THEREBY ENSURING THAT SOME OF THEIR OFFSPRING MAY SURVIVE TO ADULTHOOD.

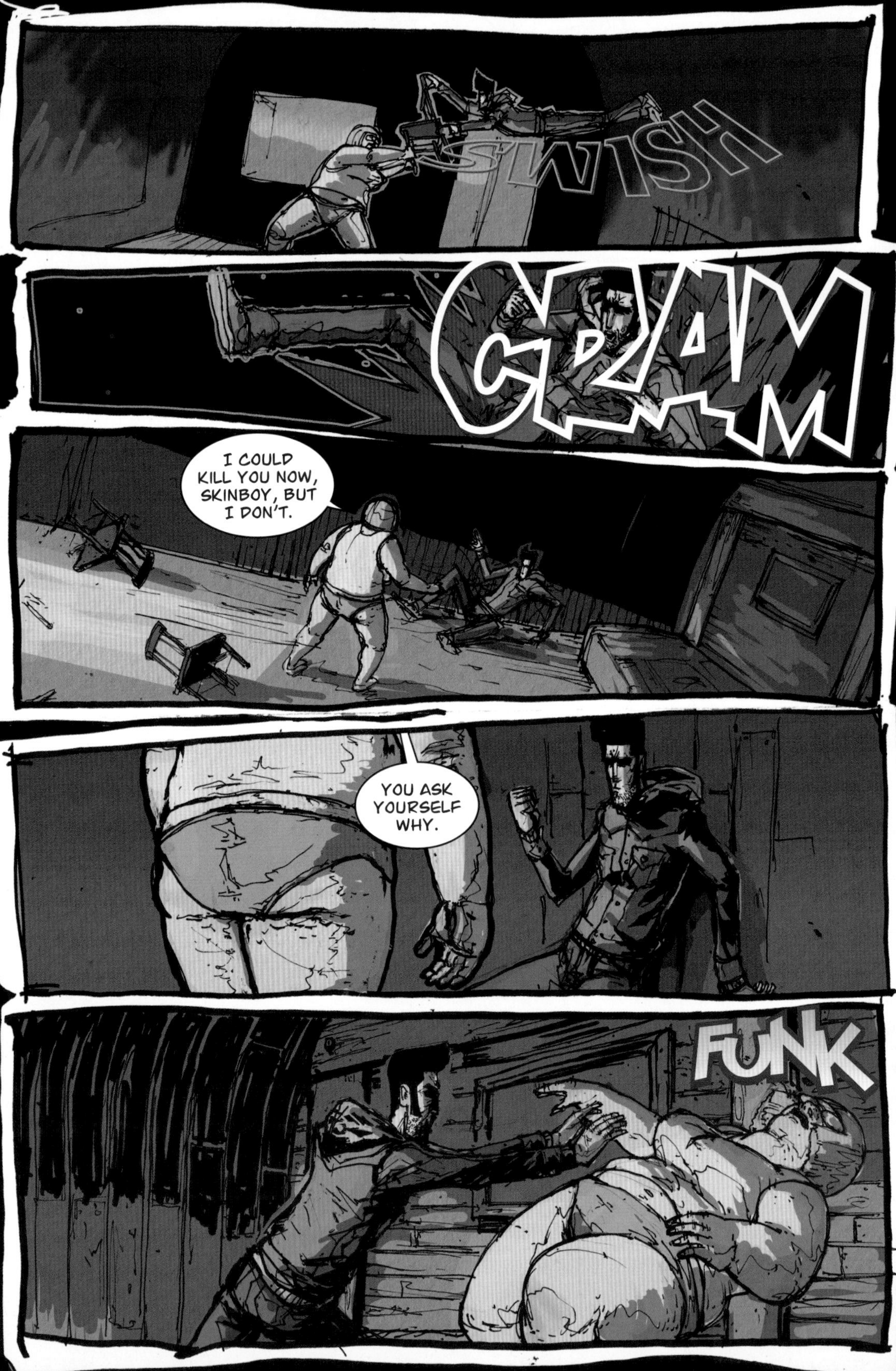
SWISH
CRAM
I COULD KILL YOU NOW, SKINBOY, BUT I DON'T.
YOU ASK YOURSELF WHY.
FUNK

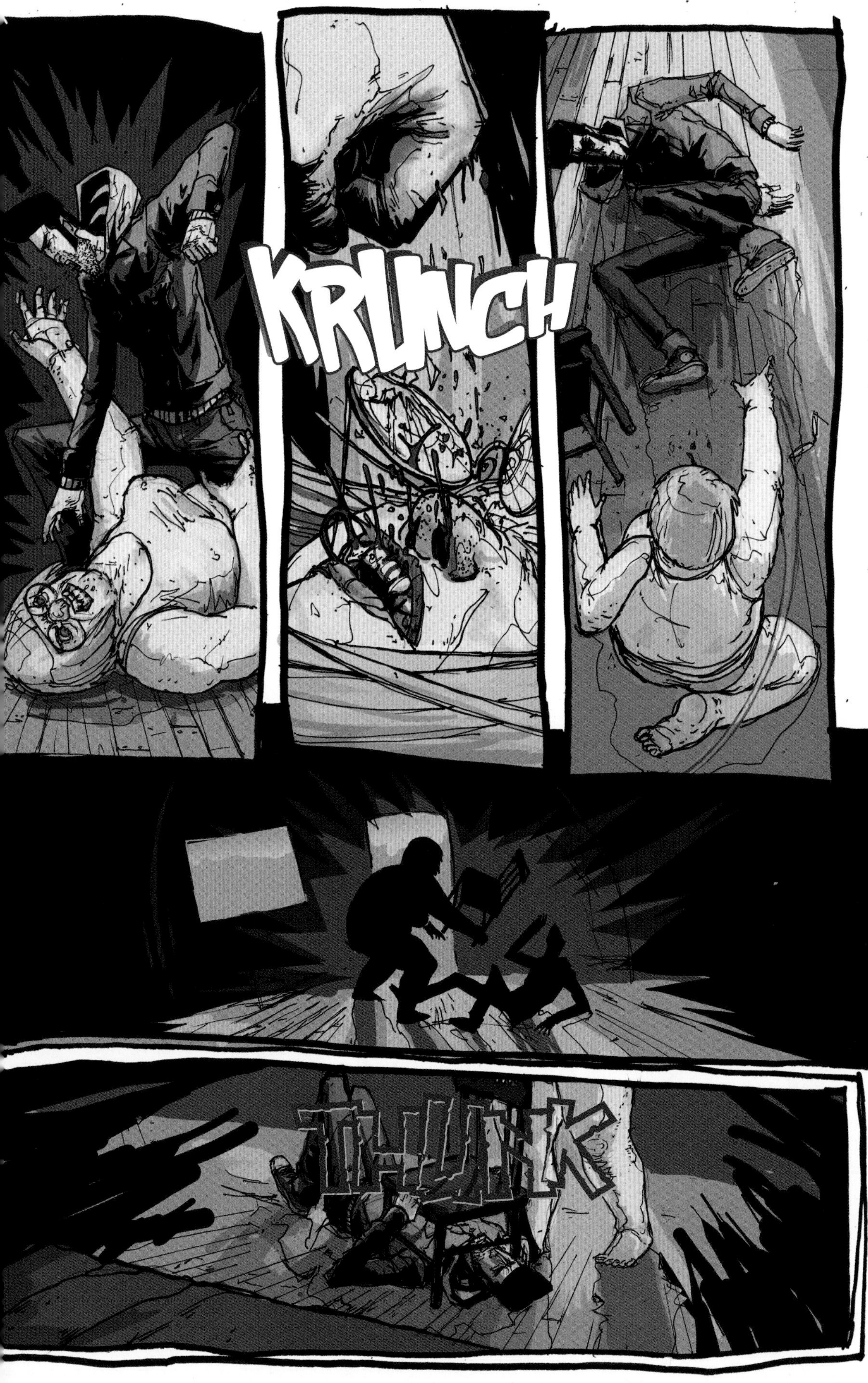
KRUNCH
THUNK

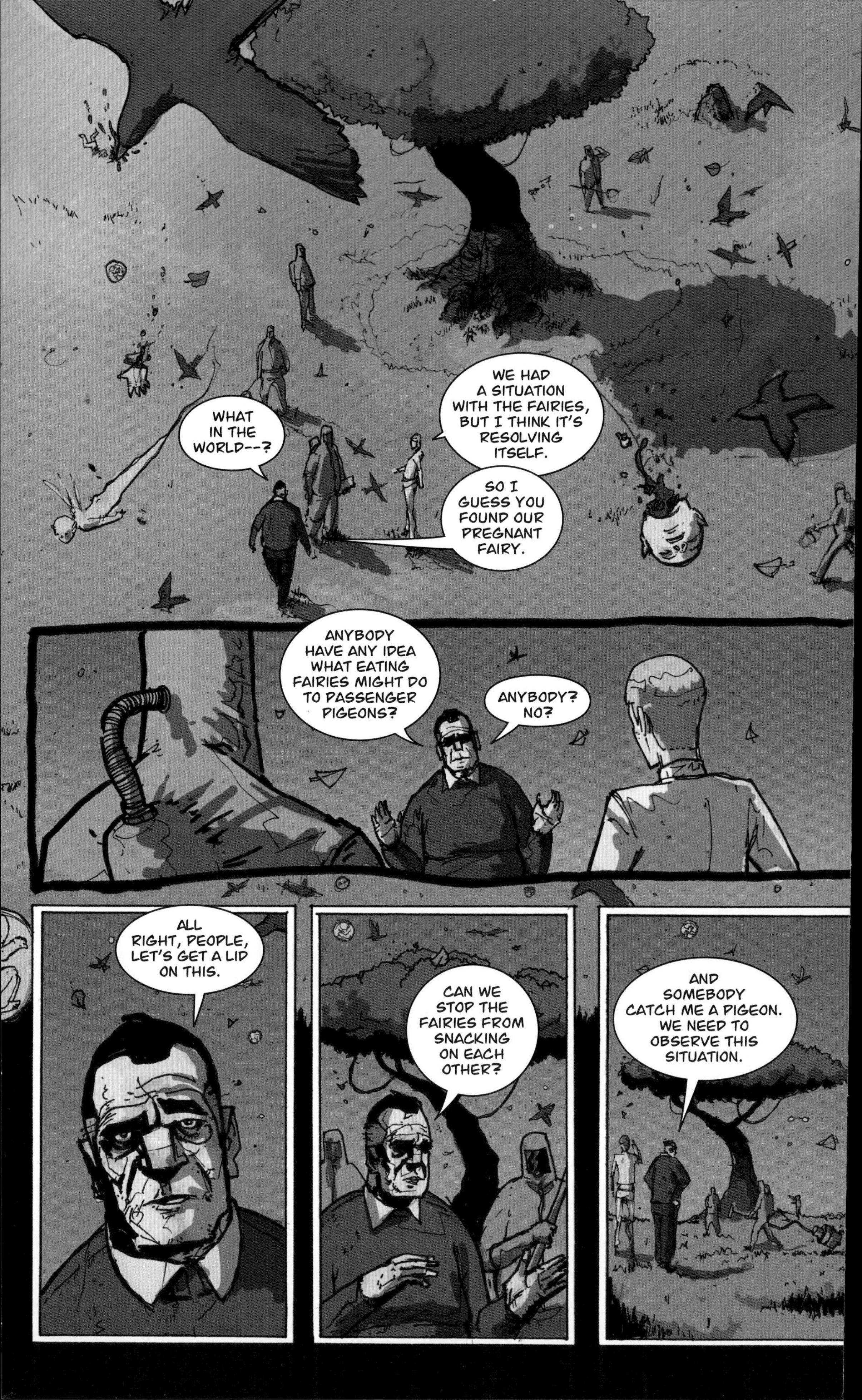
WHAT IN THE WORLD--?
WE HAD A SITUATION WITH THE FAIRIES, BUT I THINK IT'S RESOLVING ITSELF.
SO I GUESS YOU FOUND OUR PREGNANT FAIRY.
ANYBODY HAVE ANY IDEA WHAT EATING FAIRIES MIGHT DO TO PASSENGER PIGEONS?
ANYBODY? NO?
ALL RIGHT, PEOPLE, LET'S GET A LID ON THIS.
CAN WE STOP THE FAIRIES FROM SNACKING ON EACH OTHER?
AND SOMEBODY CATCH ME A PIGEON. WE NEED TO OBSERVE THIS SITUATION.

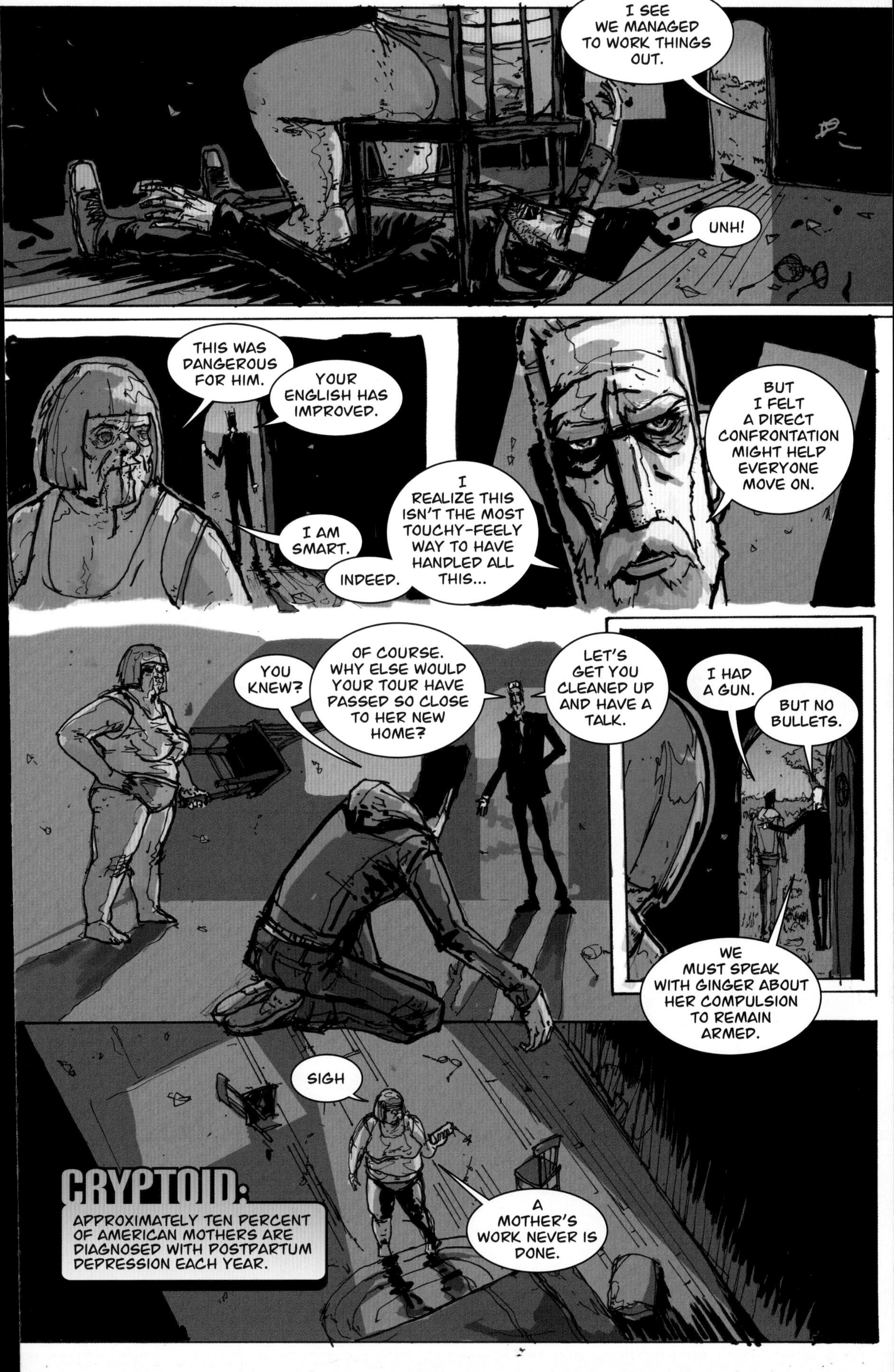
I SEE WE MANAGED TO WORK THINGS OUT.
UNH!
THIS WAS DANGEROUS FOR HIM.
YOUR ENGLISH HAS IMPROVED.
I AM SMART.
INDEED.
I REALIZE THIS ISN'T THE MOST TOUCHY-FEELY WAY TO HAVE HANDLED ALL THIS...
BUT I FELT A DIRECT CONFRONTATION MIGHT HELP EVERYONE MOVE ON.
YOU KNEW?
OF COURSE. WHY ELSE WOULD YOUR TOUR HAVE PASSED SO CLOSE TO HER NEW HOME?
LET'S GET YOU CLEANED UP AND HAVE A TALK.
I HAD A GUN.
BUT NO BULLETS.
WE MUST SPEAK WITH GINGER ABOUT HER COMPULSION TO REMAIN ARMED.
SIGH
CRYPTOID:
APPROXIMATELY TEN PERCENT OF AMERICAN MOTHERS ARE DIAGNOSED WITH POSTPARTUM DEPRESSION EACH YEAR.
A MOTHER'S WORK NEVER IS DONE.

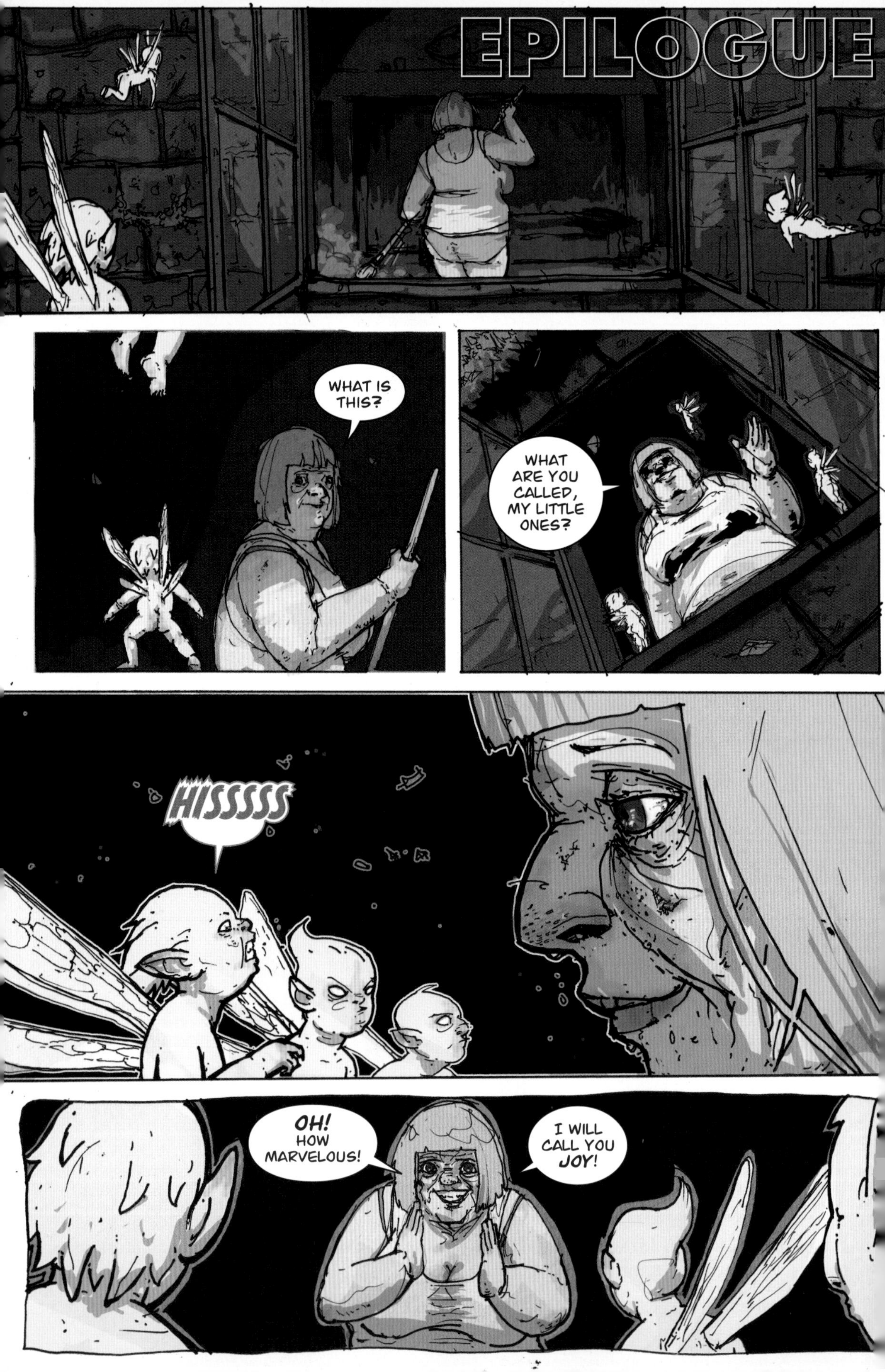
EPILOGUE
WHAT IS THIS?
WHAT ARE YOU CALLED, MY LITTLE ONES?
HISSSSS
OH! HOW MARVELOUS!
I WILL CALL YOU JOY!

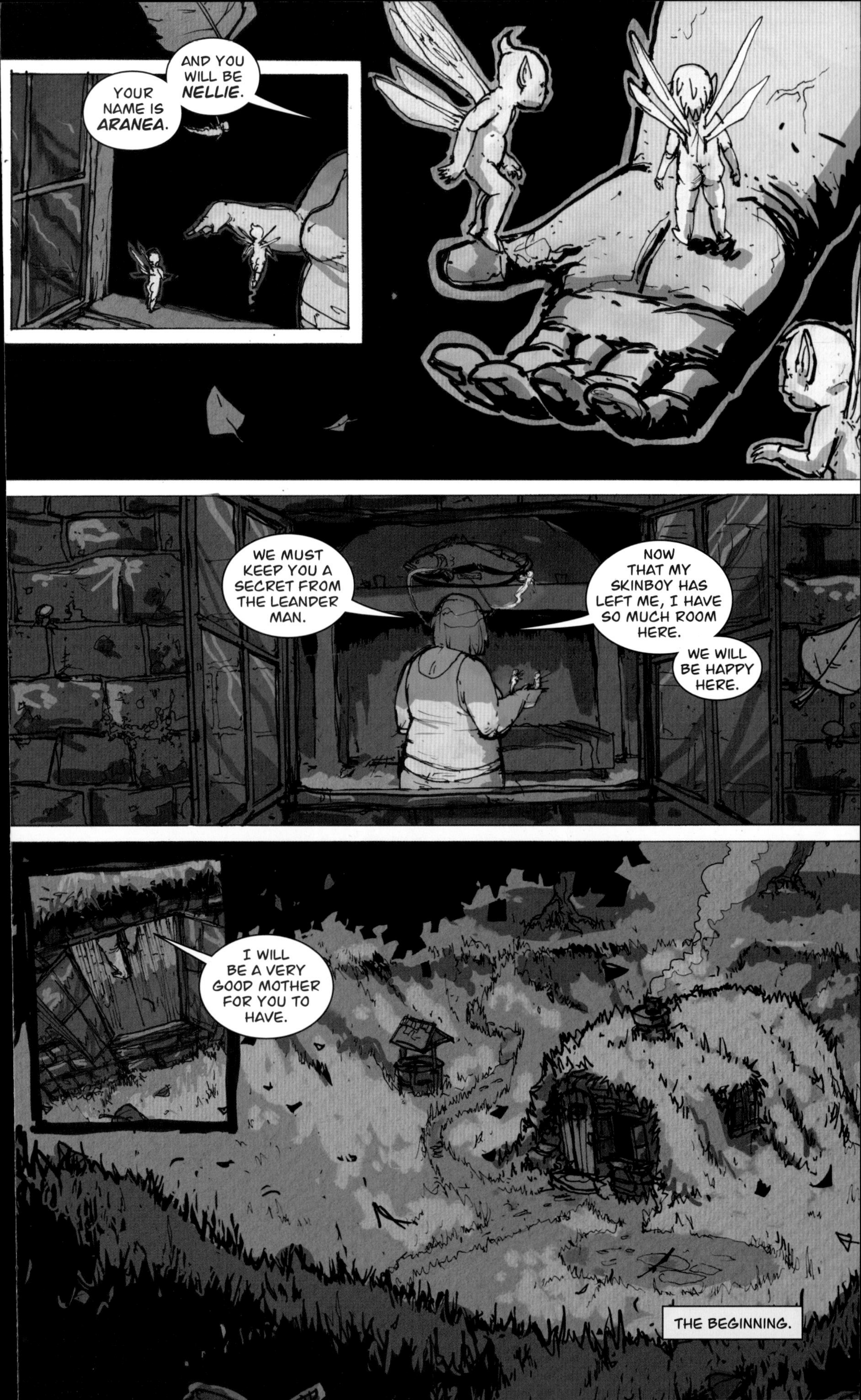
YOUR NAME IS ARANEA.
AND YOU WILL BE NELLIE.
WE MUST KEEP YOU A SECRET FROM THE LEANDER MAN.
NOW THAT MY SKINBOY HAS LEFT ME, I HAVE SO MUCH ROOM HERE.
WE WILL BE HAPPY HERE.
I WILL BE A VERY GOOD MOTHER FOR YOU TO HAVE.
THE BEGINNING.

PROOF™

VOL. 1: **GOATSUCKER** – ISBN-13: 978-1582409948
VOL. 2: **THE COMPANY OF MEN** – ISBN-13: 978-1607060178
VOL. 3: **THUNDERBIRDS ARE GO!** – ISBN-13: 978-1607061342
VOL. 4: **JULIA** – ISBN-13: 978-1607062851
VOL. 5: **BLUE FAIRIES** – ISBN-13: 978-1607063483

ALEXANDER GRECIAN
and RILEY ROSSMO

BOOK 1:
GOATSUCKER

ALEXANDER GRECIAN
AND RILEY ROSSMO
WITH FIONA STAPLES AND ADAM GUZOWSKI

BOOK 2: THE
COMPANY
OF MEN

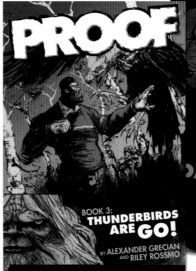

BOOK 3:
THUNDERBIRDS
ARE GO!
BY ALEXANDER GRECIAN
AND RILEY ROSSMO

THE ADVENTURE CONTINUES IN...

BY ALEXANDER GRECIAN
AND RILEY ROSSMO

BOOK 4:
JULIA

—BOOK 5: BLUE
FAIRIES
BY ALEXANDER GRECIAN
RILEY ROSSMO AND CHRIS GRINE

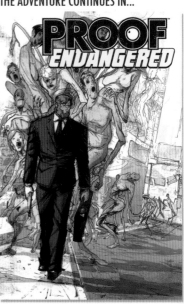

PROOF™
ENDANGERED

ENCORE...

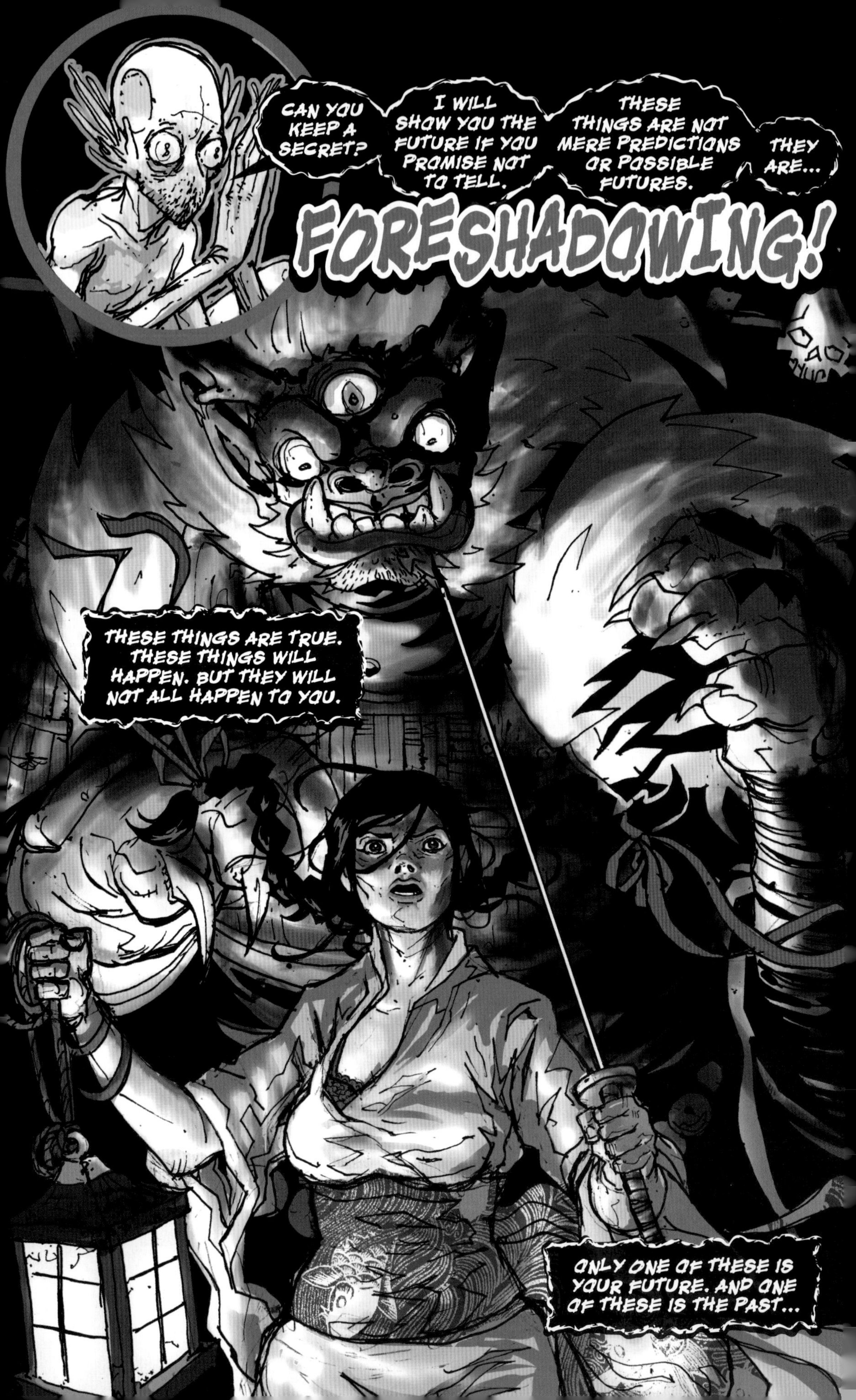

CAN YOU KEEP A SECRET?
I WILL SHOW YOU THE FUTURE IF YOU PROMISE NOT TO TELL.
THESE THINGS ARE NOT MERE PREDICTIONS OR POSSIBLE FUTURES.
THEY ARE...
FORESHADOWING!
THESE THINGS ARE TRUE. THESE THINGS WILL HAPPEN. BUT THEY WILL NOT ALL HAPPEN TO YOU.
ONLY ONE OF THESE IS YOUR FUTURE. AND ONE OF THESE IS THE PAST...

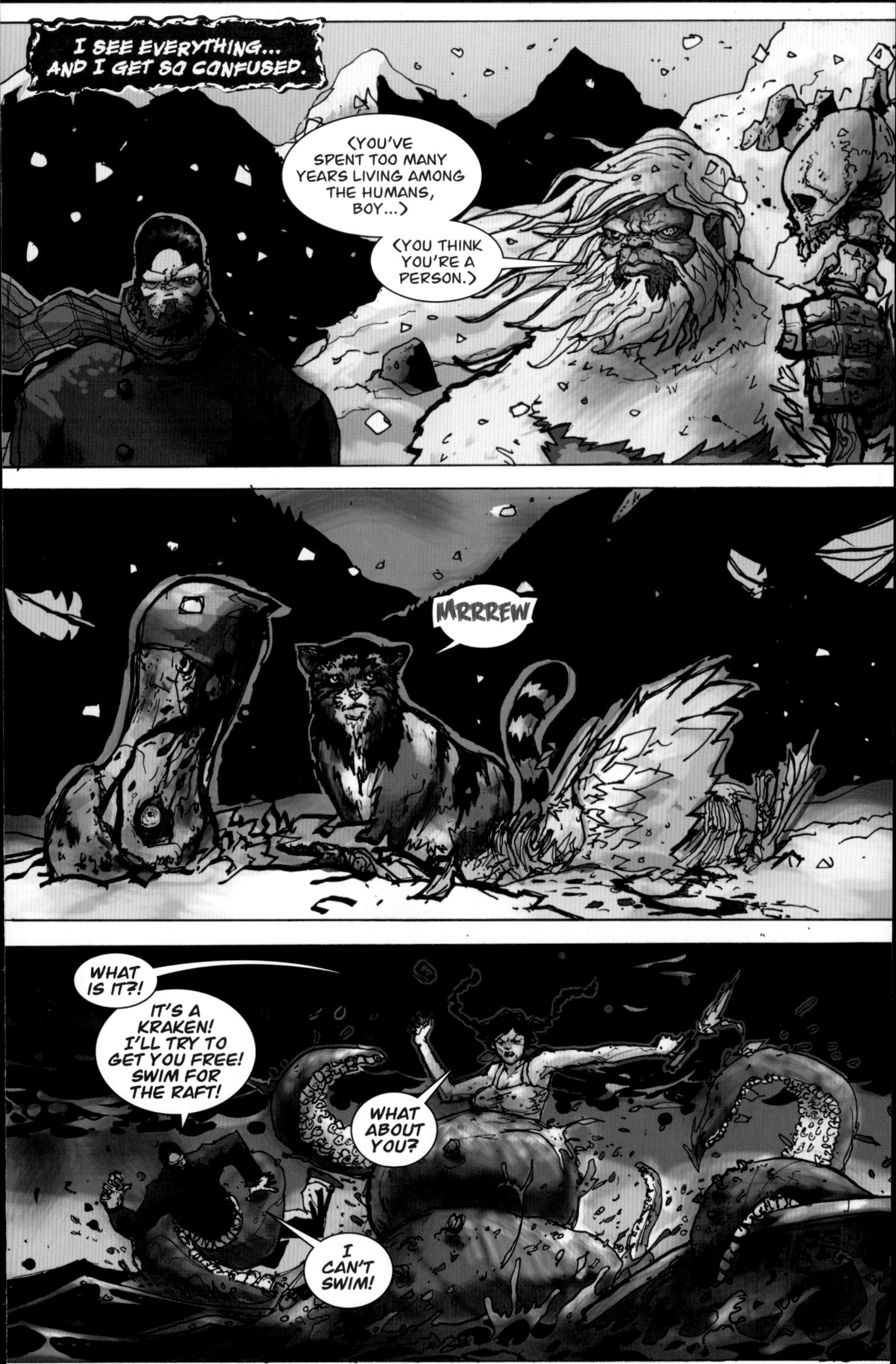
I SEE EVERYTHING... AND I GET SO CONFUSED.
<YOU'VE SPENT TOO MANY YEARS LIVING AMONG THE HUMANS, BOY...>
<YOU THINK YOU'RE A PERSON.>
MRRREW
WHAT IS IT?!
IT'S A KRAKEN! I'LL TRY TO GET YOU FREE! SWIM FOR THE RAFT!
WHAT ABOUT YOU?
I CAN'T SWIM!

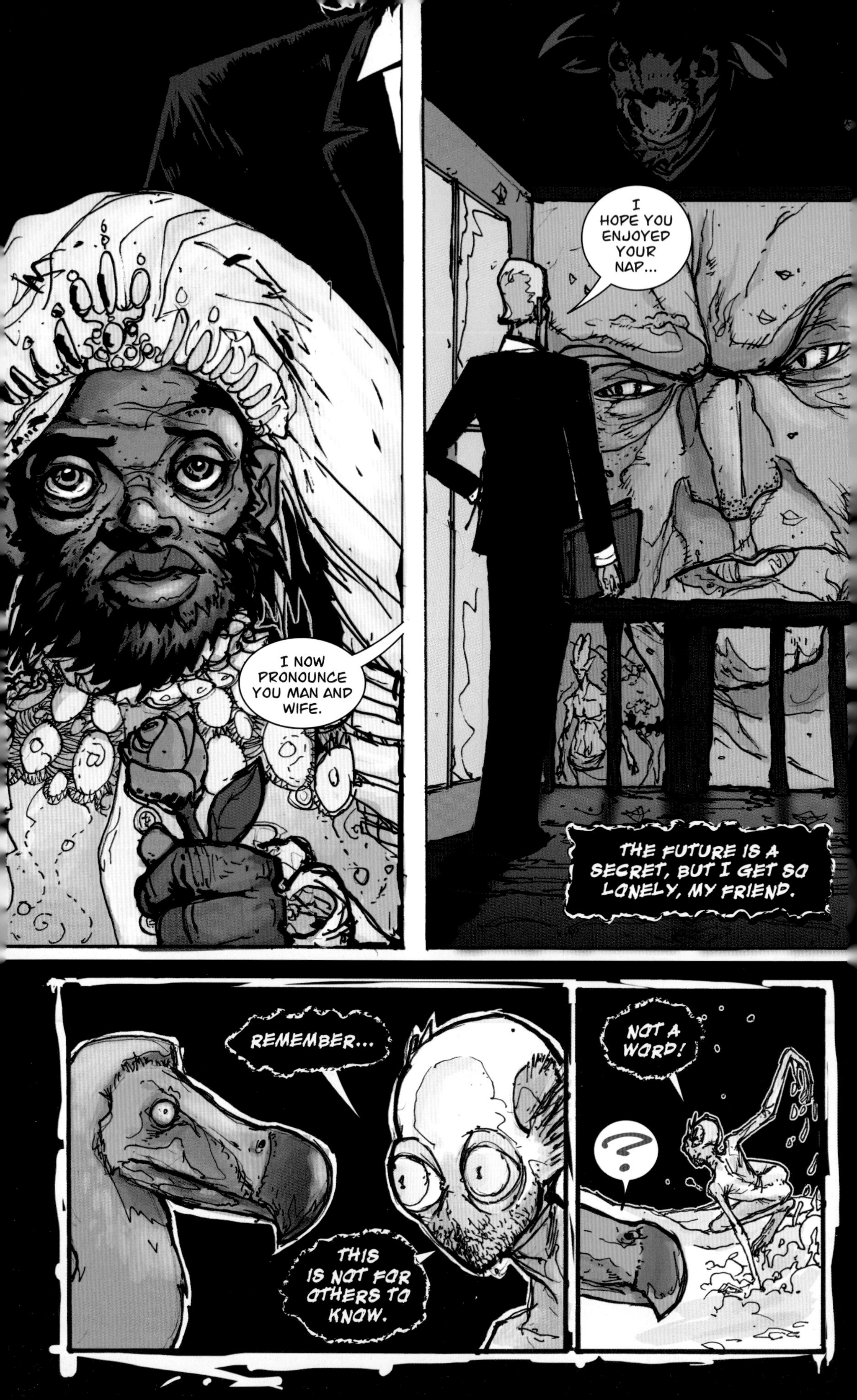
I NOW PRONOUNCE YOU MAN AND WIFE.
I HOPE YOU ENJOYED YOUR NAP...
THE FUTURE IS A SECRET, BUT I GET SO LONELY, MY FRIEND.
REMEMBER...
THIS IS NOT FOR OTHERS TO KNOW.
NOT A WORD!
?